AQ# 2446

220.9
Mat

AQ# 2446

Matthews, Victor

AUTHOR

Manners & Customs In

TITLE

The Bible

DATE DUE

MANNERS & CUSTOMS

IN THE

BIBLE

An Illustrated Guide to
Daily Life in Bible Times

THIRD EDITION

VICTOR H. MATTHEWS

HENDRICKSON
PUBLISHERS

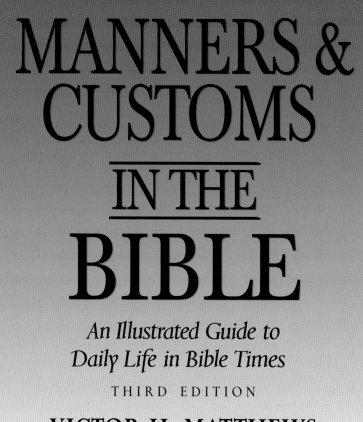

MANNERS &
CUSTOMS

IN THE

BIBLE

An Illustrated Guide to
Daily Life in Bible Times

THIRD EDITION

VICTOR H. MATTHEWS

HENDRICKSON
PUBLISHERS

Manners and Customs in the Bible
Third Edition

© 2006 by Victor H. Matthews
Hendrickson Publishers, Inc.
P. O. Box 3473
Peabody, Massachusetts 01961-3473

ISBN 978-1-56563-704-7

Second Printing — February 2010

Library of Congress Cataloging-in-Publication Data

Matthews, Victor Harold.
    Manners and customs in the Bible : an illustrated guide to daily life in Bible times / Victor H. Matthews.— 3rd ed.
    p. cm.
    Includes bibliographical references (p.   ) and indexes.
    ISBN 1-56563-704-6 (alk. paper)   1. Jews—Social life and customs—To 70 A.D.
  2. Palestine—Social life and customs—To 70 A.D.   3. Bible—Antiquities. I. Title.
    DS112.M33 2006
    220.9′5—dc22

              2005037764

Design copyright © 2006 LionHudson plc/Tim Dowley and Peter Wyart trading as Three's Company

Worldwide co-edition produced by
Lion Hudson plc
Mayfield House
256 Banbury Road
Oxford, OX2 7DH, England

Tel: +44 (0) 1865 302750
Fax: +44 (0) 1865 302757
e-mail: coed@lionhudson.com
www.lionhudson.com

Printed in Singapore

To Carol, Peter, and Samuel

Illustrations

Contents

Preface to the Third Edition

It is remarkable that new discoveries about the biblical world continue to be made some four thousand years after biblical stories began to be told. Even since the first printing of this book in 1988, significant changes in the methods of biblical study and new archaeological finds have refocused our view of life in ancient Israel. This third edition of *Manners and Customs in the Bible* is produced in hopes that old and new readers alike will benefit from the new material included.

This edition contains formatting modifications aimed at providing readers with tools to navigate the long span of Israel's history. First, when important terms are introduced in the text, they are printed in bold to alert the reader to their significance. A glossary has been added for quick reference to unfamiliar terms. Second, cross-referencing throughout the book will help readers connect the manners and customs of one period with similar practices performed in other generations. Third, photographs and maps provide a visual guide to geographical features and place names.

The bibliographies provided for each chapter have been updated and expanded to incorporate ongoing research in the fields of biblical studies, archaeology, and sociology. As in the revised edition of this work, special emphasis is placed upon sociological and anthropological methods of studying the Bible as they are particularly adept at identifying and comparing the everyday practices of those living in the Near East in ancient and modern times.

Abbreviations

General

A.D.	anno Domini
B.C.	before Christ
ca.	circa
ch(s).	chapter(s)
LXX	Septuagint (the Greek Old Testament)
n.	note
NRSV	New Revised Standard Version
v(v).	verse(s)

Primary Sources

Old Testament/Hebrew Bible

Gen	Genesis
Exod	Exodus
Lev	Leviticus
Num	Numbers
Deut	Deuteronomy
Josh	Joshua
Judg	Judges
1–2 Sam	1–2 Samuel
1–2 Kgs	1–2 Kings
1–2 Chr	1–2 Chronicles
Neh	Nehemiah
Esth	Esther
Ps	Psalms
Prov	Proverbs
Eccl	Ecclesiastes
Song	Song of Solomon
Isa	Isaiah
Jer	Jeremiah
Lam	Lamentations
Ezek	Ezekiel
Dan	Daniel
Hos	Hosea
Mic	Micah
Zeph	Zephaniah
Hag	Haggai
Zech	Zechariah
Mal	Malachi

Apocrypha

1 Esd	1 Esdras
1–2 Macc	1–2 Maccabees
3 Macc	3 Maccabees
Sir	Sirach/Ecclesiasticus

New Testament

Matt	Matthew
Rom	Romans
1–2 Cor	1–2 Corinthians
Eph	Ephesians
Col	Colossians
1 Thess	1 Thessalonians
2 Tim	2 Timothy
Jas	James
Rev	Revelation

Pseudepigrapha

T. Reu.	*Testament of Reuben*

Talmud

b. B. Bat.	Babylonian Talmud, *Baba Batra*
j. Ta'an.	Jerusalem Talmud, *Ta'anit*

Rabbinic Works

Pirqe R. El.	*Pirqe Rabbi Eliezer*

Other Ancient Sources

Eusebius

Eccl. hist.	*Ecclesiastical History*
Prae. ev.	*Praeparatio evangelica*

Josephus

Ant.	*Jewish Antiquities*
J.W.	*Jewish War*

Juvenal

Sat.	*Satires*

Herodotus

Hist.	*Histories*

Macrobius

Sat.	*Saturnalia*

Philo

Opif.	*On the Creation of the World*

Plutarch

Quaest. rom.	*Questiones romanae et graecae*

Tertullian

Cor.	*The Crown*

Secondary Sources

ANET	J. Pritchard, *Ancient Near Eastern Texts Relating to the Old Testament* (Princeton: Princeton University Press, 1969).
ARMT	A. Parrot and G. Dossin, *Archives royales de Mari* (Paris: Impr. Nationale, 1950–).
OTPar	V. H. Matthews and D. C. Benjamin, *Old Testament Parallels: Laws and Stories from the Ancient Near East* (Rev. and exp. ed.; New York: Paulist, 1997).

Introduction

One of the joys of studying the Bible is attempting to reconstruct the manners and customs of the peoples of ancient times. The gulf of thousands of years that separates us from them can be bridged, at least in part, by insights into their everyday life. Such insights can be garnered through close examination of biblical narratives and through comparison of biblical data with written and physical remains from other ancient civilizations. Modern anthropological research and the discoveries and interpretations of archaeologists and art historians are also of prime importance to the reconstruction process.

RECONSTRUCTING THE SOCIAL WORLD FROM CONTEXT

In attempting to recreate the social world of ancient Israel, scholars draw on several sources of information. Written records from this period include the biblical text and a few extrabiblical documents that parallel, but do not always corroborate, the biblical narrative. Physical remains are limited to what has been uncovered by archaeologists. These remains— tomb paintings, garbage heaps, the ruins of conquered and/or abandoned cities, bits and pieces of life that have almost miraculously survived the elements and the centuries— provide only a partial picture of life in ancient times. Finally, the social setting can be reconstructed in part from the biblical text itself and partly from the study of analogous ancient and modern cultures. To be sure, not every aspect

of life is described in detail by the ancient sources. Individual tastes in clothing, diet, and even worship practices are simply impossible to recover due to our lack of information or understanding.

It is fortunate, however, that many of the manners and customs of ancient Israel persist over long periods of time. New anthropological methods of studying the Bible seek to describe how Israel adapted in response to changes in its environment and population, and in its technologies (such as water collection and storage methods). Studies of this sort propose that many of the traditions operative before the monarchy period continued into later periods of Israel's history. For example, tribal systems that sustained the ancestors carried over into the conquest and settlement periods, when the tribes assisted one another in securing land. Tribal affiliations continued in significance as identity markers throughout the monarchy period (see 1 Sam 10:20–21). This kind of cultural continuity suggests that, in certain instances, the customs of one era can be used to illuminate the lifestyles of other generations.

This should be considered when reading the biblical text, which contains a wealth of information from many periods in Israel's history. Subjects range from civil and religious law to building codes and harvesting techniques. The text contains everything from the proper procedure for dealing with a delinquent son to the requirements for purifying a priest after he comes in contact with a corpse. Other passages specify times, places, and procedures for performing sacrifices to God, as well as injunctions regarding the slaughtering of animals.

While impressive in its quantity and breadth, the sheer amount of data acquired through careful study of the Bible can also cause confusion. Jargon associated with professional groups often requires additional explanation for the reader. For example, *selah* appears quite frequently in the Psalms and appears to be a technical term used in community worship or as a guide for religious professionals. Unfortunately, the meanings of some biblical terms are still mysteries that require further research and the careful use of extrabiblical materials. For instance, the poetic texts found at the ancient seaport of Ugarit and composed between 1400 and 1200 B.C. are similar in style and vocabulary to the Psalms and the epic sections of the biblical narrative. Comparative study of these texts has, in some cases, provided the key to understanding a word that has long remained obscure.

Occasionally, the text includes the smallest and seemingly most insignificant details, monotonously droning on with a series of "begats" or the dimensions of the pilasters and recesses of the temple. In other cases, however, the narrative may skip over the entire reign of a king, dismissing him with the phrase "he did what was evil in the sight of the Lord" (see 1 Kgs 15:26). The narrator then summarizes the remainder of the king's life in the tantalizing footnote, "Now the rest of the acts of _____, and all that he did, are they not written in the Book of the Annals of the Kings of Judah?" (see 2 Kgs 8:23). Allusions to this and other lost works, such as the "Book of Jashar" (2 Sam 1:18), demonstrate that a great deal of information was available to the ancient writers that we, as of yet, are unable to consult. These citations of lost works are a ready reminder that we have only an editorialized version of events from which to draw a picture of life in biblical times.

> O Lᴏʀᴅ, how many are my foes!
>   Many are rising against me;
> many are saying to me,
>   "There is no help for you in God."
>   *Selah*
> But you, O Lᴏʀᴅ, are a shield around me,
>   my glory, and the one who lifts up my
>   head.
> I cry aloud to the Lᴏʀᴅ,
>   and he answers me from his holy hill.
>   *Selah*
>   —Ps 3:1–4

The book of Judges is a section of the biblical text from which large segments of the narrative appear to have been edited out, perhaps because the stories were so well known to contemporary readers. For the modern reader, however, the biblical account of the activities of the judges and other people of this time period leaves many questions unanswered. For example, why is this society so violent and accepting of violence? Why do the judges have to rely on primitive weapons like ox goads and animal bones? Why is obedience to hospitality laws deemed more important than the life of the host's virgin daughter (Judg 19)? And should we read such stories as acceptance of, or indictment against, particular behavior? Because this culture is so foreign to our own, it is sometimes only through the use of comparative materials from non-biblical sources, such as texts from Ugarit or the cities of Mesopotamia, that a better understanding of life in ancient times can be obtained.

Each of these alternate sources of information, however, provides a slightly different picture of life in the biblical period than is found in the biblical text. The perspective of many extrabiblical writings is secular with no religious framework. An eagerness to draw conclusions from documents that offer some parallels to biblical narrative can therefore lead to wishful thinking and incorrect interpretations. For instance, the ancient letters from the

Mesopotamian city of Nuzi (ca. 16th to 15th cent. B.C.) describe family customs regarding marriage and the adoption of an heir. Superficially at least, these customs resemble those reflected in the stories told about Abraham, Isaac, and Jacob in Genesis. However, the Nuzi texts are legal documents that record familial matters. They do not attest to a covenant with God or any concern to maintain the cultural purity of a chosen people, two prominent features of Genesis. Without more complete evidence, one must exercise caution when using parallel materials to explain or clarify the biblical narratives.

Archaeological evidence provides some of the most illuminating information on life in ancient times. When archaeologists apply careful methods in their excavation of ancient city and village sites, information that can aid our understanding of ancient cultures slowly emerges from the ground. Such methods include the systematic recording of finds by means of photographs and written descriptions, and the sharing of this material with a wide range of experts who can draw on their specialized fields of knowledge to extract more information from the finds than the archaeologist working alone. For instance, the carbonized remains found in storage jars and on excavated threshing floors, when examined by teams of microbiologists, botanists, and paleobotanists, can reveal what ancient human beings regularly ate. Their general level of health can thus be surmised, and their methods of agriculture and animal husbandry can be at least partially ascertained. Careful records of archaeological finds also allow future scholars to return to the evidence and perhaps, using new technologies or applying new knowledge gleaned from other finds, to draw new conclusions.

At the same time, to expect archaeological discoveries to prove conclusively "the truth of the Bible" is unreasonable. The findings of archaeologists offer only mute evidence of

Part of the excavations at Jericho.

ancient life and cannot be forced into alignment with biblical narratives. In other words, to say, as John Garstang did in the 1930s, that a particular wall found in the excavations at Jericho was the one that fell to Joshua's trumpet blasts, without examining all of the surrounding evidence (pottery, building styles, the relative depth of artifacts within the mound), is unfair to the student as well as to the text. Improved methods of excavation later proved that even Garstang's identification of the stratigraphic level of Joshua's Jericho was incorrect, and this mistake led to controversy concerning the proper role of archaeological research in relation to the study of the Bible.

Finds must be interpreted in the context of the mound as a whole. The sites of ancient cities are layered, with each level (**stratum**) representing a different phase in the life history of the city. Since objects found lower in

13

the mound can generally be assumed to be older than those found closer to the surface, archaeologists can establish a relative chronology of the various levels or strata.

Some confusion of the strata does occur, however, due to earthquake activity and the digging of pits and foundations by later inhabitants of the site. Moreover, archaeologists can only determine the approximate age in years of the artifacts they uncover and the strata in which they lie. To resolve the confusion of strata and to establish a fixed or absolute chronology for a city site, archaeologists study pottery types and other artifacts from each layer. They then compare these artifacts with finds from sites whose chronology is understood. Carbon 14 dating, as well as other scientific dating methods, aids in this process of constructing an absolute chronology by establishing the approximate age of organic remains.

Due to the limitations of time and money, archaeologists seldom uncover an entire mound. They carefully map out squares for excavation or dig exploratory shafts in those portions of the mound that surveys have shown to contain the most important structures (temples, palaces, gates) or a representative selection of objects of interest.

The most recently developed archaeological techniques do try to obtain a broader perspective on the entire mound, but it is unlikely that every shovelful of dirt will be turned or every object uncovered. The fact that many sites were excavated before modern methods were developed magnifies the difficulties of obtaining a complete occupational picture. A great deal of valuable information is thus forever lost, while many artifacts now lie (without any record of their historical context) on museum shelves. Archaeology is a destructive process; each level must be recorded and then removed to get to the level below it, and what has been removed can never be replaced. As a result, we learn through archaeology some, but not all, there is to know about life in these ancient

> *Abraham said of his wife Sarah, "She is my sister." And King Abimelech of Gerar sent and took Sarah.*
> *—Gen 20:2*

cities. Thus, responsible archaeologists today intentionally leave some portions of a mound untouched for later generations and their more advanced excavation methods.

To complete this cautionary survey of aids to the reconstruction of life in the biblical period, it should be noted that modern anthropological research can be of great value to the student of the Bible. Until the beginning of the twentieth century, tribal peoples continued to live in the Near East in much the same way that their ancestors had thousands of years ago. In more recent times, anthropologists and ethnologists study tribal peoples whose manners and customs are very similar to those found in the biblical text. These peoples still engage in seasonal migration with their flocks and herds. The mutual suspicion that led Abraham to deceive Abimelech (Gen 20) is still evident in the relations between nomadic groups and sedentary peoples.

The student who engages in comparative work, however, should understand that no parallel is likely to be totally exact. Customs and traditions can remain unchanged for centuries, but each successive group of people inhabiting the same area and practicing the same basic economy is different in some way from its predecessors. Therefore it is necessary to qualify most statements made when comparing ancient and modern peoples.

DEVELOPMENT OF BIBLICAL LITERATURE

Understanding the history of the biblical text is also important in exploring the information it reveals concerning the manners and customs of biblical people. The text as we have

The Kidron Valley

it is a compilation of **narratives,** or stories, that most likely began as **oral traditions,** stories passed from one generation to the next by telling them rather than writing them down. In their final written forms these stories represent not only early memories of Israel's history, but also the political situations and religious claims of later editors. To fully appreciate the complexity of these traditions and texts spanning at least two thousand years, a reader must understand that there were very different historical settings of the authors, editors, and audiences of these books. The sometimes grand, sometimes subtle variations in the pictures painted by different authors and editors speak to the concerns of many generations. These writings are the products of writers and editors trying to make sense of their national history in light of their beliefs about their national deity.

HISTORICAL GEOGRAPHY OF BIBLE LANDS

Before moving on to the history of ancient Israel, it is necessary to sketch out the geographical character of the area in which this

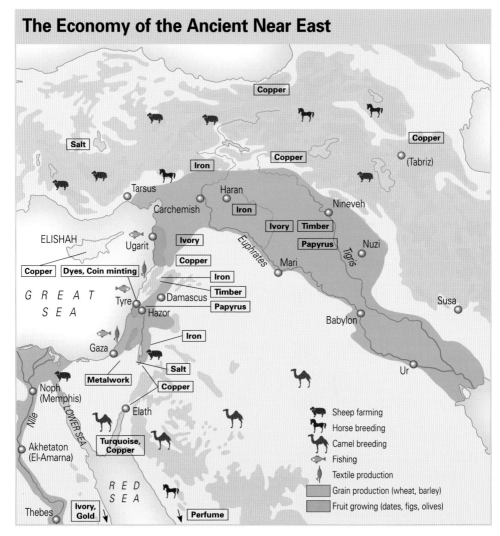

The Economy of the Ancient Near East

Highways of the Ancient Near East

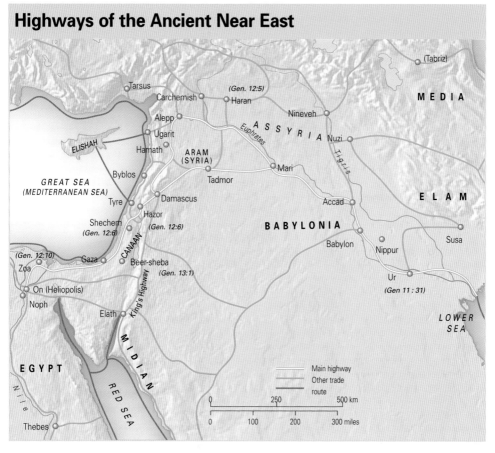

Map labels:

(Tabriz)

Tarsus
Carchemish
(Gen. 12:5)
Haran
MEDIA
Alepp
Nineveh
Ugarit
A S S Y R I A
Nuzi
Euphrates
ELISHAH
Hamath
ARAM
(SYRIA)
Byblos
Mari
GREAT SEA
(MEDITERRANEAN SEA)
Tadmor
Tigris
Tyre
Damascus
Accad
E L A M
Hazor
Shechem
(Gen. 12:6)
(Gen. 12:6)
BABYLONIA
Babylon
Nippur
Susa
(Gen. 12:10)
Gaza
Beer-sheba
Zoa
(Gen. 13:1)
CANAAN
On (Heliopolis)
Ur
Noph
(Gen 11:31)
Elath
King's Highway
LOWER
SEA
M I D I A N
EGYPT
Nile
RED SEA
Thebes

Main highway
Other trade
route

0   250   500 km
0   100   200   300 miles

ancient people was shaped. Ancient Israel lay in the midst of the so-called **Fertile Crescent,** which begins on the eastern shore of the Mediterranean Sea and curves like an inverted quarter moon ending at the Persian Gulf. This area includes the major cultures of Egypt to the west and Mesopotamia to the east. Both of these river valley cultures developed high civilizations around 3000 B.C. Major cities, with huge palace complexes and temples, as well as the large-scale commercial activity needed to support them, are hallmarks of their achievements. Very early in their history the Egyptian and Mesopotamian city-states established trade contacts, and succeeding periods saw a growth in these connections and in competition for ultimate supremacy within the region.

Trade routes to the south of the Tigris-Euphrates river valley of Mesopotamia were hampered by the Arabian desert, and sea travel to Egypt was limited to the Mediterranean coast or to the southern route down the Red Sea, touching points along the Arabian peninsula. The northern maritime trade routes were controlled in most periods by middleman states such as Byblos, Ugarit, and the Phoenician ports of Tyre and Sidon. Highways, such as the Via Maris, or "coastal road," which connected Egypt to Mesopotamia along the Fertile Crescent, and the King's Highway, which ran from the Red Sea north to Damascus, made overland trade easier. These routes connected the major population centers and helped to promote travel between regions. As a result, the land inhabited by the Israelites served as a crossroads from the beginnings of

17

civilization in this region. This area also turned into a center of conflict between the superpowers as they vied for control of the ancient Near East, and it often experienced the ravages of conquering armies. Ancient Israel thus became both a beneficiary and a victim of its geographical location.

The land inhabited by ancient Israel, situated between the eastern shore of the Mediterranean Sea and the Jordan River, is relatively small, measuring 250 miles long and 60 miles wide at its broadest point. Several spectacular geographical features, however, dominate the terrain and affect the people who live there. Moving from west to east in our geographical survey, it should be noted that ancient Israel had excellent sandy beaches, but no deep-water harbors. This prevented large-scale sea trade, and made the region more dependent on the ships and merchants of Phoenicia. Immediately inland from the coast, however, is a plain that gradually merges to the east with a hilly region known as the **Shephelah** ("lowland"). Settlement was relatively heavy in this area (especially after the coming of the Philistines), and the Via Maris ran along the coast bringing trade as well as the armies of conquering nations.

Paralleling the Jordan Valley and bisecting the country north and south is the central hill country. While it is not a precipitous range of hills, the swift plunge eastward into the Jordan Rift (an area known as the "slopes") causes a spectacular drop in elevation. Jerusalem and Jericho serve as one example of the differences in elevation that occur within a relatively short distance in this region. Lying in the southern portion of the hill country, Jerusalem's elevation is over 2,500 feet above sea level. However, Jericho, just 15 miles to the east, in an oasis near the Jordan River, has an elevation of 840 feet below sea level. Such massive shifts in the earth's surface make travel difficult and tend to cut off direct communication and cultural interaction.

Three distinctive areas further divide the central hill country. In the north the Galilee region enjoys the advantages of the highest annual rainfall and of the most fertile soil. The central portion of the hill country, once called Samaria, with its important population centers at Megiddo, Shechem, and Bethel, supports wheat farming along with fruit and olive orchards. The southernmost section of the hill country, known as Judea, is dominated by the city of Jerusalem. At one time, irrigation farming was common here as well as terraced agriculture on the slopes of the hills. Further south is the most uncertain and fragile environment in ancient Israel, with low annual rainfall in

Cross section of Palestinian Topography

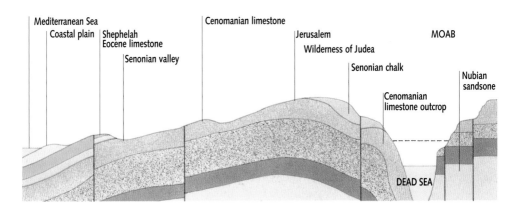

Mediterranean Sea
Coastal plain | Shephelah
Eocene limestone
Senonian valley
Cenomanian limestone
Jerusalem
Wilderness of Judea
MOAB
Senonian chalk
Nubian sandsone
Cenomanian limestone outcrop
DEAD SEA

Relief Map
of Palestine

Tyre

PLAIN OF PHOENICIA

Dan

Mt. Hermon
(9,232ft / 2,184m)

Lake Huleh

SYRIAN DESERT

Hazor

ARAM

Acco

GREAT SEA
(MEDITERRANEAN SEA)

Mt. Carmel
(1,732ft / 528m)

Tiberias

SEA OF CHINNERETH
(SEA OF GALILEE)

River Yarmuk

Mt. Tabor
(1,929ft / 588m)

VALLEY OF JEZREEL

Megiddo

PLAIN OF SHARON

Mt. Gilboa
(1,630ft / 497m)

Pella

GILEAD

River Jordan

Mt. Ebal
(3,083ft / 940m)

Samaria

Shechem

Mt. Gerizim
(2,889ft / 881m)

HILLS OF EPHRAIM

River Jabbok

ISRAEL

THE ARABAH

AMMON

Joppa

Lod

Bethel

Gibeon

Jericho

Gezer

Mt. of Olives
(2,723ft / 830m)

Heshbon

Jerusalem

hkelon

PLAIN OF PHILISTIA

SHEPHELAH

Bethlehem

WILDERNESS OF JUDEA

Mt. Nebo
(2,630ft / 802m)

JUDAH

HILLS OF JUDEA

SALT SEA (DEAD SEA)

Gaza

Lachish

Hebron

Dibon

River Arnon

MOAB

Beer-sheba

THE NEGEB

metres   feet
1,000   3,281
500   1,640
200   656
0   0
below sea below sea
level   level

0   25   50 km

0   10   20   30 miles

River Zered

THE ARABAH

EDOM

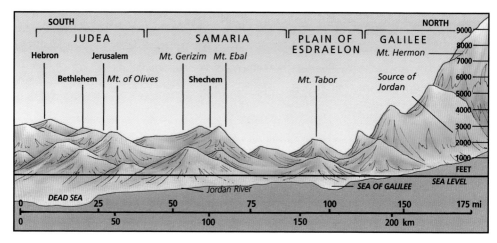

Rivers and Streams

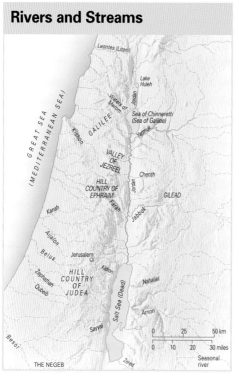

providing water for crops and livestock. The further south the Jordan flows, the more saline it becomes, thereby contributing to the country's agricultural division, with wheat being planted in the north and more salt-resistant barley being grown in the south. What little water does finally reach the Dead Sea (1275 feet below sea level) is so clogged with brine that plant life along its banks is limited to poplars and the tamarisk tree.

Because of the dominating geologic character of the central hill range and the Jordan Rift, the climate of ancient Israel is also influenced by a north-south pattern. Temperatures follow a basic Mediterranean range, though snow does fall on the peaks of the mountains and occasionally in Jerusalem. Average annual rainfall (concentrated in the months from November to March) ranges from as much as forty-five inches in the Upper Galilee region to eight inches in the Negeb desert around Beersheba and Arad. There are also years when these latter areas have no rainfall at all. Rainfall also declines from west to east since the hill country blocks the path of storms moving in from the Mediterranean. The result is an extremely arid region known as the Judean wilderness where rain may not come for years. This barrenness has made it synonymous with pain, trial, and death. The southern portion of the Transjordanian plateau, east of

the areas bordering on this wilderness and in the Negeb desert.

The heart of the landscape is dominated by the Jordan Rift, part of a massive fissure in the earth that runs from the Lebanon Mountains down into Africa. Within Israel the rift contains the Jordan River valley. The river meanders south along its course toward the Dead Sea,

Mean annual rainfall

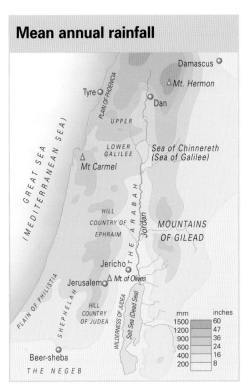

the Jordan River, also tends to be semi-arid, especially in the regions formerly called the kingdoms of Edom and southern Moab.

Transjordan, while located on the east side of the river, contained several kingdoms that had dealings with the Israelites. Running from north to south they were Bashan, Gilead, Ammon, Moab, and Edom. In some periods they were adversaries of the Israelite tribes, while in others they were vassal states of Israel or its enemies. These kingdoms were also a part of the Jordan ecosystem, drawing water from the river and its tributaries and sharing in its climatic shifts. A major trade route, the King's Highway, ran from the Gulf of Aqaba northward through Transjordan.

Each of the regions and geographical features described above figured in the development of the various cultures that inhabited the region that eventually became Israel. They will be referred to repeatedly in the text of this volume, and thus it is advisable to become familiar with them and their places on the map in order to understand the history and social life of the Israelites.

It is also important to note that the names assigned to the land in question change from one period of history to the next. The land originally called Canaan becomes Israel during the settlement and early monarchy periods. When the monarchy divides, the land becomes Israel and Judah. During the exilic period, the land under Assyrian and Babylonian rule was again divided and renamed Judah, Samaria, and Megiddo. These names, which change yet again under Persian, Hellenistic, and Roman rule, reflect the various political entities that governed the land during its long history. There are other, geographical names, such as the **Levant** (the lands from modern Turkey to Egypt that border the Mediterranean Sea), Palestine, and Syria-Palestine, which designate areas of the land regardless of which political entities govern them at any given time.

In modern times, the names Israel and Palestine are associated with a violent and prolonged conflict over land ownership. As a result, care must be taken when applying these names to different areas of the land as it is currently divided. For example, some modern Israelis reject the name Palestine when it is applied to any portion of the land. Conversely, some modern Palestinians deny use of the name Israel to identify the land on which they live. Sensitivity should also be used when applying the names Israel and Palestine when speaking about the land in ancient times. In this text the term Israel will be used in three ways: (a) to designate the particular group of people who settled in the land of Canaan; (b) as a label for the independent political entity established by these people; and (c) as an indicator of the land on which this group lived. The terms Palestine and Syria-Palestine will be used as geographical terms, designating the land that Israel, as well as other peoples, occupied during various periods.

In speaking about the people of Israel, it is necessary to distinguish between the terms Israelite, Israeli, and Jew. The first term, Israelite, designates the ancient peoples that made up the nations of Israel and Judah and who worshipped the national God, Yahweh. The second, Israeli, is the name given to modern inhabitants of the State of Israel. The third term, Jew, is used in the modern day to speak of someone who believes in and practices Judaism. In antiquity, however, the term had a series of meanings that changed over time. Before the second century B.C., the term applied to the ethnic group that inhabited the land of Judah; in other words, to a Judean (*Ant.* 11.173). In the mid-second century, the term began to be applied to those who did not necessarily have an ethnic or geographic connection to Judah, but who believed in the God of the Judeans, Yahweh (2 Macc 9:13; *Ant.* 20.38–39). It is this definition that developed into the one used today.

APPROACH OF THIS BOOK

Before attempting to reconstruct the social world of ancient Israel, a few preliminary questions must be raised. First, why must such an attempt be made at all? Is not the biblical text sufficient to answer any question that may arise on this subject? Would not a careful reading of the text supply all the information anyone would need? Second, is it really necessary to write yet another book to serve as an aid to reading the biblical material?

The biblical text is in fact a storehouse of useful information. It describes many aspects of everyday life in ancient times, written in many cases from the perspective of the people of that period. Questions such as "What did they eat?" "What did they wear?" and "How did they worship?" can be partially answered by simply reading the Scriptures. Having a mass of information and being able to relate it to our own time and situation is not always an easy task, however. Nevertheless, in many cases our interest in ancient times is sparked by our desire to understand the roots of our own culture. Furthermore, in the case of the biblical world, our concerns expand to include how God established a covenant with a particular people and how they lived under that covenant.

The place to begin this study of biblical manners and customs is the environment. Under what conditions did the people live? What physical, economic, and social demands did geography, climate, physical resources, and neighboring groups place on the people? How much of what the culture said about itself can be traced to borrowings from other cultures or to an insulated or prejudiced attitude? In the case of ancient Israel, all of these questions must be raised. The answers may vary according to the particular time period examined and its level of cultural development. Israel did change its social attitudes and customs over the two millennia of its existence before the common era.

With these questions in mind, this volume is designed to be useful to both the layperson and the scholar in their study of the Bible. The biblical material is presented in chronological order, with chapters on each of the major periods of biblical history: ancestral, exodus settlement, monarchic, exilic, postexilic, and intertestamental/New Testament. This arrangement allows the examination of biblical peoples according to stages of their social development, starting with the pastoral nomadic culture of the ancestors, and concluding with the subjugated, urban-based culture of Judea and Samaria in Roman times.

Each chapter provides a basic introduction to the historical and physical settings of the time period and sketches the basic elements of its social world. This is accomplished by examining specific scenes in the biblical text with an eye toward what they can reveal about everyday life in Bible times. Following the every example, or every event in the biblical text as it relates to the social world of ancient Israel. As a result, material has been selected to give a clear picture of everyday events while avoiding repetition, and to provide comparative evidence when the Bible descriptions of events or situations can be complemented or clarified by extrabiblical material.

Bedouin in the Judean wilderness, near Mar Saba.

historical sketch are selected units dealing with specific social customs. These are divided into sub-headings using examples from the biblical text, from modern anthropological data, and from archaeology. The archaeological periods referred to in the text are listed below.

Additional aids in this volume that will allow the reader to locate discussions of particular topics and examples include indexes of subjects, personal names, place names, and biblical passages and extrabiblical sources. Footnotes and citations, other than to the Bible or certain extrabiblical texts, have been omitted. However, at the end of the book are select bibliographies for each chapter, containing the major works consulted in writing the chapter, as well as suggested additional readings.

A word now needs to be said about the choice of material. It will not be possible in this volume to examine every piece of information,

Introduction Review

1. What role does archaeological evidence play in reconstructing the social world of the Bible?
2. How do the geographical characteristics of Bible lands contribute to the development of the social and economic structures in Scripture?
3. Which archaeological periods correspond to the movements of Abraham's children throughout the Bible?
4. How can studying extrabiblical details of life in Bible times contribute to an understanding of Scripture?

1. Ancestral Period

HISTORICAL INTRODUCTION

The book of Genesis portrays Abraham and the other ancestors as pastoral nomads who travel throughout the regions of Canaan and west into Egypt with their flocks and herds. Along the way they engage in the normal pursuits of pastoral nomadic peoples, seeking pasturage and interacting with the settled population. The efforts of historians and the excavations of archaeologists have yet to provide incontrovertible evidence for the historical reality of the ancestors. This leads some scholars to argue that the narratives are literary recreations of tribal history compiled by court employees or priests during the monarchic or the postexilic period to provide the nation of Israel with a claim to Canaan. According to this view, the ancestors were either folk heroes or composites of many tribal leaders from the nation's past.

While the history of this period is hazy, the episodes in the ancestral narratives contain quite convincing and poignant descriptions of itinerant herders and their families. The attention to detail and the importance attached to certain customs suggest that this material is more than a literary attempt to recreate an ancient era. Certainly the text contains some **anachronisms** (elements that fit into a different time period than that of the story). For example, a rival of Abraham is said to be a Philistine king even though the appearance of the Philistines in Canaan is traced to a period some eight hundred years after Abraham's time (Gen 21:32; 26:1; see also Gen 10:14; Judg 3:31). Further, there is evidence in many places of later editing of the text. Genesis 12:6 notes, for example, that "the Canaanites *were* in the land" at the time of Abraham's sojourn, distinguishing this from the writer's or editor's time (see also Gen 13:7). Nevertheless, the narratives give the overwhelming impression of a period when the Hebrews were new to the land and still dependent on the tribe, not the nation, for their identity.

The exact dates of the ancestral period are still uncertain. Ancient cuneiform tablets found at the northern Mesopotamian city of Mari and dated to the eighteenth century B.C.E. do contain descriptions of tribal groups whose activities and interactions with the urban community are surprisingly similar to those of the biblical ancestors. As noted in the introduction, parallel information such as the Mari documents must be used with care when drawing conclusions about the Bible. The similarities between the social conditions and economic pursuits described in Genesis and in the Mari texts, however, make it possible to suggest this time period as the setting for the ancestral stories.

The eighteenth and seventeenth centuries B.C. were a time of flux and development in the cultures of Mesopotamia. Under the leadership of King Hammurabi and his successors, Babylon conquered all of the city-states and kingdoms in the region. The kings of Babylon subjected the inhabitants of the entire Tigris-

Semites pictured in a painting found in the nineteenth-century B.C. Egyptian tomb at Beni-Hasan.

Euphrates valley to centralized rule and placed them under the benefits and constraints of Babylonian law and administration. After 1600 B.C., the Babylonian empire went into decline and was eventually replaced by a group of smaller states, including the Kassites in the south and the Mitanni in north-central Mesopotamia.

During the period from 2000 to 1800 B.C., Egypt experienced internal disorder. This is demonstrated in the epic narrative of Sinuhe, a political refugee who fled to Canaan in order to escape being implicated in the murder of a pharaoh (*ANET*, 18–22). Furthermore, in the eighteenth century B.C., **Hyksos** raiders invaded Egypt, leaving the country little time to deal with its political and economic contacts in Canaan. Instead, the Hyksos set themselves up as pharaohs at Avaris, their Delta region capital. Archaeological and textual evidence suggests that these foreign rulers were of Asiatic, and more specifically Western Semitic or

Amorite, origin. Discovery of scarabs—images of the dung beetle that carried inscriptions on their flat side—amulets, and other Egyptian merchandise in Jericho, Megiddo, and other sites in Canaan indicates active trade between the Hyksos and the Levant during this time.

While Babylon's kings built and lost an empire in Mesopotamia and Egypt suffered external rule and internal problems, the peoples of Canaan enjoyed relative freedom. For a time, until the rise of the New Kingdom (16th cent. B.C.) and its aggressive pharaohs in Egypt, the region of Canaan controlled its own fate and showed only minimal concern for the actions and desires of the superpowers. New peoples, like Abraham's household, entered and settled in the underpopulated regions of Canaan and Transjordan. New opportunities arose for building a life in other lands distant from the conflict in Mesopotamia.

With this historical background in mind, this chapter examines the basic economy and social life of pastoral nomadic peoples in the ancient Near East. Individual aspects of existence are highlighted, and special regard is given to the ancestral narratives, archaeological discoveries, and parallel written materials from Mesopotamia and Egypt.

PHYSICAL APPEARANCE AND FASHION

The ancestors and their families were Semites, the dominant ethnic group in Mesopotamia and much of Syria and Canaan. Semites in the ancient Near East had black hair and a dark complexion, burned even darker by the sun. Since there are few biblical descriptions of individuals' features, the examination of burial remains and of a few surviving paintings, such as those found in the nineteenth-century B.C. Egyptian tomb at Beni-Hasan, provide us with this picture. Dwellings with low roofs that stood not much more than five feet high suggest that Semites were short in stature. Most ate meat only on festive occasions (see Gen 18:7), and diets primarily made up of grains and dairy resulted in the shorter sizes.

In Mesopotamia, men generally wore beards that were carefully curled and squared off at the bottom. The Semites portrayed in the Beni-Hasan painting, however, have short, pointed beards with no mustaches. Both male and female Mesopotamians allowed their hair to grow. Men often wore their hair at shoulder length, holding it in place with a band of cloth or beads around the circumference of the head. Women's coiffures tended to be fairly simple. Their long hair was sometimes bound up with beaded ropes, or intertwined with combs of bone, gold, or silver. On the road or in the pastoral encampment, however, such attention to fashion would not be possible or desirable.

In Mesopotamia and other regions where the climate was dry, the complexion could be easily damaged. As a result, meticulous attention was given to skin care. Both men and women regularly oiled their skin and hair. This gave the body a glossy appearance, and also killed hair lice and other parasites.

By necessity, the clothing of pastoralists was primarily functional, though it was not that much different from the clothing worn by artisans and other commoners. Sturdy leather sandals protected the feet of both sexes. They enclosed the heel and were fastened to the ankle by a thong, which passed between the first and second toes.

Throughout the biblical period, men wore the *kethoneth,* a knee-length, wool tunic with half sleeves. This was held at the waist with a belt. A cloak or mantle (*simlah*) was also worn as protection against the sun and during storms. In the exodus account, it was used to carry bread dough and kneading bowls (Exod 12:34). A girdle (*ezor*), or loincloth, was also worn in later periods (Jer 13:2; Job 12:18). Women wore a similar tunic and robe, which concealed the figure, although some representations in art (as in the Beni-Hasan tomb paintings) portray them with the right shoulder bare. It was customary for those in mourning to wear sackcloth, as described in Isa 58:5 and Jer 6:26.

Genesis 38:14 indicates that Tamar removed her widow's garb and wore a veil to disguise herself as a harlot. The sacred prostitutes of the Canaanite goddess Asherah in 2 Kgs 23:7 were also veiled. From this it might be assumed that Hebrew women in this period generally went unveiled, and that Tamar was following Canaanite custom when she played the role of a veiled harlot. The issue is clouded somewhat by the action of Rebekah in Gen 24:65. In this passage she dons her veil in expectation of meeting her future husband Isaac for the first time. Her act of modesty is more in line with Mesopotamian custom. This is reinforced by the Middle Assyrian law code dated to ca. 1100 B.C. that required harlots to appear unveiled in public on pain of death (#40; *ANET,* 183).

Jewelry, then as now, was a common

> *She put off her widow's garments, put on a veil, wrapped herself up, and sat down at the entrance of Enaim, which is on the road to Timnah. She saw that Shelah was grown up, yet she had not been given to him in marriage.*
>
> *—Gen 38:14*

adornment for both men and women. In Genesis 24, Abraham's servant gave Rebekah a nose ring and arm bracelets, as well as unspecified ornaments of gold and silver as bridal presents (v. 47). Joseph, rising to his position as advisor to the pharaoh, was given a gold chain to wear around his neck and a signet ring as a symbol of his power and authority (Gen 41:42). After the escape from Egypt, Aaron fashioned a golden calf for the people out of their earrings (Exod 32:2–3).

CULTURAL ISSUES FACED BY IMMIGRANTS

The ancestors first appear in Genesis as inhabitants of Ur of the Chaldees in southern Mesopotamia. The designation "Chaldees" is an example of an anachronism, since the Chaldean people do not appear in Mesopotamian history until after 1000 B.C. Abraham, or Abram as he is originally known, and his father Terah plan a move to Canaan, but they stop in Haran, a city that is located on the Balikh River, which flows into the upper reaches of the Euphrates. There they settle for a while, and Terah dies (Gen 11:30–32). Since his origins were in Mesopotamia, that was the seat of Abram's cultural heritage. During this period of his life, he undoubtedly worshipped Mesopotamian gods (see Josh 24:14), and he was intimately familiar with Mesopotamian law and social customs.

Abraham's migration

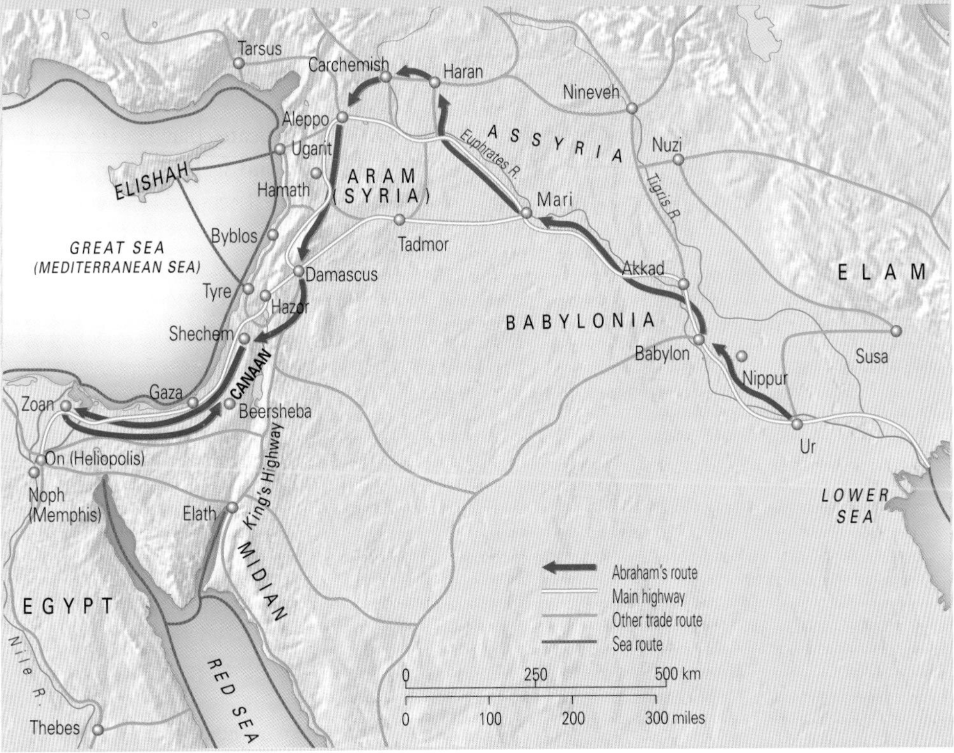

Abram's household faces a new challenge, however, when he leads them from Haran and immigrates to Canaan (Gen 12:1–4). From this point on, they are portrayed in the text as moving from campsite to campsite and from pasturage to pasturage while living in goat-hair tents. According to the biblical narrative, Abram has once again left his home, but this time he emigrates for theological reasons— God instructs him to go to a land that he will show him. The change of his name from "Abram" to "Abraham" (Gen 17:5) is designed to emphasize his new status and the covenant with his God. Whatever the reason for Abraham's departure from Haran, however, the basic psychology of being an immigrant, a stranger in a foreign land, affects nearly all of his and the other ancestors' actions during this period of Israel's history.

In the eighteenth century B.C., the northern Mesopotamian city of Haran was controlled by the king of Mari. The journey to Canaan covered several hundred miles. Abraham's route, although not described in the biblical text, probably followed the international trade highway from Mesopotamia, through Damascus and Hazor, and then down the coast of Canaan to Egypt. The southern coastal portion of this route was known as the "Way of the Sea," or Via Maris.

In preparing for his trek, he had to equip his group for survival as new immigrants in the new land. What was required of Abraham and his family was an adjustment of lifestyle from a settled, urban existence to the frequent travel of pastoral nomads. Their new world consisted of various encampments, water sources, grazing areas, and sometimes tense encounters with local villagers. As a result, they were also faced with a change in perspective about themselves and the peoples with whom they had contact. They had to accept the shift from being "part of the group" to being "outsiders."

There were undoubtedly language problems, although they are rarely mentioned in the

> *No longer shall your name be Abram, but your name shall be Abraham; for I have made you the ancestor of a multitude of nations.*
> —Gen 17:5

narratives; Gen 42:23 remarks that, in Egypt, Joseph spoke with his brothers through an interpreter. Even when the newcomers had learned the local dialect, their accent would have marked them as strangers. Over the years, they had to depend upon their own skills as herdsmen and on the produce of their flocks and herds. Life was dominated by the search for forage and water for sheep and goats and by the attempt to draw as little hostile attention to their group as possible. Abraham's ability to interact as an intermediary with the local chieftains and village elders was therefore essential to the acceptance of his household into the land and its ultimate survival (see Gen 21:22–34).

The process of walking a social and economic tightrope caused some tensions between Abraham's immigrant group and the settled communities. A newly arrived household would place additional strain on the natural resources of the land. As a result, the attempt by immigrants to acclimate themselves to the new social and economic environment required a willingness to operate within the rules set by the people who already lived there. This could well explain why so much attention is given in the biblical text to negotiations between the ancestors and the local leaders (see Gen 23).

Another difficulty faced by every immigrant group is legal helplessness. Immigrants are seldom familiar with the laws of the land, and they are often denied the legal protection which is guaranteed to citizens. This can lead to the use of deception as a defense mechanism. Assuming that survival of the group took priority over providing a potential enemy with all the facts, the morality of such a deception must not have presented a problem for the ancestors.

Wife-Sister Stratagem

Shortly after their arrival in Canaan, Abraham and Sarah (still bearing the names Abram and Sarai at that point in the narrative) are forced

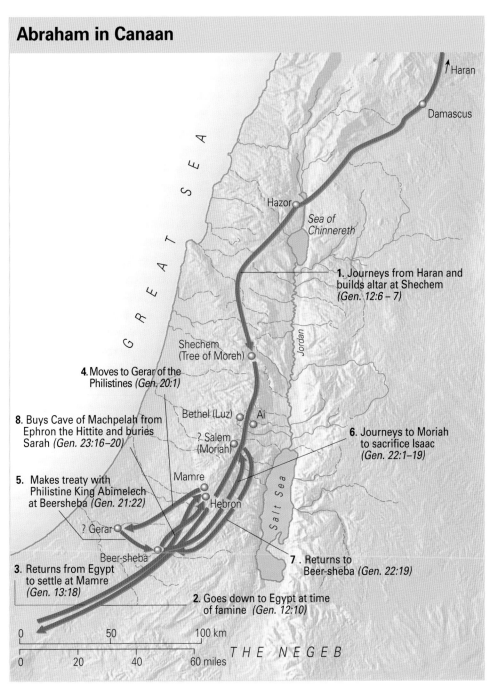

Abraham in Canaan

Haran

Damascus

Hazor

Sea of Chinnereth

1. Journeys from Haran and builds altar at Shechem *(Gen. 12:6 – 7)*

G R E A T   *S E A*

Jordan

Shechem (Tree of Moreh)

4. Moves to Gerar of the Philistines *(Gen. 20:1)*

Bethel (Luz)   Ai

8. Buys Cave of Machpelah from Ephron the Hittite and buries Sarah *(Gen. 23:16–20)*

? Salem (Moriah)

6. Journeys to Moriah to sacrifice Isaac *(Gen. 22:1–19)*

Mamre

5. Makes treaty with Philistine King Abimelech at Beersheba *(Gen. 21:22)*

Hebron

Salt Sea

? Gerar

Beer-sheba

3. Returns from Egypt to settle at Mamre *(Gen. 13:18)*

7. Returns to Beer-sheba *(Gen. 22:19)*

2. Goes down to Egypt at time of famine *(Gen. 12:10)*

| 0 | | 50 | | 100 km |
| 0 | 20 | 40 | 60 miles |

T H E   N E G E B

29

to go to Egypt to escape a famine (Gen 12:10). Since they are recent arrivals in Canaan, it would be difficult to obtain food from the economically stressed local inhabitants. This meant a further trek to Egypt, where food could be purchased and transients were tolerated and occasionally used as temporary sources of cheap labor.

In addition to his own life, Abraham's other irreplaceable asset is his wife. As they enter Egypt, he fears that she may be taken from him and added to the pharaoh's harem. He is also afraid that the Egyptian king may consider killing him as a means to possessing her. Therefore, Abraham devises a scheme in which Sarah claims to be his sister instead of his wife (Gen 20:12 indicates that she is the daughter of his father, but not his mother). This removes him from personal danger; and when she is taken into the pharaoh's harem, results in the enrichment of Abraham's household.

Thus, while the story has as an underlying theme a contest between the god/king of Egypt and Abraham's God, Yahweh, it also contains elements of immigrant psychology. This is also seen in the other two examples of the wife-sister motif (Gen 20 and 26). In these instances, the threatening authority figure is Abimelech of Gerar. As in the previous case, he is taken in by the deception. He adds significantly to the household and herds of his visitor (first Abraham and later Isaac), and, like the pharaoh in Gen 12, he eventually returns the patriarch's wife unharmed, after God intervenes.

The Purchase of Machpelah

Another example in which Abraham found himself, as an immigrant, constrained to obey the legal traditions of the people of Canaan is contained in the story of his purchase of the cave of Machpelah as a burial site for Sarah (Gen 23). His encampment at that time is near the city of Hebron in southern Canaan. In

> *And Sarah died at Kiriath-arba (that is, Hebron) in the land of Canaan; and Abraham went in to mourn for Sarah and to weep for her.*
> —Gen 23:2

order to make the purchase, Abraham goes to Hebron and engages in customary procedures, all of which favor the settled community over newly-arrived immigrants. First, he goes to the city gate, where much of the city's business and legal activities are conducted. Here he requests the elders to serve as witnesses and as advocates for him (a non-citizen) in his attempt to purchase the cave.

The owner, Ephron the Hittite, and Abraham then engage in a legal dialogue bargaining over the price and the exact parcel to be purchased. Abraham originally only wanted the cave, but eventually he is also forced to pay for an adjoining field and its trees.

The dialogue is interesting and almost comical. Ephron first offers the cave to Abraham as a gift. This gambit is designed to force the buyer into being equally gracious by asking the owner to set his own price. Once this has been done, all that remains is for Abraham to count out the four hundred shekels of silver, an exorbitantly high price (compared to Jacob's purchase of land in Gen 33:19), and to have the transaction duly witnessed by the elders.

Two pieces of information regarding this purchase are worth noting. To begin with, this is the first piece of land owned outright by a Hebrew. God had promised the land of Canaan to Abraham and his descendants, but now the patriarch had obtained legal title to a portion of it. This claim is then extended in later periods to the entire region. Second, it is rather unusual for land to be sold outright in this manner. Land was considered sacred, entrusted by a god or gods to the ruler, and he, in turn, entrusted it to individuals. In some cases its sale could even be considered a crime against the heirs of the owner (see Naboth's reaction to King Ahab's request to purchase his vineyard during the monarchic period in 1 Kgs 21:3). One way in which this customary restriction was sometimes avoided was by having the purchaser adopted into the family of the owner, a practice found in the fifteenth-century B.C. texts from the eastern Mesopotamian city of Nuzi.

That Ephron is willing to make this sale may be due to the fact that Abraham specifically wishes to use it for his wife's burial and not as a base of operations that could threaten the local people or their economy. An even more telling explanation for the sale may be found in the title given to Abraham by the city elders, "a mighty prince among us" (Gen 23:6). Rather than being a potential threat to the peace of the area like other semi-nomadic groups, Abraham may be seen as an asset. This does not, however, prevent his being taken advantage of in the bargaining.

The Rape of Dinah

Another example of the tensions between nomadic groups and the settled population occurs in Gen 34. This episode describes a request by a local prince to marry Jacob's daughter, Dinah. Jacob had settled his household near the city of Shechem. He purchased a piece of land as a base of operations for his herds, and appeared to be planning to settle down permanently. This process of sedentarization occurred among pastoralists occasionally, especially those who were wealthy and had holdings both among the tribes and in towns.

> Now Dinah the daughter of Leah, whom she had borne to Jacob, went out to visit the women of the region. When Shechem son of Hamor the Hivite, prince of the region, saw her, he seized her and lay with her by force.
> —Gen 34:1–2

> Will not their livestock, their property, and all their animals be ours? Only let us agree with them, and they will live among us.
> —Gen 34: 23

Jacob's daughter, perhaps not showing the usual caution expected of tribal women, leaves the encampment and is raped by the son of Hamor, the king of Shechem. A schoolboy's exercise tablet, written inexpertly in Sumerian and dating to the period of the eighteenth century B.C., provides a parallel to this case. According to this set of legal statements, an unbetrothed virgin could be obtained as a wife through forcible sexual relations. The woman's parents could arrange the marriage if the rapist declared, "I will marry you" (Roth, 44; #7). The woman he had abused had no say in the matter. In the Genesis account, the king's son requests that his father negotiate a marriage contract with Jacob's household. He speaks with Jacob's sons, who state that the entire male population of Shechem has to conform to their tribal custom of circumcision before the marriage can take place.

The request for such a drastic act can be seen as an attempt on the part of the brothers to discourage this marriage. It also signals the difference in social custom and lifestyle between the two peoples. Hamor and his son try to convince their fellow citizenry to accept the Hebrews' terms; like the elders of Hebron (Gen 23:6), they cite the wealth of the pastoral group and the resulting benefits this would have for the city of Shechem. Their argument is persuasive, and the citizens of Shechem agree to submit to the demand that they be circumcised.

Having undergone this painful procedure, the men of Shechem are then easy prey for a raid by Jacob's sons three days later. A massacre ensues, and the women and children are taken away as slaves by the Hebrews. Raids of

Ancient burial caves in the Carmel range near Haifa, Israel.

this type were not uncommon, although they seldom resulted in the total annihilation of a city's population. Usually they only involved the stealing of animals or women (see the capture of the dancers of Shiloh during the settlement period in Judg 21:19–23).

The justification given for this act is to obtain revenge on Shechem for the rape of Dinah (Gen 34:31). Unfortunately, it also magnifies Jacob's fear that the stigma of being labeled "immigrants" would once more haunt the group (Gen 34:30). An act such as this could once again arouse suspicions and hostilities that had been dormant for years. The story thus demonstrates underlying antagonism between settled and nomadic groups that threatened to disrupt their peaceful coexistence.

Burial Customs

Nomadic groups utilized a variety of burial types in this period. These included rock cairns, in which the body was interred within a mound of stones along the line of march, as in the case of Rachel's death (Gen 35:19–20). Similarly, some were buried near distinctive landmarks or trees, which were then given a new name to mark the event (see the burial of Deborah, Rebekah's nurse, under an oak near Bethel in Gen 35:8).

Abraham's actual purchase of a cave at Machpelah initiated its intended use for both primary and secondary burial. In **primary burial** the deceased was entombed permanently in one place, whereas in **secondary burial,** a corpse was placed in a tomb only until its flesh decomposed. After decomposition, the bones from this type of burial were gathered to the side or rear of the cave, or placed in **ossuaries** (jars for the storage of bones) along with any possessions that were left with the bodies. This method of burial created space for the bodies of those who died in subsequent generations, whose bones were in turn moved to accommodate subsequent burials. Archaeologists have discovered many tombs in this region dated to the Late Bronze period (1500–1200 B.C.) in which burial space was utilized over and over.

Upon his death, Abraham was "gathered to his people" and buried in the cave at Machpelah (Gen 25:8–10). Similarly, Isaac and Jacob were "gathered to their people" and buried in the family tomb (35:29; 47:30; 49:29, 33). This expression speaks to the significance of secondary burials. That one family member after another was laid to rest in the same place underscored the continued relationship between the dead and the living members of a family. The latter were responsible for maintaining this heritage through protection of the family holdings. This responsibility extended to all generations in a family, no matter how far removed from the actual death. While the bones of Joseph spent more than four hundred years in Egypt, they nevertheless traveled with the Israelites in the Exodus to Canaan, and were later buried at Shechem (Exod 13:19; Josh 24:32).

HERDING PRACTICES

Pastoral nomadism of the sort depicted in the ancestral narratives incorporates two types of nomadic activity. **Semi-nomadic pastoralism,** distinguished by almost constant herding activity, is marked by periodic change of pastures (see Gen 13:5–12; 21:25–34; 26:17–33). One reality of this type of pastoral life is that occasionally a group's herd becomes too large for its grazing area. In this instance, the herd must be partially sold off or the group must divide, with each segment seeking pasturage in a different area. In Gen 13, Abraham's herds significantly increased during his stay in Egypt. When he and his nephew Lot return to Canaan, they discover that the region will not support their entire herd. As a result, the herdsmen are at the point of coming to blows. They resolve the quarrel by agreeing that Lot will choose an area in which his portion of the herds will graze, and Abraham will then choose another.

A Bedouin family in their tent in Israel today.

The ancestral narratives also contain evidence of **transhumance,** in which the majority of the population leads a sedentary life and is occupied primarily with agriculture. Rather than dividing a group's herds, as often becomes necessary in semi-nomadic pastoralism, select members of a family become herdsmen and tend the family's livestock on pastures both near and far from their settlement. For instance, in Gen 37, Jacob's sons take their father's herds north from Hebron to Dothan. Jacob maintains a base camp from which his sons take the herds to seek pasturage in the hill country to the north; they return when the seasons change. That Jacob sends Joseph off in search of his brothers may reflect a delay in their return or an interruption of the normal communications through travelers or other herdsmen.

The particular combination of nomadic and agricultural activities depicted in the ancestral narratives allowed for greater flexibility in herd and land management. The area available for grazing and watering herds was broadened and the means of supporting the family were diversified. Moreover, the two activities complemented one another. The practice of allowing herds of cattle, sheep, and goats to graze in harvested fields was very common in ancient times. It provided good forage for the animals and fertilized the field in preparation for the next planting season. Additionally, if the herding cycle corresponded properly to the agricultural one, herdsmen were available to help with plowing, planting and harvesting. The dependence of both herding and farming on water, however, made for a continually unstable existence in mainly arid Canaan.

Water Rights

For a herding group to survive, access to water is essential. Sheep and goats cannot go for more than three or four days without water. Because of this, knowledge of wells, springs, and streams is among the most valuable and guarded pieces of tribal information. This knowledge and the right to use water resources are shared only among close kin and allied groups. An example of the importance that water held for pastoralists, and the cooperation necessitated by a common dependence on water sources, is found in Gen 29. Several groups of herdsmen have gathered around a well near Haran. The mouth of the well is covered by a large stone, and it is only when all the herdsmen have gathered their flocks at the well that they, working together, roll the stone away and water their animals. When Jacob arrives at the well, it is not yet the proper time of day for opening it (Gen 29:8; see also 24:11). He suggests, however, that rather than waiting until evening, it is best to water the flocks already at the well. As Rachel, his kinswoman, approaches, he single-handedly removes the large stone from the mouth of the well, enabling the young shepherdess to immediately water her flocks and run home with news of Jacob's arrival.

Although Gen 29 does not give a reason for using a stone so large it can be moved only by a group of herdsmen, other texts that tell of disputes over water rights suggest that it may have been used to ensure fair distribution of water amongst those using wells (see Gen 13:7–10; 26:19–21). An accusation that one herder was taking more than his fair share of water might have led to armed conflict. The use of force by rival shepherds is demonstrated in Exod 2:16–17, just prior to the exodus, when shepherds drive Jethro's daughters away from a well. Moses intervenes, serving as a male representative for their herding group, so that their animals can be watered.

In Gen 20 and 26, the ancestors have to negotiate with Abimelech, the king of Gerar, for the right to use wells in his region. They obtain that right as a result of the wife-sister deception; but this incident does not prevent the eventual development of friction between the herders and the people of Gerar, who also

Samaritan women carrying water.

ing a blessing (Gen 14:18); Abraham orders Sarah to prepare a meal consisting of bread made in the form of cakes, milk and curds, and roasted calf for his three visitors (Gen 18:6–8); Jacob offers a red lentil soup to his brother Esau in exchange for his birthright (Gen 25:34); and freshly killed game is apparently a favorite dish of Isaac's (Gen 27:7). This diet was spiced with a variety of fruits and nuts, considered such a delicacy that they were offered along with myrrh and balm as presents to the pharaoh's representative in Gen 43:11.

Archaeology sheds some light on the foodstuffs consumed by people in biblical times. Using new filtration methods, including botanical analysis, archaeologists have discovered the contents of ancient granaries from the settlement and monarchic periods. These underground silos contain the carbonized remains of the agricultural produce of that time, including wheat, barley, and date and grape seeds.

The cuneiform documents found at the site of ancient Nippur and dated to 1757 B.C. during the reign of Hammurabi contain menus of the food prepared for the king and his court. These include elaborate recipes for cooking stews containing various meats, leeks, and herbs like garlic and mint. The menu contained in a royal text from ancient Mari that dates to this same time period describes vast quantities of breads and cakes, bowls of dates, and a variety of concoctions made from chickpeas, semolina flour and date syrup. Few of these items would have been found on the menu of the pastoral nomadic tribesmen who inhabited the rural districts of Mesopotamia. These people, like Abraham's household, lived off their herds and the milk and meat of the sheep and goats that they tended.

need the water for their own herds and fields. Gradually, as the men of Gerar confiscate his wells, Isaac and his herds are driven further south toward Beer-sheba. Once they leave the immediate region of Gerar, however, they are left alone, and the wells that they subsequently dig are theirs to name and use.

What this narrative tells us is that there were specific zones of pasturage designated for use by urban communities. Within these zones, outsiders were only grudgingly given water rights and grazing resources. When the leaders of a city or village felt that the pastoral nomads were threatening the welfare of their economy, it was almost certain that the newcomers would be forced to leave.

FOOD PREPARATION AND DIET

The ancestral narratives provide only occasional references to food and food preparation: Melchizedek, king of Salem, offers Abraham bread and wine in welcoming him and offer-

Since bread was a staple of life for all peoples in the ancient Near East, seasonal agriculture was sometimes practiced by pastoralists; thus Isaac "sowed . . . and . . . reaped a hundredfold" in Gerar in Gen 26:12. For the most part,

> *Isaac sowed seed in that land, and in the same year reaped a hundredfold. The LORD blessed him, . . .*
> —Gen 26:12

however, grain had to be purchased from villages along the migration route. Because the pastoralists were often on the move, permanent ovens to bake their bread would have been impractical. Therefore, like their modern descendants, ancient nomadic peoples baked their bread in small, thin cakes on a heated stone or a metal griddle.

The diet of ancient, as well as modern, pastoralists primarily consisted of various breads, milk and curds, and fruits and nuts gathered along the line of march or purchased from villagers. The consumption of meat, since it involved reducing the size of the herd, occurred for the most part only on important occasions, such as the arrival of visitors. Abraham demonstrated his generosity by slaughtering one of his animals. A feast like the one Abraham prepared for his guests in Gen 18 can therefore be compared to a banquet described in a text from the ancient seaport of Ugarit (*ANET*, 146; dated to ca. 1400–1200 B.C.). In this epic poem, the legendary King Keret orders his wife Hurriya to have "a lamb from the flock" slaughtered to feed his guests.

The physical effects of a diet heavy in carbohydrates and disrupted by the periods of famine common to this region (Gen 12:10 and 26:1) would have caused some health problems for the people. It can be speculated that some of the difficulties and illnesses caused by a poor or unbalanced diet may have been offset by eating figs and dates, and using cooking oil made from dates and olives.

MARRIAGE CUSTOMS

Marriage customs among pastoral nomadic groups were often designed to maintain social continuity as well as to perpetuate the group. As a result, marriages were arranged by the father or other male kin to benefit the individual family (Gen 24:1–9; 28:1–5; 29:1–30). This means that marriage with non-nomadic peoples or with people outside the kinship group was generally discouraged (26:34–35; 27:46; 28:6–9; 34:14). Sometimes prospective brides and grooms never met before the wedding (24:63–7). Although no minimum age for marriage is stipulated in the biblical text, girls were required to remain virgins prior to marriage and were usually married as soon as they reached puberty (24:16). Boys often waited until they received their inheritance or earned enough to establish their own household (24:1).

Marriage within the Group

Marriage customs are highlighted in the biblical text on several occasions. The first instance recounts Abraham's insistence (in Gen 24:2–9) that his servant return to Haran to arrange a bride for Isaac. The servant is equipped with a suitable array of gifts for the bride's family, and journeys back to Mesopotamia using camels to carry his goods. Given that camels were expensive and little-used beasts of burden in the period before 1200 B.C., their inclusion in Gen 24 is either anachronistic, an assertion of Abraham's wealth, or both.

When he arrives in the vicinity of Haran, the servant goes to the most likely place to view the local girls, the well. At least twice a day the women of the villages and surrounding

> *Let the girl to whom I shall say, "Please offer your jar that I may drink," and who shall say, "Drink, and I will water your camels"—let her be the one whom you have appointed for your servant Isaac. By this I shall know that you have shown steadfast love to my master.*
> —Gen 24:14

Bedouin women cook unleavened bread on a traditional oven.

encampments come here to obtain water for cooking and washing purposes or to water their animals. The servant shows his knowledge of everyday activity by seeking a suitable bride for his master's son in this place.

The test that the servant uses to find a proper wife for Isaac is a signal to the reader of the values expected of an ideal wife in this society. His plan is to let the bride demonstrate her wisdom by offering both him and his camels a drink. Only a truly wise woman would show concern for another person's animals. If she knows the value of property prior to marriage, it can be expected that she will be a suitable mistress of his master's household afterwards (see also Prov 31:10–31). This dual concern for hospitality and property is so important that the narrative repeats the description of the test three times for emphasis.

The actual negotiations (Gen 24:34–50) that lead to Rebekah becoming Isaac's wife are conducted by the servant with her brother Laban and her father Bethuel. Her father, who is barely mentioned, plays a secondary role in this scene. Laban is quite impressed by the wealth of the servant's gifts to Rebekah, and certainly plans to get the best price he can for her. The servant, however, demonstrates his own shrewdness by refusing to accept the hospitality of Laban's house before beginning the negotiations. He does not wish to be unfavorably obligated to Laban, and thus it is only after the bargain is struck that he willingly enters the house and eats a meal (24:33).

While Rebekah has no direct role in the negotiations that will send her from her family and home forever, she is consulted before the departure (24:57–59). Undoubtedly, Laban hoped to detain the servant and thus obtain even more gifts. It is Rebekah's willingness to leave that allows the servant to depart graciously without further delay or expense. This may be evidence of the change in loyalties of a woman who must now be concerned with the wealth of her new household.

The high value placed on **endogamy,** marriage within the kinship or social group, motivates Jacob's journey to Haran to obtain his bride. His brother Esau had broken with custom and married two "Hittite" girls. This disappointed his parents (Gen 26:34–35). Esau's **exogamy,** marriage outside the kinship or social group, also fits into a literary and theological pattern designed to show how Esau disqualified himself as Isaac's heir. Jacob, on the other hand, is shown to be the upholder of tradition and thus a proper heir when he obediently travels to Paddan-aram and asks Laban for one of his daughters as his wife (Gen 27:46—28:5).

Just as Abraham's servant finds Rebekah at a well, so Jacob meets Rachel at a well. However, in Jacob's case, it is the potential groom who demonstrates his worthiness by removing the stone from the top of the well and watering her sheep (Gen 29:1–10). This shows his physical strength as well as his wisdom as a herdsman. Although it is customary for all of the herdsmen to be present before the animals are watered, there is a point when custom must be superseded by common sense so that the animals do not become dehydrated, and the day of grazing is not wasted.

Jacob's introduction to Laban is cordial enough, but it swiftly becomes evident to the crafty Laban that Jacob is only a poor relation. As a result, Jacob has to assume the role of an itinerant herdsman in the surplus labor pool of young men who contract themselves to work for wealthy livestock owners. Jacob agrees to serve Laban for seven years, and Laban agrees to count the wages due to Jacob toward the **dowry** (money or its equivalent that is contributed to the bride's personal wealth or to her family's, in this case by the suitor or his family) for his daughter Rachel. Laban's deception, replacing Rachel with her sister Leah on the wedding night, requires Jacob to make another contract with Laban if he still wishes to marry his intended bride. The new contract provides Laban with an additional seven years of labor from his nephew and son-in-law. Yet another seven years are

expended as Jacob agrees to continue to tend Laban's flocks for a percentage of the herd. It is this last contract that enables Jacob to build up his own fortunes.

Such labor contracts for herdsmen, although not ones involving the unusual wages paid in the biblical narrative, have been found among the business documents unearthed in the remains of the second millennium Mesopotamian cities of Larsa and Nuzi. In these contracts, herdsmen agreed with livestock owners to tend flocks in return for a portion of the herd's offspring, wool, and dairy products. Often the contracts required herdsmen to pay for animals that were lost or became diseased, although losses due to attacks by wild animals were not the responsibility of the herder.

Importance of an Heir

Aside from the possible monetary gain acquired by marriage into a rich or influential family, the primary purpose of a marriage in biblical times was to produce an heir. Each cycle of stories about the major ancestors shows the common theme of obtaining a male heir for the family and for the covenant with God. Long periods of infertility heighten the narrative's suspense. In one such instance, Rebekah finally gives birth to twins (Gen 25:21), and a contest for supremacy ensues between her sons Jacob and Esau. This is resolved when the younger twin, Jacob, obtains a blessing and the heirship from his father by means of a deception. The narrative justifies his actions by pointing out that Esau is "a skillful hunter, a man of the field," and apparently less concerned with the family's flocks (Gen 25:27). On the other hand, the description of Jacob is of a "quiet man, living in tents." The Hebrew word *tām,* generally translated "quiet," can mean "complete" or "blameless" as it does in Job 1:8 and 2:3. The qualities of a blameless man are extolled throughout wisdom literature (Prov 2:7; 13:6; 29:10). In

These figurines may have been used as votive offerings.

> Then she said, "Here is my maid Bilhah; go in to her, that she may bear upon my knees and that I too may have children through her."
> —Gen 30:3

addition, Jacob shows reverence for his parents by obeying their request that he adhere to the tribal marriage custom of endogamy (Gen 28:6–7).

There are accounts in the biblical text of daughters who claim inheritance rights (Gen 31:14–16; Num 27:1–11). Laban's daughters, Leah and Rachel, lament that in binding their husband Jacob to contract after contract, their father is refusing to pay his share of their dowries. Instead Laban uses both the labor of their husband Jacob and their dowries toward his own profit. As the sisters understand it, God has rectified this situation by causing Laban's flocks to dwindle while Jacob's prosper. It is the property that God has taken from their father and given to their husband that Leah and Rachel count as their inheritance (Gen 31:14–16). Additionally, Rachel steals her father's household gods (**teraphim;** vv. 19, 33–35). These gods were to be passed from a father to his heir along with paternal authority

as head of the family. By stealing them, Rachel attempts to further correct the wrong she feels her father has done to her and her family.

On occasion, when the wife of a patriarch is unable to produce a child, concubines (secondary wives) or slave women are used as surrogate mothers, and their children are then claimed by the primary wife. This is the case with Hagar, the maid of Sarah and mother of Ishmael (Gen 16:2–4). Similarly, in Gen 30:3, Rachel's maid Bilhah bears children to Jacob on Rachel's knees to create the legal fiction that Rachel has given birth to them herself. Subsequently, both Sarah and Rachel bear children of their own.

Another example of marriage customs that also centers on the production of an heir appears in Gen 38. In this passage, Judah, one of Jacob's sons, marries and fathers three sons. He arranges a marriage for his oldest son, Er, to a girl named Tamar. Er dies before fathering a son, and thus the law of **levirate marriage** comes into play (see Deut 25:5–6). According to this tradition, if the dead man has no heir, it becomes the obligation of his brother or closest male kin to marry, or at least impregnate, the widow. The male child born of this union will then be the legal heir of the dead man.

> When brothers reside together, and one of them dies and has no sin, the wife of the deceased shall not be married outside the family to a stranger. Her husband's brother shall go in to her, taking her in marriage, and performing the duty of a husband's brother to her, . . .
> —Deut 25:5

39

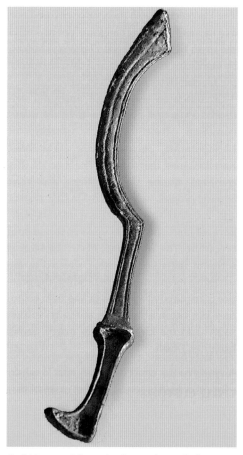

A sickle sword from the Canaanite period, designed to cut through body armor.

In Gen 18, Abraham is visited by three "men" as he sits at the door of his tent "in the heat of the day" (v. 1). The text does not say at first that these visitors are from God. Nevertheless Abraham acts according to custom by rushing out, as he did, to meet this group of strangers in order to offer them the hospitality of his encampment. In fact, his welcoming statement sounds like a formula:

My lord, if I find favor with you, do not pass by your servant. Let a little water be brought, and wash your feet, and rest yourselves under the tree. Let me bring a little bread, that you may refresh yourselves, and after that you may pass on—since you have come to your servant. (vv. 3–5; NRSV)

Each of these comforts would have been welcome to the travelers, and there is a note of respect in Abraham's address that would please anyone's ear.

The visitors' acceptance of Abraham's hospitality then obligates them to express good wishes to him and his family. Their blessings include the prediction that Sarah will bear a child within a year. Later, when they (vv. 22–32) debate the destruction of Sodom and Gomorrah, the "men's" prior acceptance of Abraham's food and of his attention seems to put the patriarch on a more equal footing with God. Men who eat together in peace and enjoy each other's hospitality can thus be said to be equals.

Genesis 19 records the visit of the angels to Sodom. In this text it is Lot, Abraham's nephew, who is sitting in the gate of the city, the physical and legal equivalent of the doorway of Abraham's tent. He also goes out to meet the visitors as they approach, and makes a statement similar to that of his uncle: "Please, my lords, turn aside to your servant's house and spend the night, and wash your feet; then you can rise early and go on your way" (v. 2).

Once they have eaten with him, Lot is forced to demonstrate just how seriously the obligations of hospitality are taken. During the night, all the men of Sodom come to his door and demand that the two visitors be sent out to them to be examined and possibly even sexually assaulted (Gen 19:4). Lot's sense of duty to protect his guests is so strong, however, that he offers instead to send out his two virgin daughters to satisfy the mob's appetite for violence. The daughters are technically his property, and he can dispose of them as he wishes, but this will involve both a financial and a personal sacrifice. He is saved from taking this action when the angels blind the crowd, and his family is able to escape.

Execution of Justice

In pastoral nomadic groups, the father is the absolute master of his own family and has complete legal control over its members. He arranges marriages, conducts all business transactions, and serves as the sole source of justice in legal matters involving his family. The principle of *pater familias,* in which the father has the power of life and death over his household, thus applies.

One example of this principle has already been mentioned. When Judah discovers that Tamar is pregnant and apparently guilty of adultery (Gen 38:24), he immediately, without trial, orders her to be burned. This is his right as head of the household.

The father's full legal control is also portrayed in the account of Hagar's flight (Gen 16:5–6). In this text, Sarah complains of verbal abuse that she has received from her servant Hagar after Abraham impregnates her. Hagar has been used as a surrogate mother in an attempt to produce an heir, but now the servant has become contemptuous of her barren mistress. Abraham settles the matter by simply turning all punishment of the insolent servant over to Sarah.

WEAPONS AND WARFARE

Since they had limited resources and manpower, war as practiced by the ancestors generally took the form of raids or small-scale battles. The instances in which combat are mentioned in the text point to the use of surprise attacks, such as the raid of Shechem by Jacob's sons in Gen 34:25, or night assaults, such as Abraham's rescue mission in Gen 14:15. Abraham is able to muster the largest group of men assembled by any of the ancestors. He divides his forces and attacks the camp of Chedorlaomer and his allies with 318 "trained men, born in his house" (v. 14).

The raid on Shechem contains the only specific mention of weapons in the ancestral narratives. The sons of Jacob take swords and kill the male inhabitants of that city. The swords used during the ancestral period had short sickle-shaped blades that were half the size of their hilts, or handles. This gave the sword an axe-like appearance. Sickle-shaped swords like those described in Gen 34:25 have been found in the nineteenth-century B.C. stratum of the excavations at Shechem. Such swords probably evolved during the second half of the third millennium from the duck-billed war axe, which was the most common weapon of that time. Axes of this type, with curved hilts and a narrow-edged blade, were designed as an effective armor-piercing instrument. They are depicted in the hands of Semitic caravanners in the Egyptian Beni-Hasan tomb paintings from the nineteenth century B.C.

Ancestral Period Review

1. How did the ancestors dress?
2. What sorts of problems did the ancestors face as they migrated to and in Canaan?
3. What is the difference between semi-nomadic pastoralism and transhumance? What nomadic methods did the ancestors practice?
4. What did the ancestors and their households eat?
5. Describe the marriage practices of the ancestors.
6. Who inherited family property and customs during the ancestral period? Why was an heir important?
7. In what ways did the ancestors worship God? How were these similar or different from other groups' religious practices?
8. How did the ancestors settle legal matters?
9. What weapons did the ancestors use in battle?

2. Exodus-Settlement Period

HISTORICAL INTRODUCTION

The second major historical era described in the biblical text is the period of the exodus and settlement. It includes the escape from Egypt, the wilderness wanderings, the conquest, and the period of the judges. Throughout this time manners and customs change as the Israelites make the transition from pastoral nomadic tribes to a settled existence in the village culture of Canaan.

Israel was not alone in its exodus and resettlement during this period. The second millennium saw mass migrations of peoples throughout the ancient Near East. Among the tribal groups that relocated themselves early in the millennium (ca. 2000–1500 B.C.) were the Amorites (who would eventually rule Assyria) and the Hurrians and various Indo-European groups that in time formed nation states like Mitanni and Hatti.

The social factors that contributed to the mass migrations of people in the second half of the second millennium are many. As city-states developed throughout the Near East, and their populations were put under tighter economic control in order to support centralized administrations, debt and slavery became serious problems. The poor were no longer allowed to survive on whatever land they could work; now land fell under the control of tribal chiefs who were quickly becoming rulers over larger and larger areas. Moreover, emerging city-states did not often codify laws to protect their citizenry, who were at the whim of those in power. These circumstances led peoples throughout the Near East to seek out lands still uncontrolled by larger powers.

By the second half of the millennium (ca. 1500–1200 B.C.), groups of people who did not wish to live under the control of these emerging city-states began another set of mass migrations throughout Canaan and adjoining regions. Israel, lacking the strength to capture walled cities, settled primarily in the hill country of central Canaan. Like the other groups migrating during this period, Israel had to adjust to life within the Canaanite cultural sphere.

To make sense of Israel's adjustment, archaeological evidence must be considered. Periods of Syro-Palestinian archaeology are usually divided by major military conquests and by the changes in language, culture, and religion that accompanied the conquests.

Beginning in the **Middle Bronze Age** (2000–1500 B.C.), political and social upheaval throughout the ancient Near East affected migrant groups like Israel. The exact length of the Middle Bronze Age and the circumstances of the transition into the **Late Bronze Age** (1550–1200 B.C.) are not entirely clear. Shifts in **material culture** (archaeological discoveries that reflect a people's beliefs and practices), which generally distinguish one archaeological period from another, are not pronounced during this transition. As a result, identifying

A horned altar.

his death. Egyptian sources do not explain this awkward succession. But, if the exodus occurred around 1447 B.C. during the reign of Amenhotep, the succession of his younger son could reflect the death of the first-born sons of Egypt described in Exod 11:1—12:32. This "tenth plague" is interpreted in the minds of the biblical authors as the event that eventually led to Israel's escape.

On the other hand, the strength of Egyptian presence in Canaan during this period makes the early date of the exodus problematic. Egyptian sources do not mention the exodus, although there is evidence of the use of forced labor gangs to construct the Egyptian storehouse cities of Pithom and Rameses in the time of Seti I and Rameses II (ca. 1300–1250 B.C.). These construction gangs may have included the Israelite slaves or groups of itinerant laborers (Exod 1:11). The "**late date**" theory—that the exodus occurred in the thirteenth century B.C.—is also supported by thirteenth-century layers of destruction found in some Canaanite sites (on this destruction, see pp. 47–48). Such destruction may be attributed to the conquests by Joshua and, later, by the Israelites who are described in Judges.

While Egyptian evidence of specifically Hebrew migration is scarce, evidence of group migrations in the second half of the second millennium is found throughout Egyptian literature. Records most often refer to these groups using social categories rather than particular group names. For instance, Egyptian records describe the **Shasu,** not in terms of their origins, but as tribes of lawless nomadic herders and sedentary farmers known to be rebellious and quarrelsome. The "Shasu-land" inhabited by this social group ran from the eastern Delta region to Gaza, and it was the site of a series of conflicts between the Egyptians and the Shasu between 1500 and 1150 B.C. (*ANET*, 247, 254, 259 n. 2).

The settlement of so-called Hapiru tribes in the Delta region is also mentioned in Egyptian

the differences between cultures is difficult. What is clear is that the upheaval of the Middle Bronze Age extended into the period of Israel's exodus and settlement that straddled the Late Bronze Age and the **Early Iron Age,** or **Iron I** (1200–1000 B.C.).

Such questions regarding archaeological periods are not the only problems that make a clear historical setting for the exodus and conquest difficult to establish. Extra-biblical sources that might indicate a clear date are scarce; the evidence of archaeology is incomplete and in some cases contradictory. The biblical account places the exodus in the fifteenth century B.C., 300 years before the period of the judges (Judg 11:26), and 480 years before the fourth year of Solomon (1 Kgs 6:1). This "**early date**" for the exodus is perhaps supported by the ascension of Pharaoh Amenhotep II's younger son, rather than his older one, after

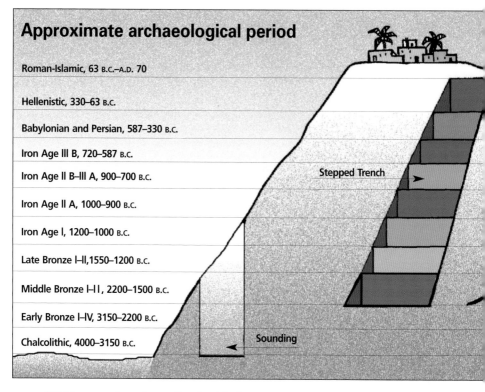

Approximate archaeological period

Roman-Islamic, 63 B.C.–A.D. 70

Hellenistic, 330–63 B.C.

Babylonian and Persian, 587–330 B.C.

Iron Age III B, 720–587 B.C.

Iron Age II B–III A, 900–700 B.C.

Iron Age II A, 1000–900 B.C.

Iron Age I, 1200–1000 B.C.

Late Bronze I–II,1550–1200 B.C.

Middle Bronze I–II, 2200–1500 B.C.

Early Bronze I–IV, 3150–2200 B.C.

Chalcolithic, 4000–3150 B.C.

Stepped Trench

Sounding

texts (*ANET,* 255, 261, 483, 486). The label 'Apiru, **Hapiru,** or Habiru appears to be a generic term for stateless people or tribal groups who lived on the fringes of the settled areas of the ancient Near East. They sometimes served as surplus labor or as mercenaries, but they appear in texts from several historical periods (from 2000 to 1200 B.C.,) and are mentioned in different areas as brigands and raiders. One large group of Hapiru congregated around Nuzi in northeastern Mesopotamia. There, private contracts have been discovered binding Hapiru to citizens of Nuzi as servants, suggesting that this refugee group did not become members of the societies into which they moved (*ANET,* 220). Migration did not always solve such problems, however, as Hapiru slavery at Nuzi suggests. The numbers of migrants also posed problems for the states into which they moved. As a result, treaties regulating migration, including agreements on extradition of members of groups like the

Hapiru, were made between states (see the 13th cent. treaty between Egypt and Hatti in *ANET,* 199–203). While there is no direct linguistic connection between Hapiru and Hebrew, the description of a people without roots who live on the fringes of society and sometimes infiltrate into poorly-defended areas does fit the biblical description of the Israelites.

The only documentary evidence from Egypt of Israel as a people is found in a victory stele of Pharaoh Merneptah dating to ca. 1208 B.C. This inscription lists the peoples and cities that the pharaoh conquered in an expedition into Canaan. One line states that Israel (specified in the text as a people, not a nation) was laid waste. This mention of Israel occurs in the systematic description of the destruction wrought by the pharaoh's armies in the area. There is a difficulty with this interpretation, however. The language of the inscription is typical of many other similar victory

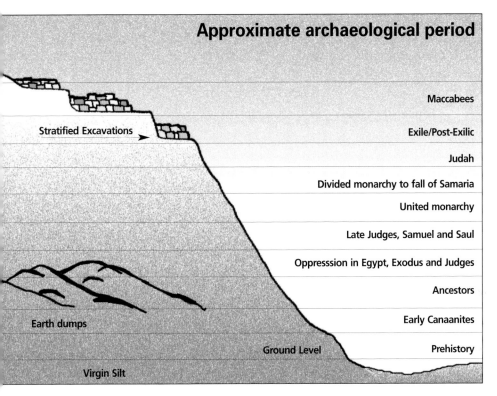

Approximate archaeological period

Maccabees

Stratified Excavations ➤

Exile/Post-Exilic

Judah

Divided monarchy to fall of Samaria

United monarchy

Late Judges, Samuel and Saul

Oppresssion in Egypt, Exodus and Judges

Ancestors

Early Canaanites

Earth dumps

Ground Level

Prehistory

Virgin Silt

announcements, and the inclusion of Israel in the list of defeated enemies may reflect some knowledge of its existence, but no actual contact with it. The pharaoh may simply be boasting that he has subdued all of the peoples in the area. Still, it is the first extrabiblical mention of the name Israel, and thus provides us with the best available evidence of its existence in the thirteenth century B.C.

Evidence for the chronology of the conquest period, as described in the book of Joshua, is just as scarce and problematic. The only discussion of this holy war is found in the biblical text. Archaeological investigations of the major sites said to have been destroyed by the Israelites have provided mixed results. Jericho, the first city listed as being conquered by the Hebrews, has been extensively excavated three times during the twentieth century; John Garstang and Kathleen Kenyon led the first scientific investigations of the site. Despite some early claims by Garstang that he had

found the remains of the walls of Joshua's Jericho, it has generally been determined that the level of the city that he identified with the conquest is actually to be dated to the third millennium B.C. Kenyon's work in the 1950s was able to demonstrate that those levels within the mound that do correspond to the fourteenth and thirteenth centuries are too badly eroded to provide explicit evidence of destruction in that period.

Ai has also proven to be a puzzle. Excavations conducted at this site by Joseph Callaway between 1965 and 1975 demonstrated that the mound was unoccupied from 2400 to 1200 B.C. It is possible that it was used as a military outpost by the nearby city of Bethel, which does show evidence of destruction in the thirteenth century, but there was no settlement at Ai such as that described in Joshua. Its name, which means "the ruin," may have led the Israelites to attach it to Joshua's list of conquests.

47

> *The LORD was with Judah, and he took possession of the hill country, but could not drive out the inhabitants of the plain, because they had chariots of iron.*
> —Judg 1:19

Other cities, including Hazor, Lachish, and Tell beit Mirsim, do have destruction levels that date to the thirteenth century. However, it is unclear whether their destruction is the work of the Israelites. The destruction levels could just as easily be evidence of Merneptah's expedition as he tried to reestablish Egyptian control in the area, or of the conquests by the Sea Peoples who raided much of the Near East around 1200 B.C. Another site, Tell deir-'Alla, possibly the biblical Succoth, was destroyed in this period (although a little after 1200 B.C.), but its demise is attributed to an earthquake.

With so many conflicting pieces of information, it is best to take a cautious view of the Israelite conquest of Canaan. Several theories have tried to explain the disparities between the archaeological evidence and the description of a nearly total victory sweep by the Israelites in Josh 1–12. One possible explanation is that the book of Joshua is not as interested in historical details as it is in making the theological point that victory is engineered by the divine warrior, Yahweh. Each battle is won because of the direct intervention of God. For instance, the fall of Jericho is not achieved by the Israelites through conventional siege warfare, but through the opening given their forces when God destroyed the city walls.

A certain selectivity may also limit the number of events described in the conquest account. There is no clear indication of the time it took to complete the conquest. Possibly some cities fell to one wave of migrants while others succumbed to later attacks. The Israelite tribes may have entered Canaan over a fairly long period of time, with each successive wave of arrivals adding to their numbers

and achieving new victories. Other migrating groups or even Canaanite villages (for example, the Gibeonites in Josh 9:3–15) may have joined forces with the Israelite tribes as they began to settle in the hill country. Such allegiances could have undermined the authority and strength of the Canaanite culture and eventually allowed the Israelites to dominate some areas, while engaging in a minimal amount of armed conflict.

Initially, the Israelite tribes may have settled in the under-populated areas of the Central Hill Country and then assimilated themselves into the Canaanite culture. As they learned the technologies and social customs of the Canaanites, they gradually and, for the most part, peacefully merged with the dominant culture. Over time, the Israelites came to control larger areas and some cities. By the time of King David, only the Philistine city-states along the coastal plain and inland in the Shephelah provided a major opposing force.

This explanation of gradual infiltration seems to fit the description of a partial conquest and settlement found in Judges 1–2. These chapters list those cities and regions that the Israelite tribes were not able to conquer. Conquest through forced entry may have augmented ongoing infiltration in cases like the destruction of Lachish (Josh 10) and Bethel (Judg 1). The lack of evidence at other sites, such as Ai, could be attributed to a later chronicling of the events or to overly enthusiastic battle reports.

However it happened, it is apparent that groups of Israelites did eventually settle in Canaan and in portions of the Transjordan in Gilead and in territories associated with Moab. Engaging in a mixed economy of agriculture and herding, most of the Israelites would have lived in small, unwalled villages. Life, as described in Judges, was somewhat uncertain. Villages had to endure frequent raids by Philistines and other Canaanite groups that used their superior weapons to harass the

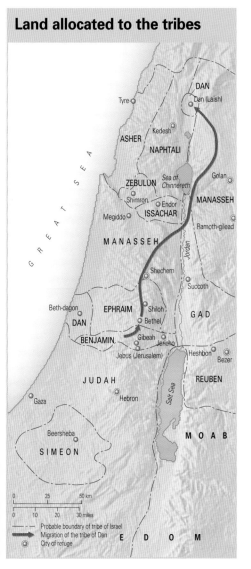

Land allocated to the tribes

DAN
Tyre
Dan (Laish)
Kedesh
ASHER
NAPHTALI
Sea of
ZEBULUN Chinnereth
Golan
Shimron
Endor
MANASSEH
Megiddo
ISSACHAR
Ramoth-gilead
MANASSEH
Jordan
Shechem
Succoth
Beth-dagon
EPHRAIM
Shiloh
GAD
DAN
Bethel
BENJAMIN
Gibeah
Jesus (Jerusalem)
Jericho
Heshbon
Bezer
JUDAH
REUBEN
Gaza
Hebron
Salt Sea
Beersheba
MOAB
SIMEON

0   25   50 km
0 10 20 30 miles

- - - Probable boundary of tribe of Israel
→ Migration of the tribe of Dan   E D O M
Ⓞ City of refuge

VILLAGE LIFE

The allotment in Josh 13–17, which lists the areas of Transjordan and Canaan assigned to the tribes of Israel, includes a list of towns and their adjacent villages or "encampments." These latter settlements, sometimes referred to as "daughters" (Num 21:25, 32), contained the vast majority of the population during the early settlement period (ca. 1200–1050 B.C.). The "iron chariots" of the Canaanites are said to be responsible for bottling up the Israelites in the inhospitable, under-populated regions of the country (Judg 1:19). This was the case even though, as the biblical writer says, "the hill country is not enough" (Josh 7:16) to support the needs of the people as the population expanded. Very likely, the higher technology and tighter political organization of the Canaanites held the new immigrants in check for some time.

Recently, archaeologists have conducted surveys of the settlements in the hill country that date to the period after 1200 B.C. They discovered that in the "hills of Ephraim" only four or five sites had existed during the Late Bronze period (ca. 1550–1200 B.C.). However, during the Early Iron Age (ca. 1200–1000 B.C.) over one hundred had appeared, especially after 1100 B.C. Some additional settlements were built on the abandoned ruins of ancient cities, such as Ai and Gibeon. These findings suggest: (a) that there was no economic need or political impetus to promote settlement in the hill country during the Late Bronze period; and (b) that rapid population growth occurred as the Israelites and other settlers entered the highlands of central Canaan at the beginning of the Iron Age.

Depending on their inaccessibility and on their poverty for protection, the new settlers did not build walls around their small villages. Extended family groups lived in multiple family compounds. These complexes may have been styled after the settlements in which the Hebrews lived while in Egypt, or perhaps after

Hebrews. For most of this period, social and political organization remained on the tribal level, and village elders had authority over local issues (see Ruth 4).

The manners and customs of this era indicate Israel's shift from an enslaved people to an independent and loosely organized group of settled tribes and villages. This transition required some fundamental changes in social life, and eventually formed the basis for the covenantal community of ancient Israel.

the nomadic encampments of the wilderness period. Villages in the hill country consisted of closely packed rows or clusters of 15–20 dwellings that could house perhaps 100–150 people. The primary building materials were rocks and sun-dried mud brick. Situated as they were on the hill tops, these villages seldom covered an area of more than five acres.

Life in the village centered around agricultural pursuits and maintaining small herds of sheep and goats. Some domestic industries, such as the making of pottery, garments, and tools, were necessary for every household. Each settlement was isolated and therefore strove to be self-sufficient with regard to the basic necessities of life. Natural resources, such as clay for pots and copper deposits, were available nearby (Deut 8:9). Even by the end of the settlement period, more advanced technology and styles of workmanship, as well as rare raw materials, could be obtained only from traveling craftsmen or in the larger cities of Canaan. For instance, 1 Sam 13:19–20 states: "Now there was no smith to be found throughout all the land of Israel; . . . so all the Israelites went down to the Philistines to sharpen their plowshare, mattocks, axes, or sickles." Adjoining fields provided food for the villagers and commanded the bulk of their work day.

> He dug it and cleared it of stones, and planted it with choice vines; he built a watchtower in the midst of it, and hewed out a wine vat in it; he expected it to yield grapes, but it yielded wild grapes. And now, inhabitants of Jerusalem and people of Judah, judge between me and my vineyard. What more was there to do for my vineyard that I have not done in it? When I expected it to yield grapes, why did it yield wild grapes? And now I will tell you what I will do to my vineyard. I will remove its hedge, and it shall be devoured; I will break down its wall, and it shall be trampled down.
> —Isa 5:2–5

Stone terraces on a hillside near Bethlehem.

Because there is little level ground in the hill country, a great deal of labor went into the building and maintaining of stone terraces on the slopes (see Isa 5:2–5). Vines and some cereals were cultivated on these artificially constructed plots. The flatter areas of the plains allowed for more conventional farming methods, but they were not settled by large groups of Israelites until the monarchic period. The uncertainties of rainfall in the hill country, hungry birds, and insects also plagued farmers and severely cut into their harvests.

Each village possessed flocks of sheep and goats that were pastured some distance from the settlement. The herdsmen sometimes kept the animals up in the higher elevations for a season, but it was also quite common to bring them back to the village for the night. The open "square" in larger settlements was sometimes used to shelter the flocks. However, primitive enclosures were more often used to prevent the animals from wandering away and from attacks by night predators.

Israel in Canaan

AMURRU

Byblos
Aphekah
Lebo-hamath

Sidon

Damascus

Dan

Achzib
Kadesh
Hazor
Acco
Ramah
Chinnereth
Rehob
Sea of Chinnereth
Nahalol
Aphek
Ashtaroth
Kitron

Megiddo
Dor
Jezreel
Taanach
Beth-shan
Ibleam
Ramoth-gilead
Jabesh-gilead
Mount Ebal
Shechem
Succoth
Mount Gerizim

Jordan

Aphek
Shiloh
AMMON

Gezer
Bethel Gilgal
Gibeon
Heshbon
Ashdod
Ekron
Aijalon
Jebus
(Jerusalem)
Beth-
shemesh
Bethlehem
Medeba
Ashkelon
Gath
Dibon
Gaza
Lachish
Hebron
Aroer
Debir

Salt Sea

Beer-sheba

G R E A T   S E A

P H I L I S T I A

M O A B

0   25   50 km
0   10   20   30 miles

Mount Halak
Zoar

Tamar

Kadesh-barnea

E D O M

Border of Canaan —·—·—
Philistine city ◎
Area controlled
by Israelites ▢

f Egypt

Domestic Architecture

Poorer village sites, such as that excavated at Tell Raddana (near Ai), provided only minimal comforts of home and living space. In this small village of six closely-packed houses, the basic design is a simple, windowless rectangle divided into two living areas by a row of four roof-supporting pillars. These pillars are usually placed within five feet of one long wall, thereby creating a "great room" in the remaining ten-foot-wide living area. This great room, illuminated by the fire pit and sputtering oil lamps, served most of the family's indoor cooking, entertaining, and sleeping needs.

Wooden beams, set in niches cut into the walls and supported by pillars, held up the roof. Slats were made from smaller pieces of wood, brush, or thatching, which were sealed with a layer of clay. The resulting ceiling was about six feet from the floor, with the beams lowering that height by five or six inches in places.

With living space at a minimum, there was no room for luxuries or privacy. Cooking was done outside the front door in small clay ovens or in a courtyard shared by two or three other households. There was no furniture, only stone ledges built along the wall and a few flat stones spaced around the central fire pit. Bathrooms were not a convenience of these dwellings. Bodily needs were taken care of outdoors. If the villagers continued the pattern prescribed in the wilderness (Deut 23:12–13), they utilized latrines outside the immediate area of the village. Some may have gone into the fields where their excrement could serve as fertilizer.

The only innovation and a true convenience designed into these homes was an interconnected cistern system that brought rainwater into the house. Chiseled out of chalk and limestone, which forms the bedrock under these hill-top settlements, bell-shaped cisterns provided a continuous supply of water. It was unnecessary to put additional lime plaster on the cisterns in the Ai/Raddana area because of the impermeability of the rock strata. Elsewhere, however, this "waterproofing cement" was used to retain the moisture.

Rainwater ran off the roofs and into the cisterns. Rocks were placed at the bottom to trap larger impurities and a hole was drilled in the side, allowing water to travel into a series of adjoining cisterns and eventually into the house. This system also filtered the water as it passed from one cistern to the next.

There are few natural springs on the hilltops, and so it was the cistern system that made life possible here. Springs and rivers of the plains and coastal areas supported Canaanite cities and villages. Therefore, the Israelites made do with the resources in the areas where initially they could settle. Later, when judges and kings began to conquer the Canaanite strongholds, Israelites were able to move down into more hospitable and better-watered areas of the land.

Another style of house that was very common in ancient Israel during this period and into the time of the monarchy was the **pillared house,** also called the four-room house. Its basic design may have evolved from earlier structures built around an animal enclosure. Houses of this type have been excavated at Tell el Farah (Tirzah), Hazor, Shechem, and Tell beit Mirsim. They are generally two-story dwellings. The ground floor is made up of a long central room with a ceiling two stories high. This central room is surrounded by partitioned rooms on three sides. With its hard-packed earthen or plastered floor, the central room was used for domestic activities like cooking and dining. Excavations of these areas reveal clay ovens, hearths, and a small group of pottery types (more than fifty percent are storage jars and cooking pots). In some cases, storage jars have been found arranged around the walls of the central room. These might have contained water for cooking or the grain, oil, or olives that would have gone into the next day's meal.

Excavations of the Canaanite and Judaic Kingdom periods at Megiddo.

The ground floor side rooms that boxed in the central room provided secure stables for a family's livestock. During the winter, the body heat of the animals stabled on the ground floor of the house provided additional natural warmth for the upper story. The upper side rooms were sometimes subdivided into smaller rooms. They served as sleeping quarters, gathering places for the family and their friends, and storage spaces. Along with the warmth provided by the livestock, the main hearth located in the central room could provide heating to the entire house.

Walls in these simply-constructed houses were quite thick, thereby providing good insulation against the cold and some relief in hot weather. In the hill country, where uncut stone is plentiful, the foundation and the walls were made of this building material. A mud plaster, mixed with small stones, was applied to the walls to smooth them over and to protect against the weather. Houses in the plains and foothills, however, would have used sun-dried mud brick for all but the foundation. These bricks, like cut stone in larger buildings, were laid in a pattern known as "headers and stretchers," which strengthened the construction and stability of the walls. Although the archaeological record can only attest to foundation patterns and the size of the column bases, the thickness of the walls and columns indicate that the standard pattern for these Iron Age houses included a second story with a sturdy, flat roof.

The roof over these dwellings was thatched with a mixture of reeds, branches, and palm leaves, and then covered with earth or bricks. It provided extra sleeping accommodations (2 Kgs 4:10), and served as an excellent spot for

> *[Uzziah] built towers in the wilderness and hewed out many cisterns, for he had large herds . . .*
> —*2 Chr 26:10*

53

drying mud bricks or flax stalks (Josh 2:6). As a rule, access to the upper room was provided by a staircase on the outside of the wall, although ladders may have been used within the dwelling. In warm weather the breeze on the roof relieved the family from heat, and domestic tasks could be performed in more comfort under a lean-to or awning.

Another area of the house that held both functional and traditional importance is the threshold/doorway. At first, doors were simply skin coverings, but these were eventually replaced by a more permanent wattle, or wooden barrier, and were barred from within. The threshold functioned as the legal, as well as physical, entryway to the dwelling, and in some cases may have served as the site where justice was done (Deut 22:21) or demanded (Judg 19:27). Shoes were removed before crossing the threshold as a sign of respect, and hospitality obligations began at this point.

AGRICULTURAL METHODS AND TOOLS

Constrained to live in the hill country, the Israelites adapted to this environment by building terraces on the hillsides. Construction and maintenance of these terraces required a large part of the villagers' energies, but it provided them with farmable strips of land that could support the growing agricultural needs of the people. Terracing in this period was not as extensive as it was in the monarchy period, when fifty percent of the hillsides were terraced. The growth in village population, however, was one of the prime reasons for initiating such a monumental project. Since these terraces have been rebuilt and reused by villagers throughout the centuries, the primary means of determining when they might have originated is through the examination of pottery remains. This is not always a reliable test, but indications are that the conversion of the hills of Judea and Ephraim into farmland began in the early settlement period, and con-

> *Then they shall bring the young woman out to the entrance of her father's house and the men of her town shall stone her to death, because she committed a disgraceful act in Israel by prostituting herself in her father's house. So you shall purge the evil from your midst.*
> —Deut 22:21

tinued on a larger scale throughout the monarchic period (see Uzziah's emphasis on agriculture in 2 Chr 26:10).

The terraces are not designed to prevent erosion of existing topsoil. The hills have little soil to lose, due to previous deforestation (Josh 17:18) and pasturing of animals. Thus much of the soil found in the terraces was brought from elsewhere, and was usually a mixture of different soil types. Channels were sometimes dug to direct rainwater into the terraces. These terraces were constructed all the way down the face of the hill to ensure natural filtration of the water and a better distribution of moisture to every farming strip. Since significant rainfall only occurs during five months of the year (October to February), it is essential that none of it be allowed to run off.

Grain Production

Wheat and barley were the most common crops grown in the hill country by the Israelites. While it comes from the tenth century B.C., the Gezer Calendar records a pattern of the agricultural year that must go back to earlier times. This schoolboy exercise, written on a broken limestone tablet, describes the seasons.

The agricultural calendar was thus based on the division between the rainy winter months and the dry spring and summer. Once the rains had loosened the ground, plowing and planting of various crops began in November and continued until January. Wheat and barley were the first to be planted, while crops like

A shepherd minds his flock in fields near Bethlehem.

sesame, millet, and lentils, and garden vegetables like cucumbers, garlic, onions, and leeks were planted from January until March. Harvest seasons varied according to the temperature ranges of specific regions, with the Jordan valley being the first to harvest and the cooler mountain areas the last. This meant that barley, which ripened before the wheat, was harvested from April to May, while the latter was harvested from May to June (on harvest festivals, see pp. 57, 73).

To prepare the ground for planting, a wooden plow (sometimes with a metal sheath or boot attached), drawn by a team of oxen (1 Sam 11:5), opened the furrows. Smaller villages probably shared a team of oxen or per-

> *He built towers in the wilderness and hewed out many cisterns, for he had large herds, both in the Shephelah and in the plain, and he had farmers and vinedressers in the hills and fertile lands, for he loved the soil.*
>
> —*2 Chr 26:10*

haps even rented one from a nearby village. A text from Mari (*ARMT* 14:80.4–10) mentions such an arrangement, in which a village obtained the use of a team of oxen in exchange for its labor service for the government. Though the people of Gideon's village wanted to kill him primarily for destroying his father's Baal altar, Gideon's subsequent sacrifice to Yahweh of the precious work oxen he had used to tear down the altar may have contributed to their rage (Judg 6:25–28). In another instance, Saul's slaughter of his own oxen perhaps signaled the urgency of his demand that the tribes assemble for war (1 Sam 11:7).

A sower cast the grain into the furrows by hand where it was trampled into the ground by foot or by the tread of the animals. The ripened grain was harvested with sickle blades (Joel 3:13). These were made of bronze, although in the poorer villages wooden sickles with flint blades continued to be used. Later, when iron technology and tools were introduced into Israel, these improved farm implements were probably prized over their primitive predecessors.

The harvested grain was taken to a central threshing floor. This flattened area ranged in diameter from 160 to 320 feet (depending on the number of villages and fields it serviced), and it was located in an open place where the prevailing winds would aid the winnowing. To separate kernels of grain from the stalks, oxen were driven over the grain on the circular earthen floor, trampling it. Israelite concern for the animals that aided them in this important activity is reflected in the law of Deut 25:4, which prohibits a man from muzzling his ox while it treads out the grain. The ox was thus free to breathe and to eat a portion for its hire.

In later periods, a more efficient method of threshing was developed using a threshing sledge with stone and bits of metal attached to its underside. These extra edges crushed the stalks more thoroughly than the sledge could alone. A sledge like this is mentioned in 2 Sam 24:22 in the context of David's purchase of the threshing floor of Araunah, which eventually became the site of the temple in Jerusalem.

After threshing, the next step in the process of preparing grain for milling was winnowing. This was done using a long wooden fork to toss the grain and chaff into the air. Then, as Ps 1:4 says of the wicked, the chaff was driven away by the wind. Jeremiah also used this common village activity to describe God's testing of the people "with a winnowing fork in the gates of the land" (15:7). Two places associated with justice are thus alluded to here: the threshing floor, where the winnowing was done, and the gate, which was the center of legal activity in the walled cities of the monarchic period.

Sieving was the final step in separating the grain from the chaff. Small wicker screens were used to sift tiny stones or bits of pottery from the grain, which then fell to the floor where they could be collected. Amos, an eighth-century prophet from the farming village of Tekoa, used this activity to describe how God in his wrath will "shake the house of Israel among all the nations as one shakes a sieve, but no pebble shall fall to the ground" (9:9).

Once the kernels of grain were collected, a portion was ground into flour with a simple millstone on a larger stone quern shaped like a saddle. Then it was pulverized in a stone mortar with a rounded pestle. Another portion was parched to be eaten as journey provisions or pressed into cakes. The remainder was stored in plastered storage pits or in pottery jars that were stacked around the walls of homes or courtyards. Only the larger villages and towns had communal silos for the storage of large quantities of grain.

Cultivation of Vines and Olive Trees

Every village in this and later periods had its vines and trees. Terraces are actually better designed for these crops than for the cultivation of grain. This fact, plus evidence from archaeological sites and the biblical text, suggests that grapes and olives were staples in the diet and a standard portion of the farm production of ancient Israel.

As Isaiah notes in his "Song of the Vineyard" (5:1–6), the cultivation of vineyards on terraces was a time-consuming and sometimes frustrating activity. It involved the maintenance of the terrace wall, the clearing of stones from the field, and the planting of proven vine cuttings. A watchtower was sometimes constructed to guard the vines, and a winepress and vat were carved out of the rock of the hillside. In addition, a hedge or fence was also built to keep out small animals and grazing herds (Ps 80:12–13).

The vines required constant care, including pruning done from June to August to remove unproductive or old vines and thus allow for new growth (compare Lev 25:4). Supports for the vine clusters prevented bruising and rot, and the area around the vine was hoed regularly to cut back on weeds that would steal moisture needed by the fruit to ripen (Isa 5:6).

The grapes were harvested with pruning

A stone watchtower in fields near the site of ancient Bethel.

hooks (Isa 2:4) in August and September. Some were dried into raisin clusters (1 Sam 25:18), and the rest were trod into wine in a winepress. The liquid squeezings were poured or channeled into a fermentation vat and then stored in jars or skin bags. Because so much communal activity occurred at this installation, its importance is second only to the threshing floor, another center of community activity, in Israelite tradition (Hos 9:2). Indeed, on at least one occasion, a wine press was used as a threshing floor. After the Midianite raiders had ravaged his village's fields, the judge Gideon secretly ground his remaining wheat in a wine press to prevent the invaders from suspecting that he was holding out on them (Judg 6:11).

The harvesting of grapes and the production of wine was a time of celebration comparable to the grain harvest in the villages (Judg 9:27). People's joy was based on the fact that wine and bread were the staples of life (1 Sam 16:20). At times the vintage festival may have gotten out of hand, leaving the village open to attack. For instance, the decimated Benjaminite tribe took advantage of the celebration at Shiloh to steal wives from among the dancers (Judg 21:20–21).

Olive and fig trees provided the chief non-cereal crops. The fruit of these trees added spice and variety to an otherwise monotonous diet. In addition, crushed olives provided oil for lamps, cooking, cosmetics and personal grooming. The olive tree was long-lived and well suited to the hot, dry summers and cool, damp winters of Israel and the rest of the Mediterranean basin. It was seen, along with the other produce of the land, as one of the blessings provided to the people by God (Deut 7:13).

> So they said. "Look, the yearly festival of the Lord is taking place at Shiloh, which is north of Bethel, on the east of the highway that goes up from Bethel to Shechem, and south of Lebonah."
> —Judg 21:19

In the autumn, villagers gathered ripe olives by striking the tree branches with sticks and collecting the fallen fruit in baskets. The olives were then crushed under a revolving, flat stone, and the stream of oil and juice was collected in a cistern. The remaining pulp was placed in wicker baskets to be crushed again by a stone-weighted lever. Squeezings were channeled into a larger catch basin. Gradually, the finer grade of oil rose to the top of the cistern and was skimmed off for use in lamps (Exod 27:20). The remainder was further refined and used as a base for cosmetics, in cooking, and as medicine. The residue of the inedible pulp may have been used for fertilizer or hardened into cakes that served as fuel for cooking fires.

Fig trees were also among the items characteristically exploited in arid farming areas like the hill country (Jer 40:10–12). Their fruit was the last to appear in the summer, and thus figs are called the "summer fruit" in the Gezer Calendar and in Amos 8:2. Because of their high sugar content, figs could be dried and pressed into cakes that were stored for later consumption or given as gifts in the dry, fruitless summer. Fig cakes are one of the items Abigail takes to David's camp to prevent his attack on her husband's household (1 Sam 25:18).

This same passage provides a list of the foods typically eaten by people in the settlement period: Abigail takes David's men 200 loaves of bread, 2 skins of wine, 5 butchered sheep, 5 measures of parched grain, 100 clusters of raisins, and 200 fig cakes. With this list as a guide, it can be seen that the land did yield its agricultural wealth to the Israelites, although not without a struggle and not always in the abundance they desired.

WEAPONS AND WARFARE

A discussion of weapons and warfare in the conquest and settlement period must consider the differences between the historical accounts in Joshua and in Judges. The book of Joshua describes the conquest and highlights Yahweh's role as the "Divine Warrior," who provides one victory after another to the Israelite forces. This pattern of divine deliverance is manifest in the wilderness period in the battle against the Amalekites (Exod 17:8–13). Once the Israelites enter Canaan, it is demonstrated in the capture of Jericho (Josh 6) and in the defeat of the five Amorite kings when God caused the sun to stand still (Josh 10:6–13). In these battles it is God's intervention, not the strength of the Israelite tribes, which determines the outcome.

In contrast to this account of divinely achieved success, the book of Judges admits that the "holy war," or *herem*, was a failure. Many Canaanite cities were too strong for the Israelites to capture, and the iron chariots (1:19) of the people of the plain kept the Israelites bottled up in the hill country (1:34). A rationalization for this failure is spelled out in Judg 3:1–4. It states that God spared these Canaanite and Philistine cities so that "successive generations of Israelites might know war, to teach those who had no experience of it before." The plan is designed "for the testing of Israel, to know whether Israel would obey the commandments of the LORD."

Thus during much of the settlement period, the Israelites were either vassals of the more powerful Canaanite rulers, or were engaged in nearly continuous armed conflict with their neighbors and fellow tribesmen. This state of affairs can be illustrated by two passages: Judg 15:11 and 12:1–6. In the first of these texts, Samson has been pursued into the territory of Judah by an army of Philistines. Eventually, he is captured and turned over to his enemies. However, his captors are men of Judah who tell

> And the sun stood still, and the moon stopped, until the nation took vengeance on their enemies.
> —Josh 10:13a

him, "Do you not know that the Philistines are rulers over us?"

Judges 12 shows Jephthah completing a war with the Ammonites in Gilead, only to be faced with the militant jealousies of a sister tribe, the Ephraimites. Contending that they were denied their share of the glory in the recent campaign, these tribesmen cross into Jephthah's territory. Unlike Gideon, who was faced with the same charge in Judg 8:1–3, Jephthah denies the Ephraimite claim, arguing that they had failed to come when called. This precipitates a civil war; Jephthah's forces take the fords of the Jordan to prevent the invaders from escaping, and slaughter a reported forty-two *eleph* of the enemies. Though most translations render this as forty-two "thousand," an **eleph** is more likely a designation for a military unit. In either case, a large number die in the battle.

One other portion of this narrative that demonstrates the obvious differences between the tribes in this period is the so-called "*Shibboleth* Affair." As the Ephraimites attempt to sneak across the Jordan, Jephthah's men stop them and ask them to pronounce the word *shibboleth,* which means "watercourse." The Ephraimites, however, speak a different dialect of Hebrew, and therefore pronounce the word as *sibboleth.* This gives them away, and they are executed on the spot.

The Contrast in Weapons

Although the Philistines and Canaanites began to experiment with an iron-based military technology in the twelfth and eleventh centuries B.C., the metal of choice throughout this period remained bronze. Israelites also used bronze weapons, but their lack of metallurgical knowledge, and the Philistine monopoly over the tin trade, probably forced many of their soldiers to use slings and farm implements to defend themselves. Some iron weapons were undoubtedly captured during raids by Israelite forces, but without the knowledge of metallurgy to repair and fabricate new weapons out of scrap metal, they would have become useless eventually. This may explain why the forces

Bronze weapons from Shiloh from about the thirteenth century B.C.

*And Joshua did to them as the LORD
commanded him; he hamstrung their
horses, and burned their chariots with fire.*
—Josh 11:9

under Joshua chose to burn the chariots of the
northern coalition of Canaanite kings rather
than use them themselves (Josh 11:9). The
Israelites could not repair the chariots, and
they did not want to leave them behind for
Canaanites to use against them in the future.
Also, the chariots would have been of little use
to Israelite bands operating out of the rugged
hill country.

An apparent Israelite lack of skill in working
metals is repeatedly mentioned in the narratives. The Israelites were deliberately denied
this knowledge by the Philistines lest they
"make swords or spears for themselves"
(1 Sam 13:19). As a result, Hebrew tribesmen
were ill-equipped for war, and were constantly
forced to rely on inferior weapons and the element of surprise. For instance, the Joseph
tribe's attack on Bethel was successful because
a man of that community was captured, and
he showed them "the way into the city" (Judg
1:22–25).

In an episode involving the Benjaminite
judge Ehud, the hero resorts to assassination
(Judg 3:15–26) to free his people from the tribute demands of Eglon of Moab. Concealing a
specially-designed dagger on his person before
his interview with the Moabite king, Ehud
then tells Eglon that he has a message for him
from God. This causes the greedy monarch to
send away his guards, and gives left-handed
Ehud the opportunity to draw his dagger, stab
the king, and escape to rally his forces against
the leaderless Moabites.

Gideon is another Israelite judge who uses
trickery rather than force of arms to achieve
his goals. When faced with overwhelming odds
in a war against the Midianites, he divides the
three hundred men that God has allowed him

to bring into three companies. They surround
the Midianite camp, and in the dead of night
raise such a racket by smashing pitchers,
shouting, and blowing horns that the confused
enemy soldiers begin fighting among themselves (Judg 7:19–22).

Other weapons mentioned in the text
include very primitive items. For example,
Shamgar, in Judg 3:31, kills 600 Philistines
with an ox-goad—not an unusual weapon
for a hill country farmer. A Kenite woman
named Jael kills the sleeping general Sisera
by driving a wooden tent peg through his
skull (Judg 4:21). Samson, judge of the tribe
of Dan, victimizes the Philistines using a
"fresh" (non-brittle) jawbone of an ass to slay
a thousand men (Judg 15:15). His exploits
also include burning the Philistine fields of
standing grain with torches tied to the tails
of foxes (Judg 15:5), and carrying away the
doors of the Gaza city gate (Judg 16:3).

When Israelite forces were marshaled
against walled cities, the siege was never prolonged and generally included fierce fighting.
Once the gates or walls were breached, the ultimate goal of the besieging army was the
citadel tower. Gideon tears down the tower of
Penuel. This leaves its people without a rallying point for their forces (Judg 8:17). In Judges
9, his son Abimelech captures the city of
Shechem by ambushing men as they come out
to the fields and by rushing a segment of his
army through the open gate (vv. 44–45).

Shechem's survivors seek refuge in the city's
citadel tower, but Abimelech then builds a fire,
weakening its masonry, and forcing the citizens to abandon it lest they be buried in col-
lapsing rubble. The remnant are slaughtered
by Abimelech's men (vv. 48–49). Later, this wily
general tries to use the same strategy at

*He also broke down the tower of Penuel,
and killed the men of the city.*
—Judg 8:17

> *So on the day of the battle neither sword nor spear was to be found in the possession of any of the people with Saul and Jonathan; but Saul and his son Jonathan had them.*
> —*1 Sam 13:22*

Early Iron Age bronze dagger from Dor.

Thebez, but he gets too close to the wall of the tower and is struck by a millstone that a woman flings down from above (vv. 50–53). Disheartened by the death of their leader, the Israelites give up the siege.

Even after the monarchy was established and Saul provided the centralized leadership that the people had lacked since the death of Joshua, iron weapons were scarce. First Samuel 13:22 records that only Saul and his son Jonathan have spears and swords (most likely bronze spears and swords). The remainder of the troops face a Philistine army with only those weapons they can swiftly acquire—probably slings, bows, clubs and farm implements. As in the Gideon narrative (Judg 7:19–22), this battle is eventually won through a raid that throws the enemy camp into confusion. Saul's son, Jonathan, and his armor bearer secretly enter the camp, causing a large enough disturbance to give his father's army the opening they need to gain the victory.

The contrast between military technologies is also graphically portrayed in the David and Goliath episode, where a heavily armored knight confronts a more mobile auxiliary fighter. Goliath is described in 1 Sam 17:4–7 as a giant soldier, clothed in a bronze helmet, bronze chain mail, and bronze greaves that protect his legs. He carries a huge spear with an iron head and is accompanied by a shield-bearer. Saul offers David the use of his armor, but David has never used armor before, and complains that he cannot wear it and walk (vv. 38–39). Thus he relies on a sling and five stones as his only weapons (v. 40).

Again, victory for the Israelites seems impossible, and the text ascribes it to God's intervention (v. 47). In any case, slingers could hurl stones with incredible force and were an important part of every army's attacking force. Stones flung by slingers have been found in great quantities by archaeologists in the levels of the city of Lachish, associated with its capture by the Assyrians around 700 B.C. David uses his sling to good effect and opens the way for an Israelite victory.

Similarities in the Practice of War

The rules of warfare which were practiced by the Israelites and their enemies seem to be very similar. Each side strove to either exterminate or subjugate the other. Goliath's challenge states that the winner of the single combat between himself and his opponent would enslave the loser's people (1 Sam 17:9). The principle of winner-take-all is quite typical of this violent age and is even found in the

Babylonian version of creation, the *Enuma Elish* (*ANET,* 67), when Marduk, the god of Babylon, challenges the chaos beast Tiamat to single combat.

Taking spoils from the bodies of the vanquished foe and their animals was an accepted and anticipated practice. In Judg 5:28–30, the mother of Sisera, general of the Canaanite city of Hazor, rationalizes that her son is late in returning because of the rich spoils he is collecting from the defeated Israelites: "A girl or two for every man; spoil of dyed stuffs for Sisera, spoil of dyed stuffs embroidered, two pieces of dyed work embroidered for my neck as spoil?" Gideon, after defeating the Midianite kings Zebah and Zalmuna, gathers the golden earrings, pendants, and purple garments of the enemies (Judg 8:21–26). He also takes the pendants from the necks of their camels.

Mutilation of corpses, as well as of captured enemy soldiers, was also established policy for both the Israelites and the people of Canaan. For instance, David brings a hundred Philistine foreskins to Saul as a bride-price for Michal (1 Sam 18:27). In Judges, Adonibezek, king of the Perizzites, says that he cut off the thumbs and big toes of seventy kings whom he defeated. The same thing is then done to him when his forces are defeated by the tribes of Judah and Simeon (Judg 1:6–7). Following this same policy, Nahash, king of the Ammonites, tells the Israelite village of Jabesh-Gilead that he will massacre the entire population if they do not surrender. However, submitting to his demand will only cost the men of the city their right eyes (1 Sam 11:2).

SOCIAL ORGANIZATION AND ADMINISTRATION OF LAW

"In those days there was no king in Israel; all the people did what was right in their own eyes" (Judg 17:6). Written in the time of the monarchy, this observation is the theme of the book of Judges, and a powerful argument for

> And the Israelites inquired of the LORD
> (for the ark of the covenant of God was
> there in those days . . .
> —Judg 20:27

the establishment of a monarchy. The authority held by Moses and Joshua, and by the tribal elders appointed by Moses to judge the Israelites in the wilderness (Exod 18:21–22), seems to have disappeared during the settlement period. Even the ark of the covenant, the visible symbol of God's presence, is nearly absent from the Judges narrative and mentioned only in 20:27. All this points to a time of local administration of justice, not total anarchy. Individual households and village assemblies administered justice and chose to heed or to ignore the rallying calls of the judges.

The Head of Household

Israelite social organization from the time of the exodus through the settlement period was based on the extended family. A man determined his lineage first by his father, then by his clan, his tribe, and finally (if at all) by his people. Thus when a new character enters a narrative, he is usually introduced as "_____ son of _____." Social organization according to kinship groups is also presumed in the narratives that describe how the process of casting lots is used to identify Achan (Josh 7:16–18) and Saul (1 Sam 10:20–21). Each man was singled out by lot by the process of divining in sequence his tribe, clan, and family.

In the wilderness tents and in the villages of the hill country, family was the focus of life. Individual dwellings were often too small to house more than the nuclear family. Villages, however, were organized into clusters of multiple-family compounds. Thus the head of the household, in an extended family arrangement, would have been a grandfather or the oldest active male member. His home would have formed the physical and social center of a

The city gate at Dan. In later periods, the gate area was a place of judgment.

cluster of dwellings that housed his extended family. The death of the head of the family may have caused a temporary disruption of the power structures within the group, but this would have ceased as the family reorganized quickly in the traditional pattern under the eldest surviving male.

An example of the way a family adapted to new leadership is found in Judg 17:1–5, where Micah's family is portrayed as living in a cluster of houses within the village. In this passage, Micah's father has apparently died. Micah moves into the position as head of the household, installing his sons in adjacent dwellings and hiring a Levite to officiate at his private shrine.

As head of the household, the eldest male is responsible for the religious practice of the family. According to Moses, he must teach his family the proper ways to worship Yahweh. Moses tells the Israelites to take the laws given at Sinai to heart and to "give them as a command to your children, so that they may diligently observe all the words of this law. This" he reminds them, "is no trifling matter for you, but rather your very life" (Deut 32:46–47).

Methods for teaching one's children are exemplified in a series of questions that begin, "when your children ask you," and end with "you shall say to your children . . ." (Exod 12:26–27; 13:14–15; Josh 4:6–7; 21–23; Deut 6:20–24). Following the law and thus acting as the head of a household should, Elkanah takes his two wives and his children on a yearly pilgrimage to his local shrine at Shiloh, and provides portions of the sacrifice for them to offer (1 Sam 1:3–5).

Each family's head, in his capacity as a village elder, also represented the members of the family in the assembly and in worship. In matters of law, the head of the household exercised the powers of the *pater familias* in much the same way as in the ancestral period. It was his right to punish or to reward the members of his family without the interference of the

This man Micah had a shrine, and he made an ephod and teraphim, and installed one of his sons, who became his priest.
—Judg 17:5

other villagers. For instance, in Judg 6:28–31, when Gideon is accused by his village of destroying the Baal altar, his father refuses to punish him, saying it is a dispute between Gideon and the god. This power of the father was protected by the commandment to "honor your father and your mother" (Exod 20:12), and by the tradition of respect that was due both parents (Prov 30:17). Under extreme circumstances, the death penalty could be imposed upon a man who struck his father or his mother (Exod 21:15).

The responsibilities of leadership and the guarantees of respect given to the head of a household, however, also brought with them an element of danger. If a man willfully broke the law, thereby endangering the survival of the community, his crime could bring destruction to the entire family group. This occurred when Achan stole from the spoils of the *herem* at Jericho. The result of his crime against God's command to totally destroy the city, its inhabitants, and its property is a defeat in the next battle at Ai. As for Achan, he and his entire household are stoned for his sin (Josh 7:24–25).

Village Elders

Beyond the level of the household, authority in the village was vested in the hands of the elders. It is clear that in these small villages each individual's and each family's actions had an effect on the entire community. When the elders were called upon to represent their households, they did so in the interests of the village and for the good of the whole body of people. These men, all of whom were heads of households and property owners, represented the collective wisdom of the community (Prov 31:23). As individuals within an assembly, they were responsible for formulating legal policy based on the legal traditions and customs of the group. The **Decalogue** (Exod 20:1-17), which was given to the covenant community at Sinai, would have formed the basis of their traditional legal knowledge, especially its injunctions against theft, murder, and adultery.

In the small, unwalled villages of the hill country, the elders probably met on the cleared threshing floor. Because grain was distributed to villagers at the threshing floor, it eventually became associated with the well-being of the community and with the administration of law. This circular, open space, hallowed by its association with the harvest and the survival of the people, was the first "courtroom." In the Ugaritic legend of Aqhat (*ANET,* 151), Danil, the hero's father, sits on the threshing floor of his village deciding the cases of widows and orphans (compare Deborah's activity in Judg 4:5). In the Laws of Eshnunna #19 (*ANET,* 162), the statute requires that "the man who gives (a loan) . . . shall make (the debtor) pay on the threshing floor." These ancient Near Eastern texts may then shed light on the case of the widow Ruth, who goes to see Boaz at the threshing floor. He happens to be spending the night there to guard his grain, but it is nevertheless fitting that Ruth should approach him at this site to make what is in essence a legal petition regarding her pending marriage (Ruth 3:6–13).

During later periods, as villages acquired walls or grew into towns, the gate area became the place of judgment where cases were brought before the elders. Thus after Ruth confronts Boaz at the threshing floor, he goes to the gate and calls on the elders to sit with him and decide her case (Ruth 4:1–2). The judicial process included restating the legal situation, hearing testimony, and resolving the problem before the witnessing elders (Deut 21:18–21).

> *Her husband is known in the city gates, taking his seat among the elders of the land.*
> —*Prov 31:23*

> *Then the LORD raised up judges, who delivered them out of the power of those who plundered them.*
> —Judg 2:16

The Judges

After the deaths of Moses and Joshua, the only other authority figures during the settlement period were the judges. They are portrayed in the book of Judges as charismatic leaders chosen by Yahweh to liberate the people from oppression. For the most part, the judges were military leaders, not judicial or religious figures. Their role was to carry out a God-directed campaign against a Canaanite, Philistine, or other enemy group. The combined intervention of Yahweh and the judge then relieved the people of the burden of taxes, slavery, or oppression, which they had originally brought upon themselves by their sin (Judg 2:11–19).

Individual skills as a military leader, however, were not the chief qualification for a judge. Gideon, who was reluctant to serve and considered himself unqualified to lead men (Judg 6:15), defeats the Midianites with a force of only 300 men and an unorthodox strategy (Judg 7:19–23). In preparing for a battle against the king of Hazor, Deborah relied upon the generalship of Barak and a promise of victory from Yahweh to inspire the troops (Judg 4:6). Samson, the most unusual of the judges, took on the Philistines, single-handedly killing thousands of them. Eventually, however, he succumbed to his infatuation with Delilah and to his inflated pride (Judg 16:4–22). His failure also may be attributed to the violation of his Nazirite vows to God (Num 6:2–21).

None of the judges, other than Samuel, were national figures. They operated in specific, limited areas and dealt with local problems. Occasionally, the judge called on other tribes to aid in a military campaign, but it was apparently up to the tribal leaders to decide whether they would go. Thus when Deborah called on

Remains of a four-roomed house, Hazor.

the Israelites to join in the war against Jabin, the king of Hazor, five tribes sent their warriors. The "clans of Reuben," however, as well as Gilead, Dan, and Asher, for their own reasons, chose not to respond (Judg 5:14–18).

The twelve-tribe league, as it is described in Joshua, does not appear to have operated during the settlement period. The narrative does not include a single example of cooperation among all twelve tribes. In fact, in several instances they are described as fighting among themselves (Josh 22:10–12; Judg 8:1; 12:1–6; 20:12–48).

Some tribes are not even mentioned by name in the text of Judges. It seems likely, therefore, that several of the smaller tribes, like Simeon (mentioned only in Judg 1:3), were absorbed into larger ones. Thus when Saul was proclaimed king by the tribes of both the north and the south at Gilgal (1 Sam 11:14–15), all twelve would no longer have existed as identifiable, independent groups. However, the tradition of Israel's original twelve tribes descended from Jacob continued in use as an ideal expression of the nation's cultural roots.

> *She used to sit under the palm of Deborah between Ramah and Bethel in the hill country of Ephraim; and the Israelites came up to her for judgment.*
>
> —Judg 4:5

A description of the role played by the judges in the religious activities of the people will be dealt with in the unit on religious practices. The legal function of the judge is mentioned only with regard to Deborah and Samuel. While their legal activity is not described in detail, it is interesting to note that both operated in the vicinity of the cities of Ramah and Bethel in the "hill country of Ephraim." Deborah sits in judgment over people who bring their cases to her (Judg 4:5). In contrast, Samuel travels a circuit from Bethel to Gilgal and Mizpah, going from village to village and administering justice (1 Sam 7:15–17). His territorial authority is widened as far south as Beer-sheba when he appoints his sons to be judges over that region (1 Sam 8:1–2).

The types of cases heard by a judge would probably include those that could not be decided by the heads of households or the assembly of elders. Since both Deborah and Samuel also function as prophets, it may be that the people assumed that their judgments would be based on both the legal tradition and divine revelation.

FAMILY LIFE

Marriage Customs

First-time marriages continued to be arranged by the bride's father during this period. In principle, endogamy, or marriage within the group (i.e., the Israelite clans), was still the norm in Israelite villages. However, once the Israelites settled in Canaan, mixed marriages were probably more common. For instance, Samson's father encouraged him to marry a "woman among your kin, or among all our

people," but Samson insisted that a marriage be arranged with a Philistine woman who caught his eye (Judg 14:3). Similarly, there seems to be no stigma attached to Boaz's marriage to the Moabitess Ruth (Ruth 4:13). As in the ancestral period, polygamy was not uncommon during Israel's settlement. Gideon had seventy sons by many wives (Judg 8:30), and Elkanah, the father of Samuel, had two wives, Hannah and Peninnah (1 Sam 1:2).

In contrast to the arranged marriage for young couples, the custom regarding widows apparently allowed for more direct contact between the two participants. Ruth goes directly to Boaz at the threshing floor to obtain his aid in arranging their marriage. David simply sends messengers to ask Abigail, the widow of Nabal, to become his wife (1 Sam 25:39–42).

The economic factors associated with arranging a marriage figure in several episodes during the settlement period. Sometimes the accomplishment of some great deed could substitute for the actual payment of a dowry. A good example of this occurs when Saul offers riches and the hand of his daughter to the man who is able to slay Goliath (1 Sam 17:25). Later, though, he demands one hundred Philistine foreskins of David as an additional dowry for his daughter Michal (1 Sam 18:25). Similarly, Caleb offers his daughter Achsah to the conqueror of the city of Kiriath-sepher (Debir). Once Othniel has accomplished this deed, however, the marriage negotiations are not yet complete. His future wife encourages Othniel to ask for an additional field, thereby increasing the size of her family's dowry payment. Achsah herself then asks for water rights, since the field they are given is in the arid Negeb region (Judg 1:12–15).

Childbirth and Child Rearing

Where they were available, midwives often helped with the birth of children. Mention of the team of Shiphrah and Puah in Exod 1:15

> *Now his daughter-in-law, the wife of Phinehas, was pregnant, about to give birth. When she heard the news that the ark of God was captured, and that her father-in-law and her husband were dead, she bowed and gave birth; for her labour pains overwhelmed her. As she was about to die, the women attending her said to her, "Do not be afraid, for you have borne a son." But she did not answer or give heed. She named the child Ichabod, meaning, "The glory has departed from Israel" . . .*
> —1 Sam 4:19–21

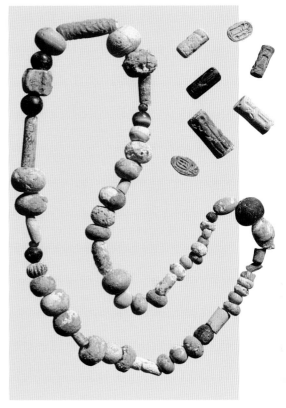

Necklace and beads from the Israelite Period.

probably reflects the assistance of two women: one who aided with the delivery, and one who supported the back of the woman on the birthing stool. Mesopotamian texts provide some insight into the elaborate set of rituals dealing with the difficulties of giving birth and the role of the midwife. One describes the fetus as a boat being steered through the amniotic fluid with the aid of the goddesses Inanna and Ninhursag. In another medical text the midwife (*ābsutu*) is required to place a necklace of stones on a linen thread around the mother's neck to help precipitate the birth.

Midwives instructed the mother on prenatal care, kept a close watch on the developing fetus, and noted any unusual discharges that might signal a problem with the pregnancy. Once labor began, she sang protective chants and cleansed the birthing room of any potential threats to mother or child. When the child was born, the midwife cleaned the infant with salt and water (Ezek 16:4), and presented it to the parents, declaring its availability for adoption. Job 3:3 contains this birthing scene, with the statement, "A man-child is conceived" followed by a "joyful cry" heralding the child's acceptance by the family (3:7).

The primitive medical practices and isolated environment of Israelite villages may have contributed to the high mortality rate among infants, as well as their mothers. Even when a midwife was present, there was no guarantee that both mother and child would survive the experience. For example, Rachel dies giving birth to Benjamin as the family travels between Bethel and Bethlehem (Gen 35:16–19). In another case, Phinehas' wife goes into premature labor after hearing the news of her husband's death in the battle against the Philistines at Aphek. The double shock to her system causes her own death, although the child survives, with the help of the women attending her (1 Sam 4:19–20).

Children grew up fast in the hill country villages. As soon as they were old enough to follow directions, they were put to work in the home or the fields. As they grew older some were sent to guard the herds (1 Sam 16:11), or

> *Then the women said to Naomi, "Blessed be the LORD, who has not left you this day without next-of-kin; and may his name be renowned in Israel!"*
> —*Ruth 4:14*

were apprenticed to craftsmen in the village. Occasionally a child was sent to serve in the religious shrines. For instance, after he is weaned at the age of three or four, Samuel is taken to Shiloh to begin his training as a priest (1 Sam 1:24).

Israelite children were expected to be respectful and obedient to their parents (Exod 20:12). They were to answer the call and orders of their elders (1 Sam 3:5). Disobedient children, like the sons of Eli (1 Sam 2:22–25), were considered a disgrace to the family and the community (see also Deut 21:18–21). The ultimate expression of obedience by a child is found in the case of Jephthah's daughter (Judg 11:34–39). She willingly submits to being sacrificed so that her father's oath can be honored.

Inheritance Practices

As in the ancestral period, during the settlement, land continued to pass from father to son. The congratulations given to Naomi upon the birth of her grandson through Ruth stress the importance of a male heir: "Blessed be the LORD, who has not left you this day without next-of-kin. . . . He shall be to you a restorer of life and a nourisher of your old age" (Ruth 4:14–15). Even for a man who had died, as Ruth's first husband had, a male heir was so important that when a widow remarried, her first-born child counted as the son of the dead man (Deut 25:5–6; on levirate marriage, see pp. 38–40).

Should the male line fail completely, provisions were also made during the settlement period for female inheritance. The five daughters of Zelophehad, who died in the wilderness without producing a son, ask Moses and the elders, "Why should the name of our father be taken away from his clan because he had no son? Give to us a possession among our father's brothers" (Num 27:4). Upon inquiring of the Lord, Moses is told that daughters are to inherit from their father if they have no brothers (vv. 5–11). Such daughters, however, must marry into the clan of their father to ensure their inheritance remains within their father's family (36:1–13).

The settling of such legal cases was often demonstrated by symbolic gestures, many involving clothing. When Ruth approaches Boaz at the threshing floor and asks that he redeem her dead husband through levirate marriage, she requests that he spread his cloak over her to signify that he accepts his responsibilities as her next-of-kin (Ruth 3:9). Later, when the unnamed man who is more closely related to Ruth declines his responsibility of levirate marriage, he removes his sandal and gives it to Boaz (4:8). His action is explained as a custom "to confirm a transaction": "The one took off a sandal and gave it to the other; this was the manner of attesting in Israel" (v. 7). For her part, Ruth does not pull off her unnamed relative's sandal, spit in his face, and state, "This is what is done to the man who does not build up his brother's house," as is her right according to Deut 25:9–10 (on clothing used as payment, see pp. 111–112).

While some families struggled to produce even one male heir, in cases of polygamous families, a father may have had too many sons claiming inheritance rights. Deut 21:15–17, a law in the Deuteronomic Code (dated to ca. 620 B.C.), deals with this matter and probably originated in the family customs of the settlement period. The law states that if a man has two wives, "one of them loved and the other disliked," and the wife whom he does not like bears his first child, he cannot choose to treat a son of the beloved wife as his first-born child with regard to the inheritance (see also the Code of Hammurabi 167, 170–171; *ANET*, 173).

Olive trees around fields outside Bethlehem. In such fields Ruth met Boaz at the threshing floor.

Burial Practices

Just as Abraham's purchase of the cave of Machpelah established his claim to a small part of Canaan, so do the narrative accounts of burials during the settlement period. Descriptions of burials from this period generally function as a means of establishing or solidifying claim to tribal territories. For instance, the bones of Joseph, which were carried by the people out of Egypt at the time of the exodus, were finally buried in a plot of ground near Shechem (Josh 24:32). This piece of land had been purchased centuries earlier by his father Jacob from King Hamor (Gen 33:18–20). By this action the Joseph tribes legitimized their claim to that area. Similarly, Joshua is buried "in his own inheritance at Timnath-serah" in the hill country of Ephraim (Josh 24:30).

The burials of Gideon and Samson, in contrast to the proprietary burials mentioned above, are in family tombs. Gideon is buried in the "tomb of his father Joash, at Ophrah of the Abiezrites" (Judg 8:32), and Samson is interred "between Zorah and Eshtaol in the tomb of his father Manoah" (Judg 16:31). As in the case of the ancestral tomb in the cave of Machpelah at Hebron, these burial places imply multigenerational residency in the area.

The burial caves or rock-cut tombs themselves were located outside the village proper. Some personal possessions were buried with the corpse, usually to serve as symbols of who the person was in life. Still, some items may have been designed as comforts in the afterlife or as charms to drive away evil spirits. Archaeological evidence from the Late Bronze tombs found at Ugarit (1400–1200 B.C.) suggests that a strand of popular religion involved communication with the dead and a sense of kinship with past generations. Superstitions about the spirits of the dead and a form of ancestor worship were strictly forbidden in biblical law (Lev 19:31; Deut 26:13–14), but legislation prohibiting its practice suggests it continued to exist. The only narrative that contains evidence of an ancestor cult and the practice of communicating with the dead, or **divination,** is found in the story of Saul's

The high place at Dan.

drastic purge of mediums and his subsequent visit to the witch of Endor in 1 Sam 28:3–19.

Israel's burial practices and participation in ancestral cults demonstrate a belief in an afterlife. Various biblical texts speak of **Sheol,** a deep and shadowy abode inhabited by the dead, both the good (Gen 37:35) and the evil (Num 16:30). It is not a place of punishment, but those in Sheol are cut off from the "living God" (Ps 6:5; 88:3–5; see Deut 5:26; Josh 3:10). Sheol is closely connected to the grave, and the dead seem to inhabit both places at the same time (Ps 49:14).

Family members performed the burial rites and, sometimes, the ancestral cult rituals described above. Caring for the tombs enabled living family members to maintain their inheritance in the land and secured their participation in ongoing society. Those whose burials went untended were not only exiled from God, but were also cut off from the inheritance of the living. This is the case with Achan, who steals from the spoils of Jericho the "devoted things" (Josh 7:1, 19, 21). After he is caught and confesses, Joshua and "all Israel" stone him to death and bury him under a great heap of stones (vv. 25–26; see 10:26). However, even in the case of crime punishable by death, bodies are not to be left unburied after death, since such exposure would constitute punishment in the afterlife, an area of authority that God has not granted to humans (Deut 21:22–23).

RELIGIOUS PRACTICES

Israelite religious practices in the exodus and settlement period range from the magnificent spectacle of thousands confirming the covenantal obligations at Sinai (Exod 19:17 and 24:3–8), to private family worship at the shrine of Micah's graven image (Judg 17:4–5). Coming out of Egypt's polytheistic environment, the Israelites were not immediately able to adapt themselves to a strict monotheism.

The signs of power displayed by Yahweh and his spokesman Moses were enough to convince the people to leave Egypt and to return to Canaan. Nevertheless, once they arrived, many found the lure of other cultures and other gods irresistible (Judg 3:5–6).

Altars

Altars served a variety of purposes. They were sometimes built as expressions of thanksgiving for a military victory (Exod 17:15–16), or as a memorial or "witness" of the faithfulness of the people to the covenant (Josh 22:10–34). For the most part, however, altars were used to make sacrifices to God. The altar built for the **tent of meeting** (**tabernacle**), in which Israel worshiped during its desert wanderings, is described with four horns, or raised areas, on its corners (Exod 27:1–2). Horned altars like this have been discovered at Arad and Beersheba, but they date to the later monarchy period (beginning in the 10th cent.; see p. 124), not to the exodus.

According to the **Covenant Code,** altars were supposed to be constructed of earth or uncut stone (Exod 20:24–26). This injunction reflects the nomadic character of the Israelites during the wilderness period. It complements the command that there should be no steps going up to the altar so as not to expose "your nakedness" (v. 26). Both instructions probably also exhibit a distinction between Israelite sacrifices and those of the Canaanites. For example, the magnificent Early Bronze circular altar uncovered at the Canaanite city of Megiddo has several steps going up to the top of the platform.

The further stipulation that their altars were to be built "in every place where I cause my name to be remembered" (v. 24), links particular altars to specific events in the nation's history and perhaps to long-used sacred sites. Thus Gideon builds an altar after experiencing a **theophany** (a physical manifestation of God's person) and a command to liberate his people from the Midianites (Judg 6:22–24). In

The remains of the Chalcolithic Period altar at Megiddo.

71

Judg 21:4–23, the tribes gather at Bethel, a site associated with Israelite worship as far back as Abraham and Jacob, build an altar, sacrifice, and ask God's guidance in preparation for battle.

Types of Sacrifices

There were two major types of sacrifices made on these altars: **burnt offerings** of animals and **freewill** or **thank offerings** of animals or cereal. Detailed instructions for these offerings are given to Moses when God tells him how to construct the tent of meeting (Exod 25–40; Lev 1–10).

The instructions for burnt offerings differ, depending on the animal being sacrificed. A burnt offering from a herd of cattle must be a male and without blemish. The person bringing the sacrifice must lay hands upon the head of the bull in order for it to be accepted as an atonement sacrifice. Once the bull is slaughtered, priests dash its blood against the sides of the altar. The bull is flayed and burned entirely (Lev 1:1–9). If the offering is from a herd of sheep or goats, the process is the same, except that hands are not laid upon the animal (vv. 10–13). Turtledoves and pigeons may also be offered. In this case, the bird's neck is wrung and its blood is drained against the side of the altar (vv. 14–17). Such "an offering by fire of pleasing odor to the LORD" (vv. 9, 13, 17) may be made to draw the attention of the deity, as in the case of Balaam's sacrifices in Num 23:1–2. However, the whole burnt offering usually serves as an atonement sacrifice, like the ones made by Job on behalf of his family in case they might sin (Job 1:5).

There are also varieties of freewill and thank offerings. A worshiper may present an unblemished animal of either sex from a herd or flock. Hands are laid upon this offering, and its blood is dashed against the side of the altar, too. Unlike the burnt sacrifice, however, only the fat of the freewill or thank offering is burned (Lev 3:1–5). The one making the offer-

> *You shall not delay to make offerings from the fullness of your harvest and from the outflow of your presses. The firstborn of your sons you shall give me.*
> —*Exod 22:29*

ing cooks and eats the remainder of the animal (7:15–18). Grain mixed with oil and frankincense, or baked into unleavened cakes or wafers, may also be given as freewill and thank offerings. A portion of these sacrifices is burned on the altar. The remainder goes to the priests performing the sacrifice (2:1–16; 7:11–14). Freewill or thank offerings do not function as atonement, but rather as celebrations brought to the Lord in joy. Such offerings seem to be the case when Elkanah distributes meat from his sacrifices between his two wives (1 Sam 1:3–5).

Some sacrifices are performed when "anyone sins unintentionally in any of the LORD's commandments about things not to be done, and does any one of them" (Lev 4:2). The same offerings are used when a person needs purification from a disease, or when a vow is fulfilled (6; 12; 15). Purification offerings are customized to the person bringing the sacrifice. For example, if it is an anointed priest who sins, he lays his hands on a male bull without blemish, whereas a ruler who sins is to lay his hands on a male goat (4:3, 24; see vv. 15, 28). After the laying on of hands, the priest slaughters the sacrifice. He dips his finger in the blood and sprinkles it seven times before the Lord. The priest pours the remainder of the blood on the base of the altar. The fat of the animal is then burned (vv. 4–10, 15–20, 24–26, 29–31). For those who cannot afford the prescribed animals, provisions for the use of other animals are given (5:1–13).

All sacrifices expressed the people's respect for the power of their God. Failure to show proper respect for the laws and rituals associated with sacrifice could be fatal. Thus Aaron's

Iron altar shovels from Dan, 9–8th century B.C.

sons Nadab and Abihu are consumed by fire after performing a sacrificial act not commanded by the Lord (Lev 10:1–3). Similarly, in stealing from a portion of the sacrifice that was set aside as God's alone (7:1–21), Eli's sons condemned themselves (1 Sam 2:12–17).

Some sacrifices are associated with national gatherings (Judg 2:5), or communal events like the Passover (Exod 12 and Josh 5:10). Such communal celebrations took shape in the context of the development of a calendar of religious holidays. Feasts centered on the major events of the agricultural year planting season, wheat harvest, and the autumn ingathering of fruit, grapes, and olives (Exod 23:14–17). The number of feasts and the rituals associated with them became more elaborate after the settlement period, as the legislation in Lev 23:1–44 and Deut 16:1–17 attests.

Spontaneous sacrifices also occur in the narrative, sometimes in the context of hospitality offered to a "visitor," who is only later recognized to be God or an angel. In Judg 6:17–21, Gideon is visited by an angel. He does not trust at first that his visitor is divine, and asks for a sign before offering him a "present" of a prepared kid, unleavened cakes, and a pot of broth, just as he might offer to a human guest. The angel instructs him to place the food on a rock, and to pour the broth over it as a libation. After the angel touches it with his staff, flames consume the offering, and he disappears.

A similar case occurs in Judg 13:15–23. Samson's parents were visited by a "man of God" who foretells the birth of their son. When he appears a second time to Manoah and his wife, they offer him a meal as an expression of hospitality and thanks for his good news. The angel refuses their food, but suggests that they offer the kid as a burnt offering on a rock. When this is done, the angel ascends in the flames from the makeshift altar.

One final example of spontaneous sacrifice occurs in 1 Sam 6:14–15. Here, the people of Beth-shemesh are surprised by the return of the ark of the covenant from its Philistine captivity. They rejoice by breaking up the Philistines' cart for fuel and sacrificing the two cows that had drawn it to their fields. Two Levites elevate the ark during the ceremony by placing it on a rock which overlooks the sacrifice.

The only example of human sacrifice by an Israelite in the settlement period is found in Judg 11:30–39. In preparing to fight a battle

The Levites took down the ark of the LORD and the box that was beside it, in which were the gold objects, and set them upon the large stone. Then the people of Beth-shemesh offered burnt offerings and presented sacrifices on that day to the LORD.
—1 Sam 6:15

against the Ammonites, Jephthah, the Gileadite judge, takes a vow that he will sacrifice the first person who comes out of his tent to greet him upon his return. This turns out to be his virgin daughter. He is probably reluctant to carry out his promise, but she insists that he fulfill his oath, although she does ask for a two-month period to mourn her unfulfilled life and untimely death.

This practice seems uncharacteristic of Israelite society (compare Gen 22:1–19), and therefore may be an example of a Canaanite practice that the Transjordanian tribes had adopted. Jephthah's oath may be another sign of cultural borrowing. His oath is similar to the one taken by Saul in 1 Sam 14:38–39—also during a war against the Ammonites.

National Places of Worship

A few sites occupied in the settlement period have national religious significance. Some, like Shechem and Bethel, have a previous history of Israelite religious and social activity. Others, like Shiloh and Kiriath-jearim, are marked as significant by the presence of the ark of the covenant, and have no pre-settlement background as an Israelite cultic site. In no case, however, is there one site that is preeminent over the others as Jerusalem was in later periods. This was probably due to the fragmented nature of the tribes during the time of the settlement. Travel to a central shrine was difficult, since they did not control the entire country.

Therefore, national gatherings at local sites signaled significant events in the history of Israel. According to Josh 18:1, the "whole congregation of the Israelites assembled at Shiloh,

> Then whoever comes out of the doors of my house to meet me, when I return victorious from the Ammonites, shall be the LORD's, to be offered up by me as a burnt offering.
> —Judg 11:31

and set up the tent of meeting there." The tent of meeting and the ark had traveled with the people during the conquest. Now that the conquest was over, the ark was brought to a central location in the hill country where distribution of the land could be made to the tribes. Since Shiloh had no previous ties to Israelite history, it was an ideal, neutral site for the distribution.

Shiloh was not the site, however, of the overriding religious event of the late conquest period. Instead, Shechem is where Joshua gathered the tribes and performed a **covenant renewal ceremony** (Josh 24). He recited the epic history of the people from the time of the ancestors through the conquest, and demanded that they put away their old gods and old religious practices and worship only Yahweh. To register their assent to the covenant, he wrote down the statutes and ordinances on a stone and placed it as a memorial stele "under the oak in the sanctuary of the LORD" (vv. 25–26). Shechem's association with the very beginnings of Yahweh worship, when Abraham constructed an altar there (Gen 12:6–7), provided the proper symbolic background for this ceremony.

Bethel also serves as a central shrine in Judg 20:27, just as it does during the monarchy period (1 Kgs 12:29). With the ark standing in their midst, the tribes gather here during a war against the rebellious tribe of Benjamin. The tribes are initially defeated by Benjamin, and now are "weeping" before the Lord at Bethel. This is reminiscent of Judg 2:5, where God tells them he will no longer drive the Canaanites out of the land on their behalf, and they weep; an action that gives their location its name, *Bochim* ("weepers"). Bethel seems to be the designated site for national weeping and repentance.

During the late settlement period, Shiloh is once again described as the residence of the ark of the covenant. The people journey here once a year to bring their sacrifices (1 Sam 1:3).

Capture of the Ark

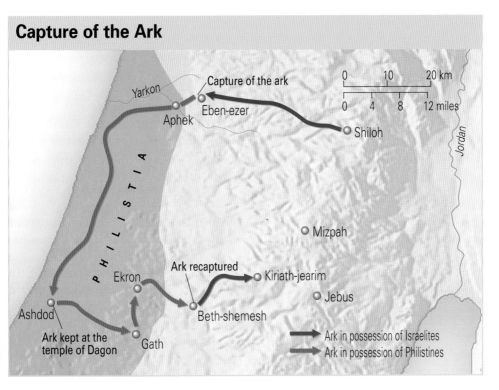

Now this man used to go up year by year from his town to worship and sacrifice to the LORD of hosts at Shiloh, where the two sons of Eli, Hophni and Phinehas, were priests of the LORD.
—1 Sam 1:3

This narrative presupposes a fairly long residence for the ark and a temple or shrine to house it (1 Sam 3:3). The yearly pilgrimage by Elkanah and his wives may reflect the injunction in Exod 23:16 to keep the feast of ingathering, and it implies that the Israelites held fairly tight control over the area around Shiloh. Even so, it seems unlikely that all of the villagers throughout the hill country would have made the trip each year.

After the Israelites were defeated by the Philistines at Aphek (1 Sam 4:5–11) and the ark was captured, Shiloh was probably destroyed. Archaeological excavations at the site show a destruction level around 1050 B.C., and the transference of the ark to Kiriath-jearim (1 Sam 6:21) implies that Shiloh no longer existed. Immediately after this, Mizpah, in the territory of Benjamin, serves as a gathering site (1 Sam 7:5). On this occasion, Samuel purifies the people through fasting and a libation of water. He completes the ritual by sacrificing a whole nursing lamb as a sin offering for the people (v. 9), and by setting up a memorial stone (v. 12).

Throughout the remainder of Samuel's career as judge, and during Saul's early kingship, Mizpah is the site for national gatherings. A different town named Mizpah is the assembly point for Jephthah's army in Transjordan (Judg 10:17). It is the place the tribes gather to hear the complaint of the wronged Levite (Judg 20:1), and it is one of the places on Samuel's judicial circuit (1 Sam 7:16). Samuel also calls the people together at Mizpah to choose a king by lot (1 Sam 10:17).

Then the Ammonites were called to arms, and they encamped in Gilead; and the Israelites came together, and they encamped at Mizpah.
—Judg 10:17

Local Shrines

Since the tribes were scattered throughout the hill country and travel was difficult at best, attendance at local shrines and observance of local religious customs were the norm for the majority of Israelite villagers. As noted in Judg 3:5–6, the Israelites dwelt among the Canaanite people, "and they took their daughters as wives for themselves, and their own daughters they gave to their sons; and they worshiped their gods."

Despite the injunction against sacred images (Exod 20:4–5), several of the narratives in Judges mention them as accepted objects of worship. In Gideon's village, his father builds an altar to Baal and sets up a sacred pole, or Asherah (Judg 6:25–26). Gideon tears this altar down, but later he has a golden ephod made from spoil taken in a war against the Midianites (Judg 8:24–28). The **ephod** was a garment worn by Israelite priests, but the term also designates a garment used to adorn idols in Canaanite worship. Gideon sets up the ephod in his hometown of Ophrah, and it eventually becomes an object of worship.

The most blatant example of the worship of sacred images within a household shrine appears in Judg 17:3–5, 7–13. Micah, a man of the hill country of Ephraim, receives a large quantity of silver from his mother; he uses a portion of it to fabricate a graven image, an ephod, and other sacred images known as **teraphim.** Micah installs these objects in a shrine in his housing cluster, and designates one of his sons as officiating priest. Later, a man from the city of Bethlehem is hired by Micah as his official Levitical priest. Micah is

sure he has done the right thing and says, "Now I know that the Lord will prosper me, because the Levite has become my priest" (v. 13).

Micah's shrine and images clearly transgressed the bounds of Israelite law. But this offense is practically excused with the statement that "In those days there was no king in Israel; all the people did what was right in their own eyes" (v. 6). This same statement (18:1) is also used to justify the subsequent theft of the images and the priest by the migrating tribe of Dan in 18:14–31.

The question then arises, why did a Levite, a man charged with teaching and maintaining the law, consent to serve a group of sacred images? Why did Micah set them up in the first place, and why did the Danites jump at the chance to steal them for themselves? The answer almost certainly is that popular religion, the religion of the local villages, was not the pure monotheism required by the law at Sinai. Recent excavations at Tell Qiri, a settlement dating to the period of the judges, revealed a similar household shrine with incense burners and a large number of animal bones. A substantial percentage of the bones proved to be the right foreleg of goats. This is reminiscent of the law in Exod 29:22, which calls for the sacrifice of the "right thigh" of the ram.

Evidence such as this suggests that the Israelites found it hard to give up household gods and were attracted to the agricultural gods and ritual practices of the Canaanites. The original ritual behind the Day of Atonement (Lev 16:7–10), with its use of a sacrificial goat upon whose head the sins of the people are placed, may have a Canaanite or pre-Yahwistic background. Driving it out into the wilderness as an offering to a demon *"Azazel"* also seems out of character for Israelite worship.

Much of what the later biblical writers described as Canaanite worship practices was also common to the Israelites throughout their

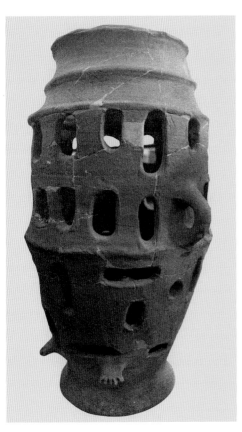

Cult incense stand.

to his friends after Gideon destroyed their Baal altar suggests as much: "Will you contend for Baal? Or will you defend his cause? . . . If he is a god, let him contend for himself, because his altar has been pulled down" (Judg 6:31). A similar henotheistic note surfaces in Jephthah's reply to an Ammonite demand that he return the land "from the Arnon to the Jabbok and to the Jordan" (Judg 11:12–24). He first recites the history of how Yahweh had given the Israelites victory over Sihon, king of the Amorites (see Num 21:21–32). Then, summing up their right to keep these captured lands, he states:

> Should you not possess what your god Chemosh gives you to possess? And should we not be the ones to possess everything that the Lord our God has conquered for our benefit? (Judg 11:24)

Circumcision
Circumcision, like sacrifice and fasting, functions within the biblical narrative as a means of rededicating the people. It is a distinctive sign of the covenant with Yahweh, differentiating the Israelites from the "uncircumcised" Philistines. However, circumcision's reintroduction at crucial points in the narrative suggests that it also has a role in ritual purification.

This practice was first introduced in the time of Abraham (Gen 17:10), and appears as part of the strategy used by the sons of Jacob to capture the city of Shechem (Gen 34:14–29). At the beginning of the exodus-settlement period, Yahweh demands that Moses circumcise his son before he returns to Egypt (Exod 4:25–26). In this case, Moses has failed to conform to Hebrew custom delaying Israel's liberation from Egypt. Zipporah, Moses' wife and the daughter of the Midianite priest, rectifies the discrepancy by performing the circumcision. She uses a flint knife to cut off her son's foreskin, and touches it to Moses' feet (a euphemism for his genitals), declaring him to be "a bridegroom of blood." This act, a parallel to the ritual of placing the blood of the

history (Deut 12:2–3, 2 Kgs 17:7–18). This is especially true of the use of the local shrines, known as "high places" (*bamôt*), for worship. For instance, in 1 Sam 9:12–13, Samuel goes to a city to bless a sacrifice being made on the "high place" (NRSV, "shrine"). In later periods, however, many of the kings are condemned for failing to outlaw the high places (2 Kgs 12:3, 16:4; on high places, see p. 41).

So many examples of idolatry and the borrowing of Canaanite rituals suggest that during this period the people were still polytheistic, or at best **henotheistic,** in their beliefs. Henotheists recognize a supreme god as well as a number of lesser divinities. Thus, the Israelites may have accepted Yahweh as their chief God, but still continued to believe in the existence of other gods. Joash's statement sacrificial lamb on the doorpost before the Passover (Exod 12:22), signals the renewal of the covenant pact. It marks the beginning of a new contractual arrangement with Yahweh that is again repeated when the Israelite males are circumcised prior to the conquest of Canaan (Josh 5:2). In this last instance, circumcision is further tied to the Passover ritual, which is performed while they wait to heal before going into the Promised Land (Josh 5:8–10).

Exodus-Settlement Period Review

1. How were houses constructed during the settlement period?

2. How did villagers grow, gather, and process grains? Olives? Grapes?

3. What weapons did the Israelites employ? How did their methods of warfare compare with those of their enemies?

4. Describe the organization and government of Israelite villages. How were legal matters settled?

5. How did Israelites marry, bear children, and bury their dead in the settlement period?

6. Where were the centers of Israelite religion during the exodus and settlement?

7. What sorts of sacrifices did the Israelites make?

8. What religious feasts did the Israelites celebrate?

9. How did the religious practices of the Israelites differ from those of the surrounding nations?

3. Monarchy Period

HISTORICAL INTRODUCTION

The transition from a loosely-formed confederation of tribes to an urban-based monarchy was the single most important political event in Israel's history. As recorded in the text, the monarchy and its attendant bureaucracy was not established overnight, nor did it begin without dispute or dissent. Once it was instituted, however, a new social and religious phase began for Israel. While Saul will be the first "king" chosen by God, he and his family will fall into abusive and corrupt practices that disqualify their rule. As a result, David, who in many ways is portrayed as an ideal king, will be the leader who establishes Jerusalem as the capital of his kingdom. His son Solomon will lay the foundations of a centralized, bureaucratic state, and constructs the temple of Yahweh as the focal point

Remains of the Jebusite tower in the city of David, possibly destroyed during David's conquest.

> *Then all the elders of Israel gathered together and came to Samuel at Ramah, and said to him, "You are old and your sons do not follow in your ways; appoint for us, then, a king to govern us like other nations."*
> —1 Sam 8:4–5

of worship and the symbol of God's presence. The covenant made at Sinai was expanded to include obedience to the king, and Yahweh's shift to Zion spelled the foundation of a priestly community that would orchestrate the rituals of sacrifice and define for all what obedience to God entailed.

It took a variety of factors to bring the monarchy into being, none of which could have been the single cause. These factors included the growing population of the Hebrew tribes, as well as continued hostilities and economic competition with the city-states of the Philistines and Canaanites. There was also a lack of outside interference by the superpowers of Egypt and Mesopotamia, due to the incursions of the Sea Peoples. Finally, the emergence of several charismatic military leaders, whose exploits built them a reputation and a following, served as a springboard for national leadership.

The elements of change that eventually led to the establishment of the monarchy began in the late settlement period, when it became evident to tribal leaders that the only way to meet the threat of Philistine and Canaanite domination was to unite the tribes under a centralized administration. As the last of the "judge figures," Samuel had had some success in joining the central hill country of Ephraim into a loose confederation. The towns and villages in this area looked to him, and to the priestly group that was previously housed at Shiloh, for leadership. The text describes his "circuit" within the region (1 Sam 7:15–17), and it may be assumed that his powers were employed to

settle tribal and clan disputes that might otherwise have torn the area apart (compare Deborah's judicial role in Judg 4:4–5).

A major indication that this arrangement would not continue to work after Samuel's time appears in 1 Sam 8:1–5. In this passage, Samuel has appointed his sons to judge the southern region of Beer-sheba. This was probably an attempt on his part to expand his effective area of administration into Judah. However, his sons, like Eli's (1 Sam 2:12–17, 22), were corrupt. They took bribes and "perverted justice" to such an extent that the elders of the tribes called Samuel to a meeting at his base in Ramah, and asked him to appoint a king to rule them instead. From that point on the text contains two strands of tradition: one which favors the idea of a monarchy (see 1 Sam 9:1—19:16), and the other that strongly opposes it (see 7:3–17; 8; 10:17–27). This dispute, which began with the inception of the kingship, continued even after the monarchy ceased to exist in the postexilic period.

Early Monarchy

Saul's rise to power, like David's a generation later, hinged upon his influence and ability as a war chief. His command of a professional force of fighters and his initial success against the Ammonites and Philistines gave him the credentials that tribal elders needed to name him as their king (1 Sam 11). The support he received from the priestly community in the person of Samuel gave his leadership position the sanction of Yahweh. Despite this, however, there were "worthless fellows" who questioned Saul's kingship from its start, demanding to know "how can this man save us?" (1 Sam 10:27). These sentiments speak to the difficulty of maintaining tribal loyalty in early Israel. Social unrest became increasingly evident when Saul ceased to win every battle (14:29–46; 18:6–9).

Moreover, Saul's relationship with Samuel began to deteriorate. This seems to result from

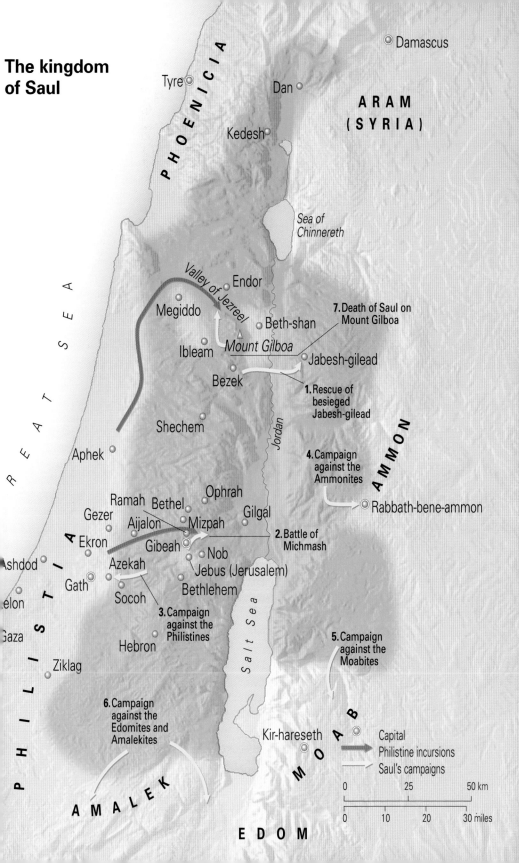

The kingdom of Saul

Damascus

PHOENICIA

ARAM
(SYRIA)

Tyre

Dan

Kedesh

Sea of
Chinnereth

Valley of Jezreel

Endor

Megiddo

Beth-shan

7. Death of Saul on
Mount Gilboa

Mount Gilboa

Ibleam

Jabesh-gilead

Bezek

1. Rescue of
besieged
Jabesh-gilead

Shechem

Jordan

AMMON

4. Campaign
against the
Ammonites

Aphek

Ophrah

Rabbath-bene-ammon

Ramah   Bethel

Gezer

Gilgal

Aijalon   Mizpah

Ekron

Gibeah

2. Battle of
Michmash

Nob

Azekah

Jebus (Jerusalem)

Gath

Bethlehem

Socoh

3. Campaign
against the
Philistines

Ashdod

Salt Sea

5. Campaign
against the
Moabites

elon

Hebron

Gaza

Ziklag

6. Campaign
against the
Edomites and
Amalekites

Kir-hareseth

M O A B

Capital

Philistine incursions

Saul's campaigns

A M A L E K

E D O M

G R E A T   S E A

P H I L I S T I A

0		25		50 km

0	10	20	30 miles

David's flight from Saul

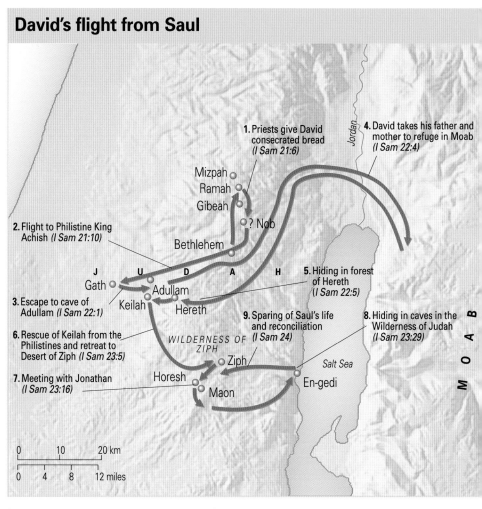

1. Priests give David consecrated bread (*I Sam 21:6*)
2. Flight to Philistine King Achish (*I Sam 21:10*)
3. Escape to cave of Adullam (*I Sam 22:1*)
4. David takes his father and mother to refuge in Moab (*I Sam 22:4*)
5. Hiding in forest of Hereth (*I Sam 22:5*)
6. Rescue of Keilah from the Philistines and retreat to Desert of Ziph (*I Sam 23:5*)
7. Meeting with Jonathan (*I Sam 23:16*)
8. Hiding in caves in the Wilderness of Judah (*I Sam 23:29*)
9. Sparing of Saul's life and reconciliation (*I Sam 24*)

Mizpah · Ramah · Gibeah · ? Nob · Bethlehem · Gath · Keilah · Adullam · Hereth · WILDERNESS OF ZIPH · Ziph · Horesh · Maon · En-gedi · Salt Sea · Jordan · MOAB

0   10   20 km
0 4 8 12 miles

his attempt to take over Samuel's cult functions. On three separate occasions (1 Sam 12–15), the narrative describes how Saul failed to follow tradition regarding sacrifice and the rules of the *herem* ("holy war"). A case is built against Saul to justify Saul's and his family's replacement on the throne by David. Several times Saul is even said to admit to David that

> *Now I know that you shall surely be king, and that the kingdom of Israel shall be established in your hand.*
>
> —1 Sam 24:20

his rival is destined to take the throne from him and his sons (1 Sam 24:20; 26:25).

Saul's peculiar admissions are just one indication that there is a political and theological agenda behind the retelling of the nation's history. This agenda can be seen in the book of Joshua. The method of history-telling in Joshua emphasizes the theological significance of Israel's conquest more than a strict recounting of historical fact.

In this record of the history of the monarchy, the successes and failures of kings depend entirely on their allegiance to Yahweh. Those kings that "do what is right in the sight of the Lord" help their nation to prosper; those who "do what is evil in the sight of the Lord" invite personal and national failure. There is a political and theological agenda to compare the kings of Israel and Judah to the pinnacle of proper kingship: David himself. In the case of Saul, for example, it is quite likely that the king did, in fact, overstep the bounds set by the priestly community. As a result, the priests chose a successor whom they thought they could control. David is described as the youngest of seven sons from an undistinguished clan of the tribe of Judah. By choosing him, Samuel and the Shiloh priesthood could not be accused of favoring the Ephraimite region. Plus, David's lack of experience and political connections would make it more likely that he would look to Samuel and the priests for support and advice.

David, however, quickly proves to be his own man, perfectly capable of acquiring the leadership and military skills necessary to become a rival chief to Saul. He initially enters Saul's royal court as a musician (1 Sam 16:18–23). David's value as a musician is enhanced by, or enhances, his status as "a man of valor, a warrior, prudent in speech, and a man of good presence." These qualities aid David in rising to the position of royal armor-bearer, and later to a leadership position in Saul's army.

Most important to later events is David's marriage to Saul's daughter Michal. This tie to the royal household gives David a claim, however remote, to the throne. Just how important she is to him becomes clear after Saul's death. David insists on Michal's return, despite that fact that their marriage was annulled by Saul many years earlier (1 Sam 25:44). He forces Abner, Saul's old general, to bring her to him as a prerequisite to his joining David's command (2 Sam 3:13). For the northern tribal leaders to join him, David needs some genealogical link with Saul's rule. This marriage will ease their acceptance of David as the legitimate successor of their former king.

The final break between Saul and David is caused by the king's awareness of David's increasing popularity (1 Sam 18:7–8). Certainly, the popular chant, "Saul has killed his thousands, and David his ten thousands" (1 Sam 18:7), must have caused royal jealousy. What results is a period of conflict between them that sees David branded as an outlaw. He eventually even joins the Philistines as a mercenary chief.

Like Jephthah in Judg 11:3–11, who became an outcast from his tribe and formed an outlaw band, David builds a following of his relatives and those discontent with Saul's rule (1 Sam 22:1–2). As a "masterless man" or banditti, David fits the complaint made by Nabal in 1 Sam 25:10 that "there are many servants today who are breaking away from their masters." David subsequently plays a cat-and-mouse game with Saul's army. Operating on the fringes of society, several of these bandits, including Joab and Abiathar, stay with David throughout his career, and form the nucleus of his advisory circle when he becomes king.

Even as an outlaw, David makes a name for himself by protecting the city of Keilah from the Philistines (1 Sam 23:1–5), and by helping shepherds guard their flocks in the hill country (1 Sam 25:7–8). Marriage alliances during this period also solidify David's position as king of Judah after Saul's death (Abigail, 1 Sam 25:39–42; Ahinoam, 1 Sam 25:43).

David's service with Achish, the Philistine king of Gath, seems to be an attempt on his part to remove himself from Saul's area of control, as well as an opportunity to acquire skills and knowledge that will help him when he becomes king. While employed by the Philistines, he builds support with the tribal chiefs of Judah by sending them portions of

> And the women sang to one another as they made merry, "Saul has killed his thousands, and David his ten thousands."
> —1 Sam 18:7

the spoil he takes in raids (1 Sam 30:26). Also during this period, David learns Philistine military tactics and strategies. Such an intimate knowledge of the enemy will prove invaluable when he leads his armies against them as king of Israel.

David's Rule

With the death of Saul and his sons in battle against the Philistines at Gilboa (1 Sam 31), David is free to establish himself as a political force within the tribes. At first, however, he does this within his own tribe of Judah. Loyalties among the Ephraimite tribes continue to center on Saul's family, and Abner successfully installs Ishbosheth as their king. Because the Philistines gained effective control over Ephraimite territory after Saul's defeat at Gilboa, Ishbosheth had to move his capital to the city of Mahanaim (2 Sam 2:8) on the other side of the Jordan. David, having been proclaimed king by the elders of Judah, chooses Hebron, long associated with the ancestors and the worship of Yahweh, as his capital (2 Sam 2:1-4).

A border war rages between the forces of David and Ishbosheth for seven years, until a falling-out between Saul's son and his general Abner leads to the unification of the two kingdoms. A series of negotiations and political assassinations then follows (2 Sam 3-4), and this removes all remaining obstacles to David's assumption of the full leadership of the tribes. The elders of Israel attend David in Hebron in order to acknowledge him as their king (2 Sam 5:1-3).

It is this acknowledgment by the elders and the tribes of Israel that ratifies David's kingship. Like Saul (1 Sam 10:24; 11:5-11), after having been chosen by Yahweh and anointed by the prophet (1 Sam 9:1—10:8; 16:1-13), David needs the support of the people in order to exercise kingly authority (2 Sam 2:4). The tribal groups that ratified the kingship of Saul and David made up a loosely-organized tribal **confederation.** This confederation provided social and political organization at the tribal level, with village elders settling local issues of law (Ruth 4). By the time of Solomon, Israel had been ruled by a central king for nearly seventy years, and had more than doubled in size. A wide range of bureaucratic institutions was required to support Israel's unification and expansion. These institutions existed in a rudimentary form, if at all, at the beginning of David's reign, and were largely developed during Solomon's rule (1 Kgs 4:1-21; 5:1—7:51; on Solomon's innovations see pp. 86–90).

Because unification of the tribes into a single kingdom remained a tenuous arrangement, they required delicate political handling by David and his court. Perhaps to remove the hint of favoritism towards his own tribe, David established a new capital at the more centralized and politically neutral site of Jerusalem. This Jebusite city, never before held by the Israelites (Judg 1:18, 21), provided a defensible location with access to trade routes and, later, a literate population from which to draw court employees to help manage the affairs of state (2 Sam 5:6–9; 1 Chr 11:4–9).

Jerusalem also served as virgin ground in which the Yahweh cult could grow and flourish. By bringing the ark of the covenant to his new capital (2 Sam 6:12–19), David signals his intent to steer an independent political and religious course to the priests of the old cultic centers at Shiloh, Shechem, and Hebron. This desire is curtailed, at least in part, when he is denied the right to construct a temple for the ark (2 Sam 7:4–16). In the next generation, however, his son Solomon overcomes any

> *So all the elders of Israel came to the king at Hebron; and King David made a covenant with them at Hebron before the LORD, and they anointed David king over Israel.*
>
> *—2 Sam 5:3*

David's united kingdom

HAMATH

Lebo-hamath

Berothah

ARAM (SYRIA)

Damascus

PHOENICIA

Sidon

GREAT SEA

Tyre

Dan

Kedesh

Acco   Chinnereth

Sea of
Chinnereth

Dor

Megiddo

Ramoth-gilead

Taanach   Beth-shan

Shechem

I S R A E

Joppa

AMMON

Gezer

Jazer

Ashdod

Rabbath-bene-ammon

Ashkelon   Gath

Jerusalem

PHILISTIA

Medeba

Gaza

Hebron

Aroer

Salt Sea

King's Highway

Beer-sheba

J U D A H

Brook of Egypt

MOAB

Zoar

Tamar

Kadesh-barnea

E D O M

25	50	75 km
15	30	45 miles

☐ Territory of Judah and Israel
☐ Vassal territory
■ Conquered territory

> *Now therefore thus you shall say to my servant David: Thus says the LORD of hosts: I took you from the pasture, from following the sheep to be prince over my people Israel;. . .*
> —2 Sam 7:8

opposition and builds the primary Yahwist temple in Jerusalem with the help of Phoenician expertise (1 Kgs 7).

Once established in Jerusalem, David and his general Joab consolidate Israel's political control over large areas of Canaan and Transjordan. Nearly continuous wars keep the sense of loyalty directed toward the capital and the king, and accelerate the decline of old loyalties to tribe and clan. However, the concept of kingship was still new in Israel, and disputes arose that threatened to rip the nation apart. The question of succession within David's household was one of the primary causes of dissension. In the last part of David's reign, Absalom precipitates a civil war in an attempt to seize the throne from his father (2 Sam 13–19). This proves to be the severest test of David's leadership, although it also unmasks some whose loyalties are questionable (Ahithophel and Mephibosheth). This gives David the opportunity to reaffirm tribal obligations to the monarchy while demonstrating the potency of his own personal army.

Solomon's Innovations

Absalom's revolt may, in fact, have smoothed the way for Solomon to succeed his father to the throne by eliminating enemies of the monarchy. Solomon begins his campaign by obtaining David's blessing (1 Kgs 1:29–30), the backing of the prophet Nathan, the support of Benaiah, the commander of the king's personal bodyguard, and of Zadok, a member of the Jerusalem priesthood. He can then argue that his power base is more legitimate and broader than that of his brother Adonijah. The tribal leaders fear that another civil war will weaken

the nation's ability to protect itself, and choose the course of continued stability by proclaiming Solomon king.

Solomon's first actions as king are designed to demonstrate that he is truly in charge of the nation. First, he ousts some of David's oldest advisers, Joab being the most conspicuous victim. The new monarch's intentions to rule as a true king, not just as the war chief of a sometimes rebellious confederation of tribes, are then shown in three extremely important actions. To begin with, by redrawing the boundaries of the twelve administrative districts of the kingdom, Solomon further

> *Solomon had twelve officials over all Israel, who provided food for the king and his household; each one had to make provision for one month in the year.*
> —1 Kgs 4:7

weakens tribal loyalties and reduces the threat of revolts (1 Kgs 4:1–21; compare Sheba's revolt against David in 2 Sam 20). Royal court employees are appointed to administer the newly created political units, to collect taxes, and to provide labor gangs for public works and defense projects. Each of these districts is made responsible for supporting the royal household one month in each year (1 Kgs 4:7). Since some districts were larger and richer, some provision must have been made to balance the financial load.

The second major action taken by Solomon is to turn Jerusalem into a true administrative and religious center for Israel. He accomplishes this with the aid of King Hiram of Tyre, who provides the building materials and architects to construct Solomon's palace and the temple of Yahweh (1 Kgs 5:7–12). The temple, built after the style of similar Canaanite temples, housed the ark of the covenant and, more

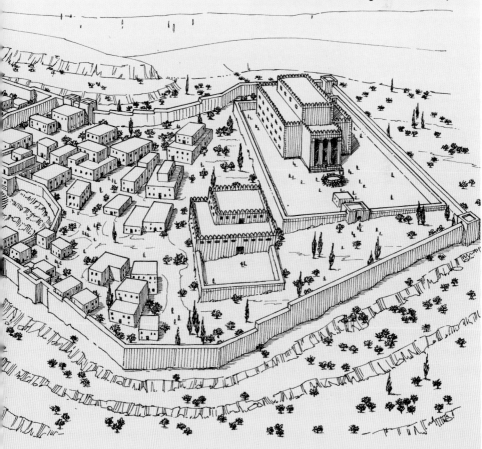

Artist's reconstruction of Jerusalem at the time of Solomon, showing Solomon's Temple.

Solomon made a marriage alliance with Pharaoh king of Egypt; he took Pharaoh's daughter and brought her into the city of David, until he had finished building his own house and the house of the LORD and the wall around Jerusalem.

—*1 Kgs 3:1*

Solomon's temple

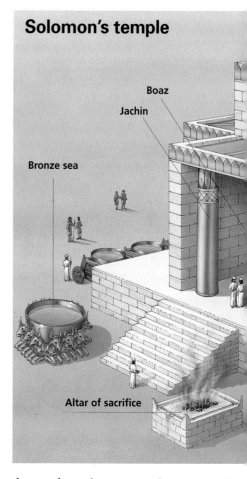

importantly, "housed" the presence of Yahweh among his people. Their God in the desert and at Mount Sinai has been transformed. His presence is now transferred to Mount Zion, and their role for him as the God of the confederated tribes is expanded to that of a national God who sanctions the rule of the king in Jerusalem, his holy city. With king and God enthroned in a well-established capital city, Israel now joins her neighbors as a legitimate nation.

As part of the process of installing the official worship of Yahweh in Jerusalem, Solomon initiates a new priesthood to serve in the temple. His ally Zadok heads this new group. Abiathar, David's old companion and a priest of the Shiloh cultic group, is exiled from Jerusalem and sent to the nearby city of Anathoth (1 Kgs 2:26). This serves the king's purpose of gaining a stronger hold over the activities of the priests. However, it also sets up a competition between the Jerusalemite and Levitical priesthoods that will continue until the fall of the temple in Jeremiah's time (587 B.C.).

Solomon's third major innovation as king is the establishment of close ties with several foreign nations. His ties to Hiram and Phoenicia are primarily economic, and are reflected by Phoenicia's aid in constructing the temple and palace complex. Political marriages also create foreign and domestic alliances, the most important of which is with a daughter of the king of Egypt (1 Kgs 3:1).

The Amarna Tablets from the fifteenth and fourteenth century B.C. (*ANET,* 483–90) confirm

that royal marriages were quite common. For example, the Hittite ruler Suppiluliumas I (ca. 1350–1325) married off his sister and two of his daughters to vassal princes, helping to assure his control over them. He himself wed a Babylonian princess, and agreed to give his son in marriage to the widow of Pharaoh Tutankhamen, but she died before the marriage could be performed. Such royal marriages gave an influential king the chance to establish political ties and alliances with other nations. Egypt during the mid-tenth century B.C. was weak and divided, and this may be why few clear records of its relations with Israel during this period have been found. Nevertheless, Solomon's marriage with Egyptian royalty, as much as anything else

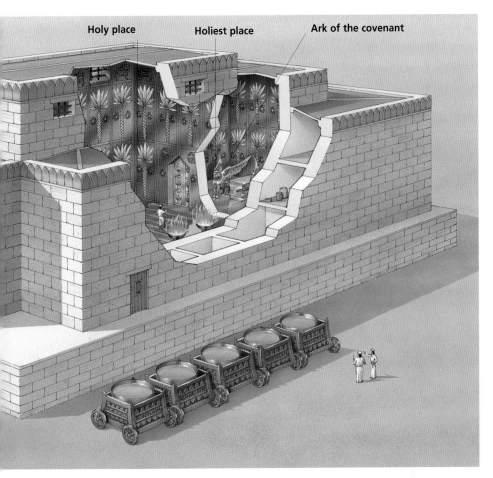

Holy place   Holiest place   Ark of the covenant

mentioned in the text, testifies to the fact that Israel had indeed become a nation to be reckoned with in Near Eastern affairs.

Whether this is an appropriate political action to be taken by an Israelite monarch or not, the theologically-minded text indicates that Solomon's wives are the prime cause of his downfall and the division of the kingdom (1 Kgs 11:1–13). In fact, Solomon's marrying foreign women and introducing the worship of their gods, coupled with the people's deep dissatisfaction over high taxes and labor service, all contribute to the schism of the next generation.

Solomon tries to establish a true monarchy on the foundation of the old confederation of tribes and their loyalty to David. He fortifies

the nation's borders with monumental defenses at Megiddo, Gezer, and Hazor (1 Kgs 9:15–19), and extracts huge amounts of the nation's produce to feed his army and labor gangs and to pay his debts. His actions justify Samuel's warnings (1 Sam 8:10–18) about the tyrannies of kings, and make it easier for the tribal leaders to dissolve the union when Solomon's son and successor Rehoboam refuses to concede to their demands for greater autonomy and shared leadership. The cry for secession goes out: "What share do we have in David? We have no inheritance in the son of Jesse. To your tents, O Israel!" (1 Kgs 12:16). The tribal elders now look to a new man, Jeroboam, who they hope will be more compliant. Jeroboam has some administrative skills,

> *So the king took counsel, and made two calves of gold. He said to the people, "You have gone up to Jerusalem long enough. Here are your gods, O Israel, who brought you up out of the land of Egypt."*
> —*1 Kgs 12:28*

having served Solomon as a supervisor of forced labor (1 Kgs 11:28). In addition, the prophet Ahijah, like Samuel in 1 Sam 16:1–13, provides divine sanction for the accession to power of a rival to the sitting king (1 Kgs 11:29–31). Although Jeroboam fled to Egypt and the court of pharaoh Shishak I (931–910 B.C.; 1 Kgs 11:40), once Solomon dies he quickly returns, and his accession as king of the northern tribes (1 Kgs 12:20) opens a new chapter in Israel's history.

It also signals an opportunity to Egypt and other Near Eastern powers to return their attention to a divided Israel. One sign of this is the campaign of Shishak I that traversed much of the country, devastating towns and stripping the cities of their wealth (*ANET*, 263-64; 1 Kgs 14:25-26; 2 Chr 12:2-12). Although Jerusalem is not mentioned as one of the 154 towns Shishak destroyed, the pharaoh's commemorative relief at Karnak notes that Solomon's son Rehoboam surrendered much of the city's wealth to him (1 Kgs 14:25–26).

Divided Monarchy

Rehoboam is left with David's original kingdom—the tribe of Judah—plus the city of Jerusalem. Jeroboam obtains the leadership over most of central and northern Israel and portions of Transjordan. However, he lacks a religious center upon which to focus the people's worship, and thus restores the old cultic centers of Dan and Bethel. In these shrines, located at either end of his kingdom, Jeroboam places golden calves to symbolize God's presence and to serve as a substitute for

The altar at Dan.

Solomon's united kingdom

Damascus

PHOENICIA

Tyre

Dan

ARAM
(SYRIA)

GESHUR

Acco

Hazor

Cabul

Asher

Naphtali

Sea of
Chinnereth

BASHAN

G R E A T   S E A

Zebulun

Megiddo

Issachar

Dor

Jezreel

Ramoth-
gilead

NAPHATH
DOR

Taanach   Beth-shan

Hepher

ISRAEL

Socoh

Shechem

Succoth

Mahanaim

G I L E A D

Joppa

Shiloh

Rabbath-bene-
ammon

Ephraim

Baalath

Gezer

Beth-horon

Gibeon

AMMON

Shaalbim

Benjamin

Jericho

Jerusalem

Gath   Beth-shemesh

JUDAH

GAD

Gaza

PHILISTIA

Hebron

Salt Sea

Beer-sheba

MOAB

Brook of Egypt

Tamar

E D O M

0	25	50 km
0	10	20	30 miles

Boundary of Solomon's empire
Boundary of administrative district
United kingdom of Israel and Judah
Vassal kingdoms
Solomonic fortification or building project

Ezion-geber

the ark of the covenant. He also supplants the Jerusalem priesthood by establishing a non-Levitical line of priests to serve in his shrines (1 Kgs 12:25–33).

Jeroboam further differentiates religion in the north by instituting a different festival calendar than the one followed at the Jerusalem temple. Specifically, he sets the Feast of Tabernacles, the year's main harvest festival, in the eighth month rather than the seventh (1 Kgs 12:32; see Lev 23:39; Num 29:12). Although it is said that this change is one that Jeroboam "alone had devised" (1 Kgs 12:33), it may be that the new monarch is reverting to an old agrarian calendar that was followed in the north before David and Solomon centralized Israel's worship in Jerusalem. Such a calendar would reflect the different harvest seasons in the Levant, which varied according to the temperature ranges of specific regions (on harvest seasons, see pp. 54–55). By realigning the Feast of Tabernacles with an older calendar, Jeroboam plays to the interests of northerners who want to see their traditional practices restored. In holding his own religious festivals, he also brings worshipers to his shrines, keeping them away from the temple in Jerusalem.

In the biblical tradition of the history of the kings, these actions became known as the "sin of Jeroboam." However, the shrines and festivals were shrewd political moves by a king who could not afford the retention of loyalties to Jerusalem. The non-Levitical priesthood also made it easier for him to control the cult. It cut short interference from priests and prophets, like Ahijah, who had helped him gain the throne. Plus, his promotion of the *bamôt* ("high places") in local villages and towns (1 Kgs 12:31) gained him the support of those tied more closely to popular or local religion than to a national cult.

Despite his attempts to consolidate power through political and religious reforms, Jeroboam still lacked one thing that his rival Rehoboam possessed. This was the sense of legitimacy that comes from multigenerational dynastic rule. Rehoboam had made mistakes, but loyalty to the Davidic line kept him in power, at least in Judah, and protected his descendants on the throne for the next three centuries. The tradition of an "everlasting covenant" with David's house (2 Sam 7:18–29; 1 Kgs 11:34–39) grew in importance and influence over the years. From the tradition grew the idea of, and hope for, a Messiah, expressed in later prophets and the postexilic period.

Without a tradition of dynastic rule, Jeroboam was subject to political pressures from the tribal leaders and the army. He also faced the wrath of the priestly community that was excluded from the central shrines of Dan and Bethel. It is not surprising, then, that the pattern of succession in the northern kingdom became one of succession by assassination. On occasion, this involved simple military coups, as in Omri's rise to power with the backing of the army (1 Kgs 16:15–22). In other cases, the prophets gave their sanction to a new claimant through the traditional means of anointing him. This was the situation with Jehu, who was anointed king by one of Elisha's associates (a "son of the prophets"), and who was commissioned to seize the throne from Ahab's son Joram (2 Kgs 9).

During the ninth century, Israel and Judah exhausted themselves in wars with other minor states in Syria, Transjordan, and Philistia. Israel also had expanded its control over Moab during Omri's reign. A resurgence of nationalism in that country during Ahab's reign is described in both 2 Kgs 3 and in the **Mesha Inscription,** a 35-line tribute praising the Moabite god Chemosh for delivering his

> *Zimri came in and struck him down and killed him, in the twenty-seventh year of King Asa of Judah, and succeeded him.*
> *—1 Kgs 16:10*

The kingdoms of Israel and Judah

Sidon

Damascus

Tyre

Dan

ARAM (SYRIA)

PHOENICIA

Hazor

GESHUR

Acco

Sea of Chinnereth

P H O E N I C I A

Dor

Megiddo

Shunem

Taanach

Beth-shan

Ramoth-gilead

Socoh

I S R A E L

Shechem

Penuel

AMMON

Shiloh

Aijalon

Bethel

Rabbath-bene-ammon

Gezer

Gibeon

Jordan

Gath

Jerusalem

Gaza

Hebron

Salt Sea

PHILISTIA

Arad Rabbah

Beer-sheba

Kir-moab

M O A B

J U D A H

Tamar

Kadesh-barnea

E D O M

E G Y P T

G R E A T   S E A

◎ Capital

★ Sanctuary city

—·— International border

➤ Route of invasion by Shishak of Egypt, c. 925 B.C.

| 0 | 25 | 50 | 75 km |

| 0 | 15 | 30 | 45 miles |

nation from its neighbor Israel (*ANET*, 320–321). While both documents claim victory over their opponent, the Moabite text probably reflects the end of effective Israelite rule in Transjordan. These conflicts often involved territorial disputes along their borders, as in the case of the war with Syria, in which Ahab of Israel and Jehoshaphat of Judah combined their forces to recapture Ramoth-gilead (1 Kgs 22:1–4). Justification for Elisha's tears, when he told Hazael that he would become king of Syria and would ravish Israel with his armies (2 Kgs 8:7–15), is found in Hazael's campaign against Gath and Jerusalem (2 Kgs 12:17–18). Hazael proved to be a very resilient king, despite pressures on his nation by the expanding Assyrian empire. Record of his sack of Israelite cities and acquisition of territory is found in the recently discovered **Tel Dan Inscription** (*OTPar*, 160–161), which also provides a reference to the "House of David."

The general lack of stability in the northern monarchy, without roots and without a tradition of smooth power transitions, played into the hands of the emerging superpower nations of Egypt and Assyria. Judah, and particularly Israel, exhausted themselves in wars with Syria (1 Kgs 20, 22 and 2 Kgs 6–7) and the nations of Transjordan (2 Kgs 3). The Mesha and Tel Dan inscriptions depict the types of defeat Israel and Judah faced at the hands of their neighbors. While Judah and Israel were engaged in local conflicts, the superpowers consolidated their control at home, and prepared to expand into this strategic land bridge between Mesopotamia and Egypt. The last period of relative independence for Israel and Judah came during the reigns of Jeroboam II (786–746) and Uzziah (782–742).

The shortsightedness of their policies with regard to other nations emerges in the prophecies of Amos and Hosea, and comes to full bloom after 740 B.C. in the face of the military might of the Assyrian king Tiglath-Pileser III (also known as "Pul," 2 Kgs 15:19). The

Mesha Stele, a Moabite inscription recounting the exploits of Mesha, king of Moab.

Assyrian war machine had first entered the area in 853 B.C. when their king, Shalmaneser III, was defeated at the battle of Qarqar by a coalition of kings, including Ahab. After the Assyrians defeated Syria in 841, however, King Jehu of Israel was forced to pay tribute to Shalmaneser III, according to the "Black Obelisk" inscription (*ANET*, 281). From that time on, the Assyrians, devastating large areas and massacring entire city populations, repeatedly forced their way south and west to the Mediterranean sea coast. Situated on the major trade route of the Via Maris, Syria, Israel, and the Philistine city-states were eventually absorbed into the growing Assyrian empire.

The campaigns of Tiglath-Pileser III

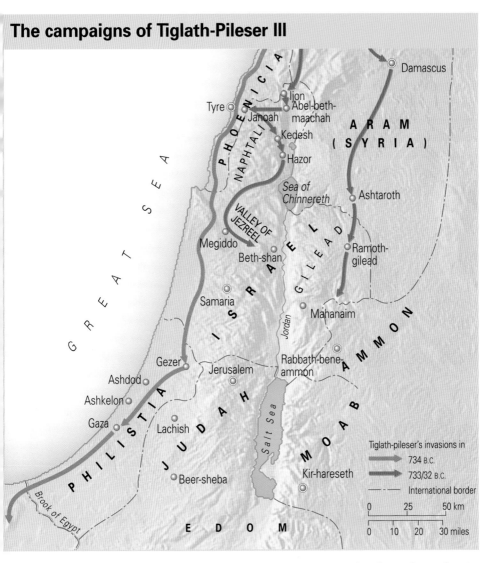

Damascus

Tyre

Ijon
Abel-beth-
Janoah maachah

Kedesh

**A R A M
(S Y R I A)**

Hazor

Sea of
Chinnereth

Ashtaroth

VALLEY OF
JEZREEL

Megiddo
Beth-shan

Ramoth-
gilead

Samaria

Mahanaim

Gezer
Jerusalem

Rabbath-bene-
ammon

A M M O N

Ashdod

Ashkelon

Gaza
Lachish

Salt Sea

Beer-sheba

Kir-hareseth

E D O M

Tiglath-pileser's invasions in

⟶ 734 B.C.

⟶ 733/32 B.C.

– · – International border

| 0 | 25 | 50 km |

| 0 | 10 | 20 | 30 miles |

These new vassal states of Assyria were restive under foreign rule and repeatedly revolted. In 736 B.C., Israel and Syria declare war on King Ahaz of Judah in order to force him to join their revolt against the Assyrians. Ahaz subsequently allies himself with the Assyrians (against the advice of the prophet Isaiah, Isa 7:1–9), and this leads to the defeat of the rebels. However, the price Ahaz pays for Assyrian help is full submission to the stronger nation. The deep anger incurred against the king is found in his portrayal by the biblical writer, who chronicles such misdeeds as paying a "bribe" to the Assyrian king Tiglath-pileser III, including the bronze Sea that Solomon had erected (2 Kgs 16:17–18), placing an altar of foreign design in the Jerusalem temple (1 Kgs 16:10–16), and making sacrifices on the "high places" (1 Kgs 16:4).

A subsequent revolt by Israel's King Hoshea in 722 B.C. causes the Assyrians to take the drastic measure of destroying Israel's capital at Samaria and deporting a large proportion of the population to remote locations in the Assyrian empire, never to return (2 Kgs 17:1-6). The kingdom of Judah also felt the effect of Assyrian displeasure with repeated invasions and the destruction of many cities. King Sennacherib recorded in his royal annals (*ANET*, 287) that on one occasion he held King Hezekiah of Judah prisoner in Jerusalem "like a bird in a cage," while he captured and enslaved the populations of forty-six other cities in Judah. The biblical account of the siege of Jerusalem credits divine intervention for the miraculous survival of the city (2 Kgs 19:32-37). Internal politics within the Assyrian Empire may have also contributed to the lifting of the siege. Second Kings 19:37 states that upon Sennacherib's return to Nineveh, his own sons murdered him.

Judah's Reforms

The traumatic effect of Israel's destruction and continuing Assyrian invasions led Judah into a state of quiet Assyrian vassalage in the period after Hezekiah's death. No prophetic voice was heard during the long reign of King Manasseh (687-642 B.C.). Only after the Assyrian Empire began to crumble under assaults from the Babylonians and Medes was Judah able to assert a measure of independence. This came in the reign of Josiah (640-609 B.C.), who inaugurated a religious and political reform designed to purge the people of foreign gods and Canaanite worship practices, and to centralize all power in the city of Jerusalem (2 Kgs 23).

Josiah's reform is instigated and carried out by a group of priests from the city of Anathoth,

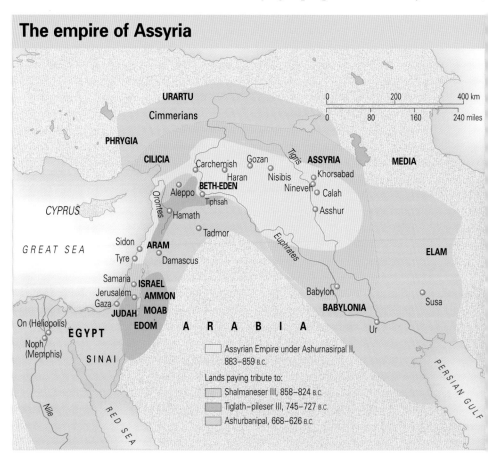

The empire of Assyria

URARTU

Cimmerians

PHRYGIA

CILICIA

Carchemish
Gozan   *Tigris*   ASSYRIA

Haran   Nisibis   Khorsabad

BETH-EDEN   Nineveh   Calah

Aleppo
Orontes   Tiphsah

CYPRUS

Hamath

Asshur

Tadmor

GREAT SEA

Sidon   ARAM

Tyre   Damascus   *Euphrates*

ELAM

Samaria   ISRAEL

Jerusalem   AMMON

Gaza   JUDAH   MOAB

Babylon

BABYLONIA

Susa

On (Heliopolis)   EDOM   A R A B I A   Ur

EGYPT

Noph
(Memphis)   SINAI

MEDIA

0   200   400 km

0   80   160   240 miles

☐ Assyrian Empire under Ashurnasirpal II,
883–859 B.C.

Lands paying tribute to:

☐ Shalmaneser III, 858–824 B.C.

☐ Tiglath–pileser III, 745–727 B.C.

☐ Ashurbanipal, 668–626 B.C.

PERSIAN GULF

Nile

RED SEA

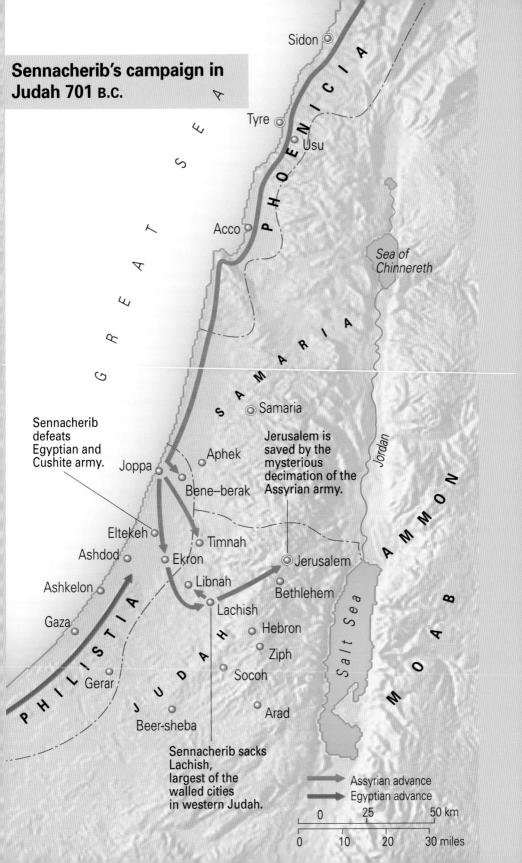

Sennacherib's campaign in Judah 701 B.C.

Sidon

T Y R E

Tyre

Usu

P H O E N I C I A

Acco

Sea of Chinnereth

G R E A T   S E A

S A M A R I A

Samaria

Sennacherib defeats Egyptian and Cushite army.

Joppa

Aphek

Bene–berak

Jerusalem is saved by the mysterious decimation of the Assyrian army.

Eltekeh

Timnah

Ashdod

Ekron

Ashkelon

Libnah

Jerusalem

Bethlehem

Gaza

Lachish

P H I L I S T I A

Hebron

Ziph

Gerar

Socoh

J U D A H

Arad

Beer-sheba

Jordan

A M M O N

Salt Sea

M O A B

Sennacherib sacks Lachish, largest of the walled cities in western Judah.

→ Assyrian advance
→ Egyptian advance

0   25   50 km

0   10   20   30 miles

The Babylonian empire

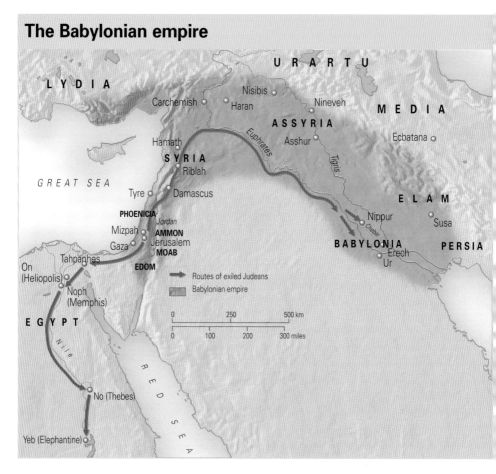

> *Take care that you do not offer your burnt-offerings at any place you happen to see. But only at the place that the LORD will choose in one of your tribes . . .*
> —*Deut 12:13–14*

including Hilkiah, Shaphan, and Ahikam. Their intent, and that of the king, is to restore the powers of the monarchy and of the Jerusalem priesthood with themselves as its leaders. To do this, they institute the legal code found in Deut 12–26, a code that sets up "the place that the LORD will choose" as the only true place of sacrifice (Deut 12:13–14), and that commands the elimination of all vestiges of Canaanite and Assyrian worship. To ensure

that this became a national effort, the high places and local altars are destroyed (Deut 12:2–4), the seasonal religious festivals are centered in the capital (Deut 16:2–17), and the Levitical priesthood is authorized to officiate only within the precincts of the Jerusalem temple (Deut 18:6–8).

Such a radical reform could not be put into effect overnight. Enforcement must have been difficult in the face of long years of polytheistic religious activity. Archaeological findings from this period include fragments of a horned altar found incorporated into a wall at Arad. That the altar was dismantled and used in the construction of a non-sacred structure suggests an attempt to eliminate sacrificial activity at Arad (on similar reuse of altar stones at Beer-sheba, see p. 126). Such finds indicate that religious reformers had some success, but the extent to which they brought about permanent change in the beliefs and practices of Judeans cannot be definitively determined. The fact is that Josiah's reform was only enforced until his death in battle at Megiddo against Pharaoh Necho II (609 B.C.; 2 Kgs 23:29–30).

Josiah's death spells the end of most of his reforms and the beginning of a new era of submission to the superpowers. Egypt claims Judah and the surrounding regions as a consequence of Josiah's failed campaign. In Judah, this means a new master and a puppet king. Josiah's son and immediate successor Jehoahaz is taken hostage to Egypt, and his brother Eliakim is placed on the throne. The pharaoh graphically portrays Eliakim's status as a servant of Egypt by changing his name to Jehoiakim (2 Kgs 23:34).

What follows are the last days of Judah's monarchy. A series of political mistakes and revolts eventually lead the superpowers to crush the nation. The sequence of events begins with a shift of masters. In 605 B.C., Babylonian forces defeat Egypt at the battle of Carchemish. Two years later, the Babylonian King Nebuchadnezzar wrests Judah from the Egyptians, and Jehoiakim suddenly finds himself a Babylonian vassal (2 Kgs 24:1). Because of a temporary reversal of Babylonian advances on the Egyptian border in 601 B.C., and promises of aid, Jehoiakim revolts, bringing the might of the Babylonian army down on his people.

During this period, the prophet Jeremiah condemns Jehoiakim's policies (Jer 36), and denounces the people's reliance on the temple

Pharaoh Neco made Eliakim son of Josiah king in place of his father Josiah, and changed his name to Jehoiakim. But he took Jehoahaz away; he came to Egypt, and died there.
—2 Kgs 23:34

of Yahweh to save them from any threat (Jer 7 and 26). The Babylonian king besieges the city and captures it in 598 B.C., taking the son of Jehoiakim back to Babylon as a hostage, along with a group of Judah's leaders and priests (2 Kgs 24:10–17). Nebuchadnezzar then installs as his puppet-king the last of Josiah's sons, Mattaniah, and changes his name to Zedekiah (2 Kgs 24:17).

Again there is a period of relative quiet as Jerusalem licks its wounds. However, in the ninth year of his reign, Zedekiah revolts (probably again under the urging of Egypt, Jer 37:7); this time Nebuchadnezzar completely destroys this source of continual irritation and rebellion. While Jeremiah urges the people to surrender to the Babylonians (Jer 38:17–18), Zedekiah continues to hold out until the city falls to Nebuchadnezzar's army. The last reigning king of Judah is forced to watch the execution of his sons, and then has his eyes gouged out (Jer 39:6–7). The only remaining member of the royal house, Jehoiachin, eventually dies in Babylonian exile without an heir, never having returned to Jerusalem.

The fall of Jerusalem and the Babylonian exile mark the end of the Davidic monarchy and the beginning of a community that was ruled by foreign officials and an increasingly rigid priesthood. The monarchy period itself witnessed the heights of its power under David and Solomon, and a slow decline to near-oblivion after the kingdom was divided. The life of the people included growth of an urban-based culture in Jerusalem and other administrative sites, and retention of agricultural village life. Both aspects of this society will now be examined.

THE ISRAELITE CITY

The transition during the monarchy period from a village culture to an urban culture brought enormous changes to the lives and religion of the people of Israel. A large

> *This is the account of the forced labor that King Solomon conscripted to build the house of the LORD and his own house, the Millo and wall of Jerusalem, Hazor, Megiddo, Gezer.*
> —1 Kgs 9:15

proportion of the population continued to live in villages, but these settlements became associated with the life and economy of their regional cities. They supplied produce for the cities' markets and men for the king's armies and labor battalions. There were some feelings of hostility concerning the vices of city rulers, such as those expressed by the prophet Micah (3:9–12). Despite this, the villagers' fate—for good or bad—was hereafter intimately tied to that of the city.

Many of the Israelite cities which were occupied during the monarchy period were built over the ruins of older Canaanite cities (Megiddo, Gezer, and Hazor). Jerusalem, David's capital, was originally a Jebusite city. When he made it his capital of the united kingdom, he built his first palace within the old citadel and the enclosure to accommodate his growing bureaucracy and to house his closest followers (2 Sam 5:9–10).

Certain considerations governed the choice of a site where a new city, such as Samaria, was established (1 Kgs 16:24). These included whether the prospective city site was easily defensible, and whether it had an adequate water supply for a growing population. In addition, its access to major commercial routes and its distance from supporting agricultural areas also were considered.

City Walls

Cities in the ancient world contained several major features. Most important among these was the wall. Cities unearthed in the region of ancient Israel had walls as much as thirty feet thick, rising to a height of fifty feet or more.

They were constructed of a mixture of stone and mud brick, with larger quantities of stone being used in hill country sites where it was more easily quarried. Also, stones from earlier cities were recycled, thereby mixing the stratigraphy of the site, and adding to the archaeologist's chronological puzzle. **Ashlar masonry** incorporated dressed stones that were worked smooth on all six sides in the Canaanite-Phoenician style. The uniform stones alternated lengthwise (**headers**) along the width of a wall and crosswise (**stretchers**) along the length of the wall for added strength. These particular styles of stone dressing, and the engraving of mason marks on the stones, do help in unraveling this problem, however.

The walls were the major defense of the city and thus were constantly maintained and refortified with towers and, in some cases, with the addition of a **glacis,** a clay and stone slope built up against the face of the wall. This was sometimes plastered over to present a smoother, less scalable surface. The glacis was also designed to prevent effective use of ladders or battering rams against the wall or city gate (see Joab's attack on Beth-maacah in 2 Sam 20:15–16).

Generally, wall construction followed the slope of the hill or promontory on which the city was built. As a result, walls were seldom straight for any great distance. Eventually, these alternating protrusions and indentations were intentionally incorporated into a defensive design called "**offset-inset,**" or **redans wall construction.** The uneven face of the wall made it difficult for attackers to use battering rams and scaling ladders. Moreover, these features provided defenders more protection, a better view, and a broader field of fire from the battlements.

Where defense was not as much of a concern, cheap construction was a higher priority, and more commercial space was needed, **casemate walls** were used. Casemate walls were made up of two parallel walls connected by short

Excavations at the Solomonic period gate at Gezer.

perpendicular walls; this construction formed a series of rooms, or casemates, between the two parallel walls. Some casemate walls were filled with rubble to strengthen the structure. Casemates could also be used for storage or as back rooms for houses built just inside the wall (Josh 2:15). This hollow-wall pattern became the standard during Solomon's more peaceful reign. Archaeologists have discovered that each of his fortress cities at Megiddo, Hazor, and Gezer (1 Kgs 9:15–19) were built with casemate walls. While not affording the protection of solid walls, they did have the advantage of a lower cost, quicker construction, and the creation of premium space within the walls for warehouses and shops.

City Gate

Among the busiest and most vulnerable features of a walled city was the city gate. The gate provided access for the inhabitants, it served as an assembly area for important governmental and religious announcements, and it functioned as the commercial and legal center of the city. However, because it was an entryway through the walls, it was invariably the focal point of any attack (Judg 9:44 and 2 Sam 18:4). The multi-use character of the gate required ingenious construction that would provide a fairly broad entrance and activity space for the population and visiting merchants. At the same time, it had to present a significant obstacle to potential attackers.

During the monarchy period, the diagonally-positioned, six-chambered gate became the norm. Archaeologists have found this type of gate at Beth Shemesh, Hazor, Shechem, Gezer, Megiddo, and Tirzah. A stepped approach, often with right-angled turns, led up to the ramparts outside a city to a multistoried

> *Abimelech and the company that was with him rushed forward and stood at the entrance of the gate of the city, while the two companies rushed on all who were in the fields and killed them.*
> —Judg 9:44

entranceway. The towered gateway would have been the first line of defense for the city. On the inside of this first gateway sat two of the gate's six chambers, one on each side of the gate's entrance. Beyond these chambers lay second, third, and fourth gateways, each separated by two chambers and protected by a set of metal-hinged wooden doors. The last of these gates was the entrance to the city. During times of war, the chambers that separated each of the gateways could be used as defensive positions against those who would try to enter the gate complex.

It may be that the gate of Mahanaim, in which David awaited word of the battle with Absalom's army, was one of this type (2 Sam 18:24). While the watchman went up on the roof of the first, exterior gateway, David sat in a chamber between two gates. A chamber in a gate discovered at Dan contained benches and a canopied platform. These structures, used by judges and kings (1 Kgs 22:10; Ruth 4:1–2), may serve as a model for David's position at Mahanaim. David's sitting between the gates signaled to the people his personal command of the city and his desire to be informed about the battle and the defense of the city. After David learns of Absalom's death, he goes "up to the chamber over the gate" to mourn the loss of his son (2 Sam 18:33). This chamber may have been located in one of the towers flanking the gate or a room in the upper story of the gateway itself. Of course, architecture varied based on the topography, wealth, and importance of the site.

During peace times the gate served as a gathering place for merchants (Gen 19:1; 2 Kgs 7:1). The stalls and booths of craftsmen and hawkers, as well as the produce market for surrounding villages, were found in the gate's chambers. Fresh produce was bartered for bread, pottery, leather goods, and clothing. Egyptian jewelry, Phoenician furnishings, perfumes from Arabia, and ingots of metal from Cyprus and Anatolia; all were available in these open-air bazaars (Gen 37:25; 1 Kgs 10:23-29).

Like the threshing floor in unwalled villages, the city gate functioned as a gathering place for legal activity (see also Ruth 3:10–14 and Ugaritic Tale of Aqhat v:5–8; on threshing floors, see p. 56). Each of these places was intimately tied to the economic and social well-being of the community, and each was large enough for a crowd to gather and a trial to be held. Deuteronomy 21:18–21 provides a good example of how the gate area served as a legal forum. In this text the parents of a "stubborn and rebellious" son are required to bring him to the gate where they testify against him to the elders. Following their testimony, "all the men of the city" stone the son to death. This type of communal execution was designed to bring home to the entire community that crime was not just an individual matter—it was a physical and religious threat to the entire population of the city.

The gate thus became the city's judicial center. Here elders habitually sat (Prov 31:23) awaiting the summons to hear testimony and make pronouncements based on the law. On a higher level of authority, the king was also supposed to listen to the cases of his people. David's failure to provide a hearing for the complaints of tribal officials gives Absalom an opening for his rebellion. He stands "beside the road into the gate" and commiserates with these men, assuring them that he would have given them a fair judgment if he were king (2 Sam 15:1–6). The legal role of the gate is also found in the period just before the fall of the northern kingdom of Israel (ca. 750 B.C.). As one of the gravest crimes of the people, Amos states that justice has been perverted "in the gate" (Amos 5:10–15).

Streets and Public Squares

Despite the protection offered by city gates, at some point in their history many cities were destroyed. Rather than abandoning a razed city to construct an entirely new one,

Artist's reconstruction of the city gate at Dan. Note the double gates.

inhabitants rebuilt what they could, using recycled materials from demolished buildings. This method of reconstruction made city planning practically impossible, because inhabitants were not building in large open spaces, but rather on top of older, destroyed layers of occupation. While many cities were originally built on hills because of the natural protection they offer, rebuilding city upon destroyed city created artificial mounds of successive layers of occupation. Such mounds are called **tells.** As cities were rebuilt time and again on the crowns of natural hills or tells, the amount of space within the citadel, or the city proper, was reduced. This made establishing open areas like thoroughfares and markets difficult.

The average size of a city site in the biblical period was five to ten acres. This meant that planning considerations were set aside when the need arose to build an extension onto the administrative complex. As a result, the city often expanded beyond its walls and down the slope of the tell. This new area was then walled in with fortifications. Such a process led to expansion of the site of Hazor to two hundred acres in the Late Bronze period (ca. 1550–1200), and Dan eventually grew to fifty acres in size.

With space at such a premium, it is no wonder then that biblical Hebrew lacks a word for street. Ḥûṣ, which literally means "outside," is often used to indicate "streets." Only in well-planned cities or neighborhoods, as discovered in certain sections of Samaria, were streets a consistent width, running in straight lines parallel and perpendicular to the city wall. In most cities and villages, streets would have

> The people of Israel secretly did things that were not right against the LORD their God. They built for themselves high places at all their towns, from watchtower to fortified city; they set up for themselves pillars and sacred poles on every high hill and under every green tree . . .
> —2 Kgs 17:9–10

> *You shall bring both of them to the gate*
> *of the town and stone them to death, the*
> *young woman because she did not cry for*
> *help in the town and the man because he*
> *violated his neighbor's wife. So you shall*
> *purge the evil from your midst.*
> —Deut 22:24

been narrow paths between buildings, many times ending in a blind alley. Often these were choked with traffic, carts, and booths, and accumulated garbage. In 1 Kgs 20:34, *Ḥûṣ* may refer to bazaars set up in the city streets of Samaria.

What little open space that did exist in Jerusalem for public assembly and market activity was in front of important buildings like the palace and the temple and in the vicinity of the city gate. A term used for these relatively open places is *reḥob,* a "broad area." In Deut 13:16 and 2 Sam 21:12, it can be loosely translated as "public square." In the first of these texts, the "square" served for the burning of loot following the capture of a Canaanite city. In the second instance, the *reḥob* was a place of execution and assembly. It functioned as the marshalling area for Hezekiah's troops in yet another text (2 Chr 32:6).

Considering the space limitations in most ancient walled cities, however, the most likely place for an assembly point would have been immediately outside the city gate. Evidence for this occurs in 1 Kgs 22. An impressive event was staged, according to this passage, involving King Ahab of Israel and King Jehoshaphat of Judah. They sat enthroned before the city gate of Samaria on what had been a threshing floor (*gôren*), surrounded by court officials and four hundred prophets. Such a spectacle would have been too cramped within the confines of the city walls, and could not have taken advantage of so many symbols of royal power and judicially-charged space.

Palace and Temple

The two city structures that did represent the worship of Yahweh and the power and prestige of the Israelite monarchy were the temple and the king's palace in Jerusalem. These buildings mark the transition from tribal to national status and from village to urban culture. Unfortunately, little remains of these monuments to indicate the power of David's and Solomon's kingdom. Despite the fact that Jerusalem is one of the most excavated ancient cities in the world, most of the physical remains have disappeared as a result of repeated destructions and the reuse of materials in later structures.

What has been revealed in the most recent excavations is evidence of the establishment of an Israelite city on the site in the eleventh–tenth centuries B.C., and a succession of expansion projects that extended the original "city of David" (2 Sam 5:7–9) over a much larger area. Further excavations, made difficult by current occupation of the site and political and religious pressures, could reveal a more complete history of the city's life.

The descriptions of Solomon's temple in 1 Kgs 6, 7:13–51, and of his palace in 1 Kgs 7:1–12, point to a drastic change of fortunes. In just two generations, the Israelites had risen from a people subject to Philistine city-states and Canaanite warlords, to a major power with control over all of Canaan and much of Transjordan. Solomon had made a marriage alliance with the Egyptian pharaoh (1 Kgs 3:1), and had a working arrangement with Hiram, the king of Tyre, to provide craftsmen and building materials for his construction projects.

One result of this reliance on foreign expertise was the use of a basically Canaanite decorative and architectural style. Although no archaeological remains of Solomon's temple have been found, its description in 1 Kgs 6–7, 2 Chr 3–4, and in Ezek 40–48 provides a good picture of its basic structure.

> *He set up the pillars at the vestibule of the temple; he set up the pillar on the south and called it Jachin; and set up the pillar on the north and called it Boaz*
> —*1 Kgs 7:21*

At the entrance to the temple stood two carved pillars, Jachin and Boaz (1 Kgs 7:21). Since they did not support the roof, their purpose is unknown, although some suggest they stood in silent witness to the presence of Yahweh. Bases for similar freestanding pillars have been found at the entrance to Canaanite temple sites at Hazor and Arad. These pillars are also represented on carved ivory plaques from Phoenicia. The pillars outside Solomon's temple may have symbolized the presence of God, like the pillar of cloud before the tabernacle (Exod 33:9), or marked the passage of worshipers from secular to sacred precincts.

Laid out on an east-west axis, with its entrance on the east, the temple was oblong, with two courtyards. The outer courtyard was made up of the "lower pavement" (2 Chr 7:3). On top of this, up a series of steps (Ezek 40:6, 26) and through a series of gates (vv. 19, 20, 24, 28), was the inner courtyard (vv. 17–19, 28). Offset-inset walls surrounded each of these courtyards (vv. 6–7; on offset-inset walls, see p. 100). Burnt offerings were performed in the inner courtyard, where the altar and its accompanying instruments were set (vv. 38–47). The innermost **"Holy of Holies"** housed the ark of the covenant (1 Kgs 6:23–28).

New forms of worship and an expanded priesthood also came into being at this time. Along with housing the ark in Solomon's temple, a group of priests was charged with its care and the maintenance of the sacrificial routine (1 Kgs 8:1–6). The religious calendar was expanded or revised. Festivals and sacrifices were now held in Jerusalem. However, people continued to sacrifice at the local "high places," despite the existence of a national religious shrine (1 Kgs 3:2).

The Islamic Dome of the Rock probably stands on the site of Solomon's Temple in Jerusalem.

Temple and palace represented a new form of government, in which the people were subject to the rule of a single king. During the early monarchy, the king took care to balance centralized rule with tribal interests. Semi-elite "people of the land" (2 Kgs 21:24) continued to exert economic, social, and military influence. However, social stratification became more pronounced as the king created a new elite comprised of his advisers, family, administrators, military officers, and those who had done him a special service (2 Sam 15:14–15; 1 Kgs 4:1–6; 2 Chr 11:23, 2 Sam 19:31–38). Unlike the semi-elite who inherited the land they owned, this class received land by royal decree. Samuel had warned that a monarch would "take the best of your fields and vineyards and olive orchards and give them to his courtiers" (1 Sam 8:14), and Saul warns his own servants that David will not provide them with these kinds of favors should they turn from Saul to follow him (22:7). Implicit in the warning is the assumption that such grants were common rewards for loyal followers.

During Solomon's reign, this growing royal bureaucracy managed the affairs of former tribal districts, collected taxes, and recruited manpower for the army and labor battalions (1 Kgs 4:1–19). The resources of the nation were expended in monumental construction projects and the enhancement of court powers. The citadel became an administrative nerve center with its offices and warehouses squeezing out previous inhabitants. An extreme example of this reorganization was found at Megiddo. In the early tenth century B.C., the city contained only two administrative buildings, leaving seventy-five percent of the city available for private dwellings. By the late tenth century, over eighty percent of the city was occupied by administrative projects, including a city wall and gate, a palace, seventeen royal storehouses, open courtyards used as campgrounds by merchants and army

> *He dealt wisely, and distributed some of his sons through all the districts of Judah and Benjamin, in all the fortified cities; he gave them abundant provisions, and found many wives for them.*
> —2 Chr 11:23

units, and a water system. By the eighth century, the commoners of the city were crowded into a few small dwellings. This zoning signaled the boundaries between the powerful and the powerless within the city. In Samaria, a wall was even built to divide these two areas of the town, and the architecture was markedly different in each. Amos refers to the lavishly decorated houses of the rich and influential as "houses of ivory" (3:15).

Such a transition from regional administration and popular religious practices was not accomplished overnight. Opposition to Jerusalem and the monarchy surfaced in the next generation and led to the division of the kingdom. However, the kingdom of Israel in the north immediately adopted a similar form of government with a monarchy and national shrines at Dan and Bethel to focus the people's worship (1 Kgs 12:25–33). Clearly, once the temple-palace process had begun, it could not be reversed.

As the kingdoms of Israel and Judah gradually fall prey to the superpowers, the temple and palace become symbols both of the sins of the people as well as of future hope and restored glory. Isaiah centers much of his prophetic message on the everlasting covenant which God had established with the house of David (2 Sam 7:18–29; Isa 11:1–3). His assurance is that Jerusalem, while punished for the sins of the people, will never be destroyed (Isa 10:24; 29:7–8). Living at this same time (late 8th cent. B.C.), Micah places the blame for destruction by invading Assyrian armies squarely on the cities of Samaria and Jerusalem (Mic 1:5). Unlike Isaiah, he has no

> *All this is for the transgression of Jacob and for the sins of the house of Israel. What is trangression of Jacob? Is it not Samaria? And what is the high place of Judah? Is it not Jerusalem?*
> —Mic 1:5

abiding tie to the city culture, and predicts that these royal capitals will "become a heap of ruins" (Mic 3:12).

After the northern kingdom had been destroyed in 720 B.C., Jerusalem and its temple became the last bastion of hope for Yahweh's chosen people. Josiah's religious and political reforms (2 Kgs 22:3–24) came at a point when Assyrian control of Judah was weakening (622–609 B.C.). Modeled on the laws in Deut 12–26, they were designed to redirect the people's political and religious focus on Jerusalem and the Davidic monarchy. Such central events as the Passover celebration (2 Kgs 23:21) were restored to prominence, and provisions were made to increase the power of the Jerusalem priesthood by eliminating all of the local shrines, and by recalling all the Levites to Jerusalem (23:8). Josiah's untimely death in battle against the Egyptians (2 Kgs 23:29) ended his reform measures.

Even after the reforms had ended, the idea of the temple as the supreme expression of Yahweh's power and presence survived. It continued to be a symbol of hope for the people of Jerusalem. Yet, just before the fall of the city to the Babylonians (600–587 B.C.), Jeremiah calls for the destruction of the temple. In the prophet's estimation it had become an idol and symbol of false hope for an unfaithful people since Josiah's time (Jer 7:8–15 and 26:4–6). Despite this, Jeremiah offers Jerusalem's inhabitants hope of a restored city, complete with a temple, after their punishment is complete (Jer 30–31, see especially 31:23).

Private Dwellings in the City

The style and size of private dwellings in Israelite walled cities varied based on available space, construction materials, and the relative importance of the inhabitants. Excavations of Iron Age (8th cent. B.C.) levels at Megiddo and Hazor reveal houses of a standard four-room style with a large central room. The fact that these are old sites with many previous occupation levels may explain why small, poorly-constructed houses are found next to much larger and more complex dwellings. These newer homes probably belonged to the new Israelite elite who now ruled these cities. Space limitations had squeezed the social classes closer together, while squeezing most of the non-administrative inhabitants out of the walled cities into surrounding towns and villages.

In newer cities like Samaria and Tirzah, however, there was a clearly defined distinction between the poorer areas and those of the elite. This latter area was usually on the western edge of the mound, where a prevailing west wind would cool the houses and carry away cooking and human odors. These houses were much larger and better built, generally showing additions and repairs made over the long periods of time that they were occupied. More hewn stone and squared corners appear in the walls than in village dwellings, though like those in the villages, they were pillared structures with stone foundations and only a few windows for ventilation (Hos 13:3). The large central room contained the oven, cooking vessels, and storage jars, and served as a gathering area for the family and its friends.

The entrance to these dwellings usually led into an alleyway, and there were stairs on the outside of the house leading up to a second

> *Do not trust in these deceptive words: "This is the temple of the LORD, the temple of the LORD, the temple of the LORD."*
> —Jer 7:4

> *Therefore they shall be like the morning mist or like the dew that goes away early, like chaff that swirls from the threshing floor or like smoke from a window.*
> —Hos 13:3

story. If the house was built next to the city wall, these stairs were built against the wall. An economy of materials can be seen in the construction of doorways at the end of the wall, so that only one doorjamb was required. The ceiling consisted of log beams thatched over with several layers of a clay and straw mixture.

Sanitary conditions within these homes continued to be unhealthy. Poor ventilation, the odor and gases arising from decaying food and waste matter, and the heat contributed to the growth of bacteria and the spread of disease. Frankincense and other sweet-smelling aromatics were burned in small incense stands in these homes to mask some of this staleness. While these stands, which have been excavated in large numbers at Megiddo, Gezer, Beth-Shan, and Shechem, may have also had a cultic purpose (Jer 19:13), their smoke helped to cover the household odors and drive away insects.

Excavations at Jericho, Bethel, and other sites have revealed stone-lined drainage systems for sewage and excess rainwater. However, these are only associated with the houses of wealthier families. References to muck and mire in the streets (2 Sam 22:43) suggest that they were still the principal areas for waste disposal. Waste was also deposited in nearby fields and in communal dung heaps.

Archaeological evidence shows that at least some houses within the city served as both dwelling places and industrial and commercial establishments. At the site of Shechem, a house was uncovered which contained dye vats and loom weights, suggesting a clothing manufacturing enterprise. Elsewhere, booths were dis-

covered attached to the outside of a house. They contained rows of clay storage jars containing the carbonized remains of grain. This may have been a shop selling grain to city dwellers. A similar shop unearthed at Hazor with a large number of small pottery bowls may have been a primitive cafe or food market.

SOCIAL LIFE

Even with an urban-centered culture emerging during the monarchy period, the vast majority of the Israelite population continued to live in small, unwalled villages and towns. Life there would have remained much the same as it was in the settlement period except for the demands and opportunities afforded by regional urban centers. Cities like Beersheba, Jerusalem, Lachish, Samaria, Megiddo, and Hazor became focal points of royal power and major defense posts for the rest of the land (1 Kgs 9:15–19). They served as regional markets for farm produce and provided a clearing-house for manufactured and imported goods. Farm families made the trek from their villages once or twice a year to sell their surplus grain and to buy new farm implements, pottery, and luxury goods (jewelry, perfumes, and cosmetics). They also came to Jerusalem and other religious centers to make sacrifices and to celebrate major religious holidays.

Until the Assyrian occupation of the eighth century B.C., those Israelites who did live within the walled cities were primarily government workers and prominent merchant families. Their "service sector" jobs made it necessary for them to live close to the

> *He bought the hill of Samaria from Shemer for two talents of silver; he fortified the hill, and called the city that he built, Samaria, after the name of Shemer, the owner of the hill.*
> —1 Kgs 16:24

Panel depicting Israelites bearing tribute, from the Black Obelisk of Shalmaneser (see p. 110).

administrative hub. However, because the inhabitants of the walled cities devoted their full time to managing the affairs of the government and the economy, these cities were not self-supporting. They depended on the rural farm belt to supply them with food and the raw materials for manufacturing. Local villages also provided surplus manpower for construction projects and military campaigns.

Social Mobility

A symbiotic arrangement between the rural and urban areas is quite common in the ancient Near East. In such a culture, the basic traditions and loyalties of extended family relationships can remain intact in the villages, but

> *The man Jeroboam was very able, and when Solomon saw that the young man was industrious he gave him charge over all the forced labor of the house of Joseph.*
> —*1 Kgs 11:28*

the opportunities of joining the royal elite or the military may dissolve old ties among city dwellers. The drive to advance in a period when social mobility is possible can lead to the abandonment of old values and the establishment of new loyalties to the state and to oneself.

One possible example of this may be Jeroboam, son of Nebat. This son of a widow from the tribe of Ephraim rises to a position of high authority, having "charge over all the forced labor of the house of Joseph" (1 Kgs 11:28). Solomon gives him this position because he has proven himself to be "industrious." Later, the prophet Ahijah singles him out to rule the northern ten tribes, because Solomon worships the gods of his foreign wives (1 Kgs 11:29–40). As a result of this prophecy, Solomon attempts to kill Jeroboam, who promptly flees to Egypt (v. 40). Whether Jeroboam began his attempt to undermine Solomon's authority prior to the king's death (as suggested by the Septuagint, the Greek version of the Old Testament; on the Septuagint, see p. 202), or simply bides his time in Egyptian exile, he leads the revolt against Rehoboam (1 Kgs 12:12–20). His loyalty to his former benefactor ends when the opportunity arises for him to become a king himself.

The monarchic period yields other examples of individuals taking advantage of a situation to advance themselves. In the ninth century, the succession to the throne of Israel was in dispute; the support of the army and assassination were the primary means to power. King Elah is murdered by Zimri, "commander of half his chariots" (1 Kgs 16:9–10), and then Zimri is overthrown after only seven days by Omri, another army commander (1 Kgs 16:15–20). In a brief civil war, Omri himself defeats a rival claimant named Tibni (vv. 21–22). The biblical narrative does not record the genealogy of either Zimri or Omri, which may indicate that these kings came from unimportant families and rose to power on the strength of their skills as soldiers.

Clothing and Personal Adornment

General style of dress did not change markedly during the monarchic period. The basic undergarment for both men and women was the *kethoneth,* a shirt-like garment that is depicted in ancient art in a variety of styles. Usually made of wool, it could reach as far as the ankles or just to the knees; it might have either long or short sleeves (2 Sam 13:18).

This garment is mentioned in the "Black Obelisk" inscription of the Assyrian king Shalmaneser III (842 B.C.). In a series of sculpted, captioned registers, Jehu, king of Israel, is depicted bowing before the king; his servants are shown carrying gifts as tribute payments. Jehu is wearing a fringed *kethoneth* tied with a girdle that also has hanging tassels. A pointed cap covers his head, and his beard, like those of the Israelite porters carved on this monument, is trimmed to a point. The porters have a slightly different costume. Each is also wearing a *kethoneth,* but a fringed *simlah,* or mantle,

> *Take the garment of one who has given surety for a stranger; seize the pledge given as surety for foreigners.*
> —Prov 20:16

which is draped over their left shoulders, covers it. Their beards are trimmed to a point like the king's, and they are wearing pointed caps and sandals with upturned toes.

An Assyrian **relief** (large, two-dimensional stone carvings) and inscription from 701 B.C. shows Judean captives from the city of Lachish. This monument to the conquests of Sennacherib comes from the period of his invasion of Judah and siege of Jerusalem (2 Kgs 18–19). The barefooted prisoners on the relief are wearing a short-sleeved, full-length *kethoneth.* They are bareheaded and have closely-trimmed beards. The variations may reflect different styles in Israel and Judah, or simply the changes in style from one period of time to the next. However, their traditional clothing continues to distinguish them from the Assyrian captors, indicating that they have not adopted the clothing of the superpowers that ruled over them.

Designed to be draped loosely around the body, garments regulated body heat and allowed for ease of movement. They were most commonly made of wool, although linen was also used. Woolen garments, however, were difficult to launder. They were nearly always moist with perspiration and soiled with food and dirt. This led to skin infections and the transmission of bacterially-based diseases (Lev 13:47–59; on skin disease, see p. 115).

Beyond their immediate physical use, items of clothing also served as social markers, indicating a person's status, occupation, and wealth. The elaborate priestly vestments signified their role as intercessors in the temple (see Exod 28). The *me'il,* or robe, was a loose, wide-sleeved outer garment worn by royalty (1 Sam 18:4; 2 Sam 13:18; 1 Chr 15:27), priests

Fourteenth century B.C. Canaanite precious stones and gold jewelry from Deir-El Balach.

(Exod 28:4, 31–32), and prophets (1 Sam 28:14; 1 Kgs 11:29). Samuel is often described wearing this garment. As a child, his mother brings him a new *me'il* every year (1 Sam 2:19). The prophet is wearing a *me'il* when he announces Saul's loss of the kingship (15:27). Later, when Saul employs the medium at Endor, the king recognizes Samuel rising from Sheol because he is dressed in his *me'il* (28:17).

The rather elaborate hems with suspended tassels found on the *me'il* and most garments in the ancient Near East symbolized the rank of kings and their advisers, as well as the mili-

> He said to his men, "The LORD forbid that I should do this thing to my lord, the LORD's anointed, to raise my hand against him; for he is the LORD's anointed." So David scolded his men severely and did not permit them to attack Saul. Then Saul got up and left the cave, and went on his way.
>
> —1 Sam 24:6–7

tary. The biblical narrative uses the association between royal robes and political status several times. Saul graphically demonstrates how God will "tear the kingdom" away from his own family when he grasps and tears the hem of Samuel's robe. After cutting off the hem of Saul's garment in 1 Sam 24:4–5, David expresses remorse for even symbolically depicting his killing of "the LORD's anointed" (1 Sam 26:9).

The girdle, which was used to tie the *kethoneth* and *simlah,* also functioned as a weapons belt and a sign of rank. In 2 Sam 20:8, Joab wears a "soldier's garment" tied with a girdle (*hagor*) through which he has sheathed his sword. David uses the same term in describing Joab's crimes to Solomon in 1 Kgs 2:5. In this case, however, the *hagor,* and thus the authority, had been symbolically soiled with the blood of Joab's murder victims.

Clothing often played a part in legal transactions. Garments were given "in pledge," or as collateral for a loan or trade. Even the poorest in society could offer their outer garment to

The "Black Obelisk" of Shalmaneser III affords invaluable glimpses into the ancient past. The second panel from the top shows "Jehu son of Omri" bowing in submission. The polished black stone was discovered on the site of the Assyrian city of Calah (Tell Nimrud) during the 1845 expedition to Mesopotamia under Henry Layard.

seal an agreement. Legislation regarding these sorts of transactions forbid confiscation of a widow's garment (Deut 24:17), and instructed one who had given a loan to be just: "If you take your neighbor's cloak in pawn, you shall restore it before the sun goes down; for it may be your neighbor's only clothing to use as cover; in what else shall that person sleep?" (Exod 22:26–27; see Deut 24:13). The seventh-century B.C. Yavneh Yam Inscription describes the hardship suffered by those whose clothing had been confiscated. In this letter, an Israelite reaper, who was accused of poor workmanship and thus lost his garment, professes his innocence and petitions a local official for intervention (OTPar, 331–32). Biblical laws regarding garments "given in pledge," and the Yavneh Yam inscription, underscore the physical and economic importance of clothing in ancient Israel (on clothing used in legal transaction, see p. 68).

Although the general style of dress did not change in the monarchic period, there were some shifts in costume, jewelry, and other personal items, especially among the well-to-do. Some of these changes were the result of increased wealth and the desire to differentiate between social classes. Other changes reflect increased contact and commercial activity between Israel and surrounding nations. Fabric brightened with expensive Tyrian purple dye, extracted from the hypobranchial gland of the murex snail (Ezek 23:6), was employed in the tabernacle (Exod 26:1, 31, 36), and the wealthy demonstrated their affluence by wearing clothing cut from this cloth.

You were adorned with gold and silver, while your clothing was of fine linen, rich fabric, and embroidered cloth. You had choice flour and honey and oil for food. You grew exceedingly beautiful, fit to be a queen.

—*Ezek 16:13*

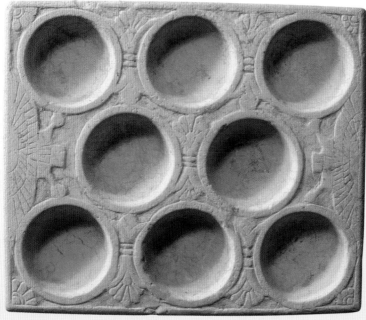

Decorated cosmetics tray carved from sandstone, ninth century B.C.

Possessing more than one change of clothes also denoted wealth and power (Judg 14:12; 1 Sam 28:2; 2 Sam 12:20; 2 Kgs 5:5).

The garments worn by aristocratic men and women are listed in Isa 3:18–24. Primarily items of the wealthy, the catalog indicates a large variety of accessories that could be found in their wardrobes. Head coverings in this list include veils, scarves, and headdresses for women, and turbans worn by both sexes. The priestly turban was a symbol of authority. Sashes, mantles, and girdles would have been used to tie the undergarments, some of which are said to be made of linen (Ezek 16:10). Special robes and festal garments, with embroidered cloth (Ezek 16:13), were used for festive occasions, weddings, and entertaining.

Jewelry and Personal Items

The list in Isa 3:18–24 also includes items of jewelry and personal care products. While some of these pieces of jewelry were worn by men, the list in Isaiah seems to be a catalog of what well-dressed (extravagant) women wore.

Various adornments covered the owner from head to foot. These included delicately-carved garlanded frontlets and moon-shaped crescents, drop pendants on twisted necklace cords, armlets (note Saul's armlet of office in 2 Sam 1:10), nose and signet rings, and tinkling anklets (Isa 3:16), all fabricated of gold or silver. Engraved signet rings, used to stamp documents or as symbols of office, were encrusted with precious and semiprecious stones (Ezek 28:12–13). Larger pieces, like the breastplate of the high priest (Exod 28:15–21), also contained mounted precious stones. A description of the clothing and jewelry worn by Jerusalem, here portrayed as Yahweh's unfaithful bride, includes bracelets for her arms and a gold and silver chain around her neck. Her head is adorned with a crown, earrings, and a nose ring (Ezek 16:10–13).

Cosmetics

Jezebel's preparations before meeting the triumphant Jehu and her own inevitable death have served as the classic example of the use of

113

> *They even sent for men to come from far away, to whom a messenger was sent, and they came. For them you bathed yourself, painted your eyes, and decked yourself with ornaments.*
> —Ezek 16:13

cosmetics by Israelite women (2 Kgs 9:30). She, of course, was a Phoenician princess who had married King Ahab. Her use of eye paint, *puk*, may have been only a Phoenician style; however, both Jeremiah (4:30) and Ezekiel (23:40) speak of women who enlarged their eyes with eye paint, which suggests that this was a common practice in Israel, as well as the rest of the ancient Near East. Analysis of black kohl eye makeup sticks from Egyptian tombs and from cosmetic palettes has shown that it consisted primarily of crushed galena mixed with gum and water (on eye paint, see p. 152).

Archaeologists have also found red dyes made from iron oxide (red ochre) or crushed leaves of the henna plant (Song 1:14) in Egyptian tombs. This mixture would have been applied to cheeks, lips, finger and toenails, and hair to add color to a woman's appearance. Other shades of color were produced with a mixture of clays or crushed plant matter. The "perfume boxes" of Isa 3:20 may refer to receptacles for these dyes as well as powdered or liquid fragrances.

Perfumes of various types were used by the Israelites to mask household odors and as incense offerings in shrines and temples. Several personal fragrances and soaps were used by women as part of their attempts to cleanse and purify the body (Jer 2:22). Along with oils and other ointments, these scents were applied to the body (Prov 27:9), as well as being sprinkled on clothes (Ps 45:8) and on room furnishings (Prov 7:17).

A number of these scents are mentioned in the Song of Songs. Among them are spikenard, taken from gingergrass root imported from

Arabia, myrrh, and saffron, extracted from crocus and turmeric (Song 4:13–14; 5:5). The spices mentioned among the gifts from the queen of Sheba to King Solomon in 1 Kgs 10:2 probably included those used for cooking as well as those that were burned as incense and used as personal fragrances.

Forms of Entertainment

The variety in Israelite entertainment would have increased during the time of the monarchy. A larger and more diverse population in the cities, the significantly greater personal wealth of some individuals, and an increase in leisure time probably ensured that this was the case. As in earlier periods, occasions for celebration such as marriages, births, religious festivals (2 Sam 6:14–15), and military victories (1 Sam 18:6) could all spark individual and mass entertainment. These might include feasts (1 Sam 20:5), singing and dancing to a variety of musical instruments, board games (many examples of which have been excavated), and riddle contests (Judg 14:12). Additional forms of entertainment were borrowed from neighboring or conquering nations. While the Assyrians were particularly fond of physical contests involving hunting, archery, and javelin and stone throwing, the Babylonians enjoyed wrestling, as well as intellectual games, including cryptograms and crossword puzzles.

During the monarchy, celebrations were probably more common and more elaborate as the king, the nobility, and the priesthood drew the people's attention to themselves and the Yahweh festivals. Many of these celebrations centered around music. For instance, when Jehoshaphat returned with his army to Jerusalem after a victory over Moab and Ammon, his victory processional marched to the temple playing harps and lyres and trumpets (2 Chr 20:28). Similarly, the wine and merriment of the feast described in Isa 5:12 was accompanied by the music of lyre, harp timbrel, and flute. The text also indicates that the royal court was entertained by professional musicians and singers (2 Sam 19:35 and Eccl 2:8). Dancing would have been a natural accompaniment to singing and the rattling of tambourines (1 Sam 29:5; Ps 30:11; Jer 31:4).

Temple rituals included music and the singing of psalms in procession by pilgrims and priests. Psalm 24 and the "songs of ascent" (Ps 120–134) are good examples of hymns that might have been used in public processions to the temple. Chronicles systematically emphasizes the cultic use of music, especially in terms of David's role as institutor. Thus, David is said to have appointed men who were "in charge of the service of song in the house of the LORD" (1 Chr 6:31–48). Choirs or pious individuals sang psalms on particular occasions (such as Ps 66, a hymn of one who has come to fulfill a vow), and as continuous praise to Yahweh (such as Ps 92, a song for the Sabbath).

Choirmasters were given specific instructions, contained in the superscriptions to each psalm, on how to orchestrate performances of these songs. For example, the superscription to Psalm 22 instructs the choirmaster to perform this song according to a popular tune of the time, "The Deer of the Dawn." These instructions also include specific instrumentation and some technical terms, such as *Selah* (Ps 32:4, 5, 7), whose exact meanings are still unknown to modern scholars.

Treatment of Disease

The text describes quite a number of medical problems that afflicted the people of Israel. Some were treated with herbal remedies (Gen 30:14). Topical salves, referred to as "balm," were used to cover or soothe a wound (Jer 46:11; 51:8), while injuries were "wrapped with a bandage" (Ezek 30:21). The more serious problems included a disease of the bowel (amoebic dysentery—2 Chr 21:15, 18–19), boils or tumors (perhaps bubonic plague in 1 Sam 5:6–12), and various plagues (2 Sam 24:13–15;

1 Kgs 8:37). The common denominator for many of these diseases was attribution to divine causes. When the Philistines captured the ark of the covenant in battle, they connected its presence in Gath to an outbreak of tumors in the citizens of the city (1 Sam 5:9). When David sinned by numbering his soldiers, God offered him a choice of punishments. He chose a plague, which subsequently afflicted the land for three days as a direct consequence (2 Sam 24:10–17).

In the case of leprosy (probably a general term for several different skin conditions, none of which were Hansen's disease), Lev 13 prescribed a complicated set of procedures in which the afflicted person went to the priest to be examined. Certain primary appearances of eruption or discoloration of the skin were listed, as well as several secondary features. A waiting period in increments of seven days was set for the disappearance of these outward symptoms. If they were still present after that time, the priest declared the individual unclean and outcast from the community and the temple. The contagion was considered transmissible through clothing, and these were burned if washing did not remove the stain (vv. 47–59; on soiled clothing, see pp. 158–159).

Physicians are mentioned in a few scattered instances in the biblical text. Even then, they seem to be associated with magicians and pagan priest-healers. This is apparently the case when King Asa is condemned for consulting physicians instead of Yahweh (2 Chr 16:12). Jeremiah 8:22, in speaking of spiritual healing of the people, mentions the "balm in Gilead," and physicians to administer it. Jeremiah 51:8

> So the LORD sent a pestilence on Israel from that morning until the appointed time; and seventy thousand of the people died, from Dan to Beer-sheba.
> —2 Sam 24:15

> *Is there no balm in Gilead? Is there no*
> *physician there? Why then has the health of*
> *my poor people not been restored?*
> —*Jer 8:22*

also indicates that herbal medicines were known and used. Isaiah, for example, prescribes a "cake of figs" poultice to be applied to a boil which is troubling King Hezekiah (Isa 38:21).

For the most part, however, medicine and the treatment of disease remained a primitive business, with the biblical writer describing some health problems as incurable (Deut 28:27). When this happened, the afflicted person or a relative sometimes sought a holy man whose intercession with a god might effect a cure. For instance, in 1 Kgs 17:17–24, a woman asks Elijah to restore her comatose son to life. The prophet lays on the boy three times and calls on God to "let this child's life come into him again" (v. 21). Once the boy is revived by this procedure, his mother testifies that "now I know that you are a man of God" (v. 24). Similarly, Na'aman, the Syrian general "cleansed" of his leprosy by Elisha's intercession, states, "I know that there is no God in all the earth except in Israel" (2 Kgs 5:15).

Conceptions of Death

Isaiah, taunting the king of Babylon (14:4–11), appeals to the common Israelite belief that the dead go down to Sheol where they, king and pauper alike, are all the same. Following the painful loss of his son, David sums up this general belief concerning the dead (2 Sam 12:21–23). As the child lay ill, the king fasted and wept, lying on the ground. But after his death, David simply states: "Can I bring him back again? I shall go to him, but he will not return to me." Likewise, Job remarks that "those who go down to Sheol do not come up" (Job 7:9–10).

Conceptions regarding Sheol, a poorly-defined region from which there was no resurrection and in which there was no reward or punishment, remained the same throughout the monarchy period (on Sheol, see p. 70). It was a place so cut off from the world of the living that "the dead do not praise the LORD, nor do any that go down into silence" (Ps 115:17–18). In the only instance in which the dead communicate with the living, Saul has the witch of Endor bring up Samuel's shade from the netherworld (1 Sam 28:8–19; on sorcery, see p. 69). Samuel complains that his rest has been disturbed, and prophesies the end of Saul's reign and the death, in battle, of his sons.

Mourning

Conventional mourning rituals were quite elaborate and expressive. For example, the messenger who brings the news of Saul's death has torn his clothing and placed earth on his head. David's reaction to the news is also to tear his robe, weep, and fast until evening (2 Sam 1:2–12). Furthermore, David composes a eulogy (2 Sam 1:17–27) for Saul as well as for Abner (2 Sam 3:33–34). Other expressions of mourning included a procession (2 Sam 3:31–32), wearing sackcloth, putting dust on the head, and shaving all the hair from one's head (Mic 1:16 and Ezek 27:30–31). Jeremiah also mentions the custom of bringing food and drink to the mourning family, and cutting oneself as a sign of mourning (16:6–8), a practice prohibited in Deut 14:1.

Burial Customs

Failure to be buried was anathema for the Israelite dead. Ahijah and Elijah spoke of a day

> *As the cloud fades and vanishes, so those*
> *who go down to Sheol do not come up; they*
> *return no more to their houses, nor do their*
> *places know them any more.*
> —*Job 7:9–10*

Ophel Hill on Zion. Rock-cut tombs found here may be royal sepulchers.

of vengeance on Jeroboam and Ahab when Yahweh would destroy their families and leave their corpses unburied (1 Kgs 14:11; 21:24). Similarly, God's unfaithful people would be defeated by the armies of Egypt, Assyria, or Babylon, and their bodies left for birds and animals to consume (Jer 16:4), or cast out to lie like dung heaps in the field (2 Kgs 9:37; Jer 8:2; Zeph 1:17).

The law required that even executed criminals be buried as soon as possible (Deut 21:23), and that bodies found beside the roadway be buried by the people of the nearest village (Deut 21:1–9). On one occasion, however, David hands seven of Saul's sons over to the Gibeonites to pay "blood guilt" for Saul's attack on this non-Israelite people (2 Sam 21:1–6). In violation of the law, David allows their bodies to remain impaled for a full season. He is eventually shamed into burying them, along with the bones of Saul and Jonathan, by the faithfulness of Rizpah, mother of two of the executed men, who stays with the bodies to prevent them from being eaten by animals (2 Sam 21:10–14).

The bodies of the dead were buried in tombs that reflected the social station of the

> *His corpse must not remain all night upon the tree; you shall bury him that same day, for anyone hung on a tree is under God's curse. You must not defile the land that the LORD your God is giving you for possession.*
> —Deut 21:23

individual. Cremation was almost unknown, although the bodies of Saul and his sons are burned after being retrieved from the walls of Beth-shan by the men of Jabesh-gilead (1 Sam 31:12). This may be because of the dismemberment and advanced state of decay. After the cremation, the bones are buried under a tamarisk tree and a seven-day fast is observed as a mourning period (v. 13).

Burial for kings and for the wealthy was in family tombs (2 Sam 21:12–14) in caves or carved into the rock of nearby hillsides. The often repeated phrase at the end of a king's reign, "[he] slept with his ancestors, and they buried him in the city of David" (1 Kgs 15:8), is used of most of the kings of Judah. Similar notices are attached to the accounts of the

> *What right do you have here? Who are your relatives here, that you have cut out a tomb here for yourself, cutting a tomb on the height, and carving a habitation for yourself in the rock?*
> —Isa 22:16

reigns of Israel's kings (2 Kgs 14:16). Excavations in Jerusalem have uncovered several tombs that would have been located within the walls during the monarchy period. It seems unlikely that these could be anything but royal tombs, because of the skill with which they were carved and the lack of space for tombs within the city.

A group of rock-cut tombs have been found on the northern end of the Ophel Hill on Mount Zion, and these may also be royal sepulchers. Perhaps this is the spot where Absalom prepared an elaborate monument tomb for himself "in the King's Valley," with a pillar to mark the spot (2 Sam 18:17–18). The mention that Manasseh's tomb (7th cent. B.C.) was located in the Garden of Uzzah (2 Kgs 21:18) may suggest that a new site was designated for royal burials after the original area was filled.

Rock-cut tombs, such as that identified by archaeologists as the tomb of the "Steward of the House," generally had a single large chamber, although there are some with more. This elaborate tomb, located in the Silwan Valley across from the City of David, contains an inscription giving the name of the owner and cursing anyone who would disturb it. It may be the tomb of Shebna, King Hezekiah's steward, who was rebuked by Isaiah (22:15–16) for carving a tomb higher up on the hill than his social status would allow.

An additional feature of the rock-cut tomb is the charnel pit in which the bones of older burials were placed (on primary and secondary burials, see p. 32). They no longer had the principal place within the tomb, but at least they were still interred with the rest of the family. Bench shelves are carved into the walls to accommodate primary burials. Rounded pillows are carved at one end, often with clay lamps placed at the head, perhaps to light the way to the underworld for the dead. Jars of wine, water jugs, and open-mouthed food jars are also found in these tombs, designed to aid the dead in their journey. Personal items like arrowheads and seals are also common grave goods.

The burial of the poor or lower classes would have been much less elaborate, perhaps involving simply the scooping of holes out of the earth. Both the Valley of Hinnom (Jer 7:32) and the Wadi Kidron (2 Kgs 23:6) may have served as common burial grounds for the poor. In some cases, their bodies may even have been placed in abandoned or pillaged tombs that once belonged to a prominent person or family (2 Kgs 13:20–21). Infants were often interred within the house itself. The large number of these domestic burial sites gives further evidence of a high infant mortality rate in the cities.

LAW

The Bible preserves several collections of laws, including the Decalogue or Ten Commandments (Exod 20:1–17; Deut 5:11–21), the Covenant Code given at Sinai (Exod 21–23), the Holiness Code (Lev 17–26), and the **Deuteronomic Code** (Deut 12–26). The last of these, collected and implemented during Josiah's late seventh-century B.C. reforms, proposed significant revisions of the laws found in earlier codes. In part, these revisions were reflections of theological differences between the Deuteronomic writer and his predecessors. Other revisions are largely matters of practicality, as the situation of those living in the seventh century was different from that of their ancestors.

One of these differences was the introduc-

You shall not charge interest on loans to another Israelite, interest on money, interest on provisions, interest on anything that is lent.

—Deut 23:19

tion of the monarchy and the movement of a large number of people into urban centers. These shifts contributed to significant changes in legal custom and the administration of justice in ancient Israel. Naturally the Israelite kings, like their ancient Near Eastern counterparts (see the preface to Hammurabi's code in *ANET*, 164), wished to exercise as much control over the law and its enforcement as possible in order to increase their own authority. This meant the king had to be identified with the dispensing of justice to all segments of society, especially the weak. The ideal, perhaps best exemplified by Solomon's judging of the two prostitutes (1 Kgs 3:16–28), was to create the perception that he was a "just king." With this accomplished, it would be more likely that people would look to him first for justice.

The other major factor at work in the transformation of the Covenant Code (Exod 20:23—23:19), with its emphasis on the village culture, was the need to meet the needs of urban legal problems. New situations arose that had not been a part of their society before, requiring regulations on aspects of commerce, making loans (Deut 23:19–20), or the accuracy of weights and measures (Deut 25:13–16). As a result, new laws or new interpretations of the law had to be made.

During the early monarchy, royal judicial authority was held as a prerogative of the king, and little delegation of authority to local judges was allowed. However, by the reign of King Jehoshaphat (ca. 873–849 B.C.), the complexity of running the nation of Judah, and the sheer number of cases, led to a major reform of the judicial system (2 Chr 19:4–11). The king, who had fortified the border regions, now used these new fortress cities as judicial centers where district courts were held and judges heard cases (vv. 5–7). Jehoshaphat also differentiated between secular and religious matters. He appointed Levites and priests in Jerusalem to hear appealed cases dealing with religious crimes, defined by the categories of "bloodshed, law or commandment, statutes or ordinances" (v. 10). To supervise this new judicial bureaucracy, Jehoshaphat set the chief priest, Amariah, over the Levitical judges, and Zebadiah, one of the king's chief officers, was made the head of the secular judges (v. 11).

Family Legal Customs

The introduction of royal authority forced changes in some legal customs, but was unable to supersede others. Early in David's career as king at Hebron, he faced a legal problem with the potential to tear apart his political hopes for a united kingdom. His general Joab murdered Abner, the commander of Ishbosheth's army (2 Sam 3:26–27). This was done in the name of blood revenge, since Abner had killed Joab's brother Asahel in battle (2 Sam 2:18–23).

The blood feud was an extension of familial responsibility to protect its own and was tied to clan affairs, since it involved a dispute between two extended families. However, it directly threatened the authority of a king trying to establish a system of royal justice. The solution (2 Sam 3:29–39) was for David to disclaim responsibility for Joab's act, and to disgrace Joab by forcing him to mourn publicly

When Abner returned to Hebron, Joab took him aside in the gateway to speak with him privately, and there he stabbed him in the stomach. So he died for shedding the blood of Asahel, Joab's brother.

—2 Sam 3:27

> And as if it had been a light thing for him to walk in the sins of Jeroboam son of Nebat, he took as his wife Jezebel daughter of King Ethbaal of Sidonians, and went and served Baal, and worshiped him.
> —1 Kgs 16:31

> In the case of a seignior's daughter, a virgin who was living in her father's house, whose [father] had not been asked (for her hand in marriage), whose hymen had not been opened since she was not married, and no one had a claim against her father's house, if a seignior took the virgin by force and ravished her, either in the midst of the city or in the open country or at night in the street or in a granary or at a city festival, the father of the virgin shall take the wife of the virgin's ravisher and give her to be ravished; he shall not return her to her husband (but) take her; the father may give his daughter who was ravished to her ravisher in marriage. If he has no wife, the ravisher shall give the (extra) third in silver to her father as the value of a virgin (and) her ravisher shall marry her (and) not cast her off. If the father does not (so) wish, he shall receive the (extra) third for the virgin in silver (and) give his daughter to whom he wishes.
> —MAL A.55

at Abner's funeral. In the fictitious case presented by the woman of Tekoa, David goes a step further and invokes royal authority to protect the accused murderer from clan vengeance (2 Sam 14:4–11).

The ultimate solution to this problem came with the establishment of six Levitical "cities of refuge" as described in Josh 21:13–40. Here, a man who had accidentally caused the death of another could flee from the vengeance of family and clan to a city of refuge. There he would be tried by the elders of the city, and either granted asylum or punished for his crime (Num 35:9–34). In the time of Josiah's reform (late 7th cent. B.C.), when all worship and royal authority were centralized in Jerusalem, the number of cities of refuge remained at six, but there was no Levitical involvement (Deut 4:41–43; 19:1–13).

Marriage and Betrothal

The more cosmopolitan atmosphere of Solomon's court, and increased contacts with other nations, led to a greater acceptance of intermarriage between Israelite and non-Israelite. Solomon solidified foreign alliances through his marriages to foreign princesses such as the pharaoh's daughter (1 Kgs 3:1), and Ahab strengthened already strong ties with the Phoenicians when he married Jezebel, the daughter of the king of Sidon (1 Kgs 16:31). In the text, these diplomatic marriages do have a dark side, where they are cited as prime causes for the adoption of idol worship (1 Kgs 11:1–8; 16:31–33) and the suppression of Yahweh's prophets (1 Kgs 18:13). Nevertheless, with such

a precedent set by the king, it is not surprising to find mixed marriages among the rest of the people. (Bathsheba's marriage to Uriah the Hittite in 2 Sam 11:3 may be a precursor of this policy.)

The parallels between Israelite marriage laws and those found in other ancient Near Eastern law codes indicate a common Near Eastern tradition that persisted over many centuries. For instance, the sanctity of the betrothal vows is found in Deut 22:23–27 and in the eighteenth-century B.C. Code of Hammurabi #130 (ANET, 171). The presumption in both cases is that the father contracts the marriage, and once a girl is betrothed, she is technically the wife of that man. Any crime against her is also a crime against both her father and her betrothed husband.

The Babylonian law states that a betrothed

virgin who has been raped will be freed while her attacker is executed. The Deuteronomic law is more specific, making provision for the location of the crime, and using this as the basis for the punishment of the couple. If the crime took place within the city, both are to be executed, since the woman could have cried out for help. However, if the rape is committed in the "open country" where no one could hear her cries, she goes free, and only the man is executed.

The Middle Assyrian Law Code (ca. 1100 B.C.) also contains similarities to the biblical criminal code. MAL A.55 (*ANET*, 185) is concerned with the rape of an unbetrothed virgin, who is still living in her father's house. The rapist must pay a fine in silver to the father for the loss of his daughter's virginity, and the father has the option of forcing this man to marry his daughter, with no possibility of divorcing her later. Deuteronomy 22:28–29 is almost an identical version of this law. Here, the rapist must pay a fine of fifty shekels of silver, and marry the girl without later recourse to divorce.

Divorce was an option for an Israelite man whose wife had committed some "indecency" (Deut 24:1–2). This was probably adultery, although other ancient Near Eastern law codes also list childlessness (CH 138) and taking a job outside the home (CH 141) as grounds for divorce (*ANET*, 172). There is no law in the biblical text allowing a woman the right to divorce her husband. However, he may not make unsubstantiated accusations of adultery or shameful conduct against her, on pain of paying a fine and being publicly whipped (Deut 22:13–19).

Inheritance Laws

Samuel's earliest arguments against the establishment of the monarchy "like other nations (have)" included the statement that the king "will take the best of your fields and vineyards and olive orchards and give them to his

These five men abandoned their territory (and) came to me because their brothers had been entrusted with wheat and a field here and were satisfied. Now on this matter I have sent their sugāgum *to you. These men should be taken and entrusted to his hand (so that) they may be brought to me. They should be given satisfaction and go with their brothers.*
—ARM

courtiers" (1 Sam 8:5, 14). Such privileges were granted by the king of Mari to reward tribesmen for military service (*ARM* IV 1:5–28). Saul did attach "any strong or valiant warrior . . . into his service" (1 Sam 14:52), and presumably

Stele of Hammurabi, depicting the king before a seated deity: the rest of the stele is inscribed with the code of Hammurabi.

he was able to do this by granting them privileges at court and tracts of land. Kings would have done this by transferring land to these advisers that was no longer being used, or whose owners were dead.

The sale of land outside the family or clan was unusual in ancient Israel. Even during the siege of Jerusalem by Nebuchadnezzar in 587 B.C., Jeremiah's cousin offered him the option to purchase a field in Anathoth. Before the land could be offered to a stranger, Jeremiah had "the right of redemption by purchase" (Jer 32:7–9). This transaction was made and signed before witnesses. Its stipulations were recorded on a legal contract that was then placed in a sealed earthenware vessel for safe storage (vv. 10–14).

On occasion, kings tried to exercise their powers in the manner of surrounding nations, so as to infringe upon inheritance traditions. Laws governing such obligatory transfers of field, orchard, and house appear in the Code of Hammurabi, where property vacated, willingly or unwillingly, because the owner did not fulfill his feudal obligations, would be given to one who did (CH, 30; *ANET*, 167). Thus, in 1 Kgs 21:1–4, King Ahab attempts to purchase the vineyard of a Jezreelite named Naboth. As was his right, Naboth refuses to sell his land to the king, citing the fact that he cannot give him "my ancestral inheritance" (v. 4). Ahab has no legal recourse, and goes home to sulk. His Phoenician wife Jezebel, however, has no qualms about taking what she wants. She is not bound by Israelite tradition or the law, and promptly trumps up charges of blasphemy against Naboth (vv. 8–12). Two witnesses, as stipulated in Deut 19:15, are brought forward to testify against him, and he is subsequently stoned to death (1 Kgs 21:13–14). Naboth's sons are apparently also executed along with their father for this crime (2 Kgs 9:26).

When Ahab, as the ultimate heir of property within the kingdom, goes to take possession of Naboth's field, he is met there by the prophet Elijah (1 Kgs 21:15–19). The king and his entire family are cursed for having "sold themselves" in order to take possession of land that is not theirs. The "king's call to justice" theme, employed here by the writer of Kings emphasizes that even the king is not above the law, and will be called to justice by Yahweh, a justice that will affect his rule and that of his descendants. This same theme also occurs in the narrative of David's adultery with Bathsheba (2 Sam 12) and of Solomon's idolatry (1 Kgs 11).

Slavery

Slavery was a part of Israelite tribal society from the earliest periods. Abraham maintained at least two slaves, Eliezer of Damascus (Gen 15:2) and the Egyptian woman Hagar (Gen 16:1). Throughout the early settlement period, the number of slaves remained quite small. However, by Saul's time, ownership of slaves had become so common that when David asks the wealthy Nabal for provisions, Nabal assumes that David and his band of followers are some of the "many slaves today who are breaking away from their masters" (1 Sam 25:10). During David's reign, numbers of slaves in Israel increased significantly as his almost continuous wars provided a steady flow of prisoners. These non-Israelite men and women became perpetual household servants, wives (Deut 21:10–14) or concubines, and construction workers (2 Sam 12:31). Not all prisoners of war, however, were spared to become slaves. In one instance (2 Sam 8:2), David executed two-thirds of his Moabite prisoners, perhaps to strike terror into the people of that nation.

Solomon's public works projects were built

When you buy a male Hebrew slave, he shall serve six years, but in the seventh he shall go out a free person, without debt.
—*Exod 21:2*

> *But of the Israelites Solomon made no slaves; they were the soldiers, they were his officials, his commanders, his captains, and the commanders of his chariotry and cavalry.*
> —1 Kgs 9.22

by forced labor battalions, drafted from the Israelite villages (1 Kgs 5:13-18). The text states that Israelites were not used as slaves, however, but served in the army and in positions of authority (1 Kgs 9:22). By whatever title, Israelite "workers" would have been required to carry out Solomon's grandiose building program along with the levies of captured Canaanite slaves (1 Kgs 9:20-21).

Poor Israelites occasionally were forced to become slaves, selling themselves or members of their family into slavery to satisfy a debt. According to the Covenant Code of law, this servitude was to only last six years for males; in the seventh they were freed and their debt canceled (Exod 21:2). Another law protecting the rights of slaves is recorded in Exod 21:26-27. This statute required that male and female slaves be freed if their masters had brutalized them. This early legal code (Exod 21:7-11) also stated that daughters, sold by their father into slavery, did not obtain their freedom in the same way as males. Many of these women became concubines or wives, and thus their position as slave or free women was determined by their marital status.

The later Deuteronomic Code (dating to ca. 620 B.C.) also required that slaves be freed after six years service (in a similar case, CH 117 mandated only three years of service; *ANET*, 170-71), and that they should not be sent away empty-handed (Deut 15:12-15). This Deuteronomic Code further simplified the law by including both men and women in this limited six-year period of servitude (Deut 15:12). The fact that these laws were not always obeyed, however, is attested to in Jer 34:8-16.

Here, the prophet complained that Hebrew slaves had been freed during the Babylonian siege of Jerusalem and then re-enslaved after the immediate danger was passed.

Provision for perpetual slavery for male Israelites occurs in the law to address the slave who decided to remain a slave. He may have done this to prevent falling back into the pattern of poverty that had forced him into slavery originally, or because freedom would have separated him from his family. The latter is explained in Exod 21:4-6, where a master gave a man a wife and they had children while he was still a slave. When his period of servitude ended he was freed, but not his wife and children. At that point he could renounce his freedom by swearing an oath to God and having an awl driven through his earlobe into the post of his master's door. A revised version of this law is found in Deut 15:16-17, without the reference to a wife. The mark of the awl branded him as a slave for life. The Code of Hammurabi prescribes mutilation or capital punishment for those who participate in the fraudulent removal of a slave mark (CH 226-227; *ANET*, 176).

The majority of the slaves mentioned in the period of the settlement and monarchic periods were Israelite debt slaves. This may explain why, according to the law, both Israelite families and their slaves were included in the covenantal community's Sabbath obligations to honor the Creator's recess by resting from all work (Exod 20:8-11). In the Deuteronomic Code, this attitude toward slaves is revised to tie directly to the memory of Israel's enslavement in Egypt (Deut 5:12-15). The tradition of their own enslavement became the basis for a generally humane treatment of slaves in the law.

RELIGIOUS PRACTICES

The establishment of the monarchy did not initially have a dramatic effect on local and family religious practices. Popular religion remained separate and often quite different from the official religion of Jerusalem and the temple. Political developments further complicated the Israelite religious scene. The Yahweh cult and its Levitical priesthood were established in Jerusalem during David's and Solomon's reigns. Shortly after the division of the kingdom, however, Jeroboam created rival shrines at Dan and Bethel where non-Levitical priests oversaw worship (1 Kgs 12:25–33). Jeroboam and later kings of Israel also legitimized the use of high places in local villages. In Judah, however, the main (if not the only) cult center was the Jerusalem temple run by Levitical priests. The history provided by the biblical text gives a picture of how the two nations understood their religious divisions. Rarely did the kings of Israel and Judah agree with one another in these matters.

During the divided monarchy, a single pattern of worship throughout a nation existed only when a king exercised strong control over the entire nation, as Josiah did in Judah. Josiah's religious reforms, based on the legal code found in Deut 12–26, forbid worship of any deity but Yahweh (Deut 12:29—13:18), outlawed shrines other than the Jerusalem temple (Deut 12:2–4), and purged Canaanite practices from worship (Deut 12:29—14:2). In the northern kingdom of Israel, uniformity of worship was rarely a concern of the kings (2 Kgs 10:18–31).

While the Assyrians and Babylonians did not impose the worship of their gods on the Israelites when they conquered the region (2 Kgs 17:24–33), their destruction of many local shrines (2 Kgs 25:9, 13–17) and their deportation of large portions of the population made performance of many religious rituals difficult, if not impossible. Those living in exile in Babylon wept when asked by their captors to sing the songs of Jerusalem's temple (Ps 137). It is not until their return from Babylon under the Persians (539 B.C.) and the reconstruction of the temple in Jerusalem (515 B.C.) that the exiles could once again fully worship Yahweh (Ezra 3).

Popular Religion

At the beginning of the monarchic period, individual Israelite homes and villages continued to engage in popular expressions of religion, most centered on seasonal festivals. For example, the New Moon festival was celebrated monthly on the first day after the appearance of the crescent moon (Ps 81:4; Amos 8:5). The day was set aside for rest, feasting (1 Sam 20:18, 29), and sacrifice (Num 28:11–15). These sacrifices and others were designed to ensure the fertility of the people, land, and herds. They were made on altars in private chapels, or collectively on the "high place" (bamah, 1 Sam 9:19). Horned altars, too small to be used in animal sacrifices, have been found at Megiddo in dig levels associated with King Solomon. They were probably used for burning incense and for grain offerings. Sacred household images (teraphim), in the form of the particular gods a household relied upon for protection and prosperity, were used in **divination,** or communication with the gods (Ezek 21:21; Zech 10:2). Despite prohibitions against household gods (2 Kgs 23:24), they remained a part of Israelite religious custom and were even mentioned in the story of David's escape from Saul's palace (1 Sam 19:11–17; on teraphim see p. 76).

Given the uncertainties of life in the ancient Near East, with drought, famine, and war real and constant dangers, it is quite likely that the Israelites chose to adopt some of the religious

> *Samuel answered Saul, "I am the seer; go up before me to the shrine, for today you shall eat with me, and in the morning I will let you go and will tell you all that is on your mind."*
> *—1 Sam 9:19*

Bronze figurine of Baal, Canaanite god of war.

> He also made houses on high places, and
> appointed priests from among all the
> people, who were not Levites.
> —1 Kgs 12:31

Exod 38:8). It is possible that by lying with these women, the priests are, in effect, forcing them to play the role of cult prostitutes, as in Canaanite religion. For this action and others, all of the adult members of Eli's priestly clan are killed (1 Sam 2:31-36). There is also evidence of prostitution as a means of paying for a sacrifice or vow made at the temple. The woman described in Prov 7 resorts to such measures because her husband has "gone on a long journey" and "took a bag of money with him" (Prov 7:10-20; see especially v. 14).

The biblical writer judges the adoption of Canaanite religious practices, including use of images and cult prostitutes, as "abhorrent" (Deut 23:18). As a result of the prostitution and other improper acts instigated by Eli's sons, all of the adult members of the Eli priestly clan are killed, and the shrine at Shiloh ceases to function (1 Sam 2:31-36). Generations later, during King Josiah's religious reforms, the king follows Deuteronomic law when he breaks down the houses of the male prostitutes that are in the temple precincts (2 Kgs 23:7; on Josiah's reforms, see pp. 96-99). To stand against adoption of Canaanite religious practices, the biblical text provides an ideal of proper behavior calling for strict adherence to Yahweh's covenant (see especially Deut 13-14). This legal prohibition was reinforced by the stern pronouncements of the prophets against idolatry, cult prostitution, and other syncretistic practices (Jer 8:19; Hos 4:13-14; 10:3-6; Mic 1:6-7).

Despite these later proclamations from the prophets, many Israelites in the early monarchic period, commoners and kings alike, combined Yahweh worship with Canaanite practices. While he is praised for

practices of neighboring peoples. This mixing of religious practices, called **syncretism,** included the use of images as well as specific rituals, prayers, and sacrifices. Among the Canaanite communities, worship of fertility gods also included the use of both male and female cult prostitutes. Sexual activity at local shrines was designed to promote the fertility of the land by encouraging the storm god Baal and his consort Asherah to engage in divine intercourse, causing abundant harvests and herds.

The extent to which Israelites incorporated this particular religious ritual is uncertain. First Samuel 2:22 suggests that Eli's sons have subverted the activities of women whose job it is to clean up the debris of the sacrifice "at the entrance to the tent of meeting" at Shiloh (see his construction of the Yahweh temple in Jerusalem, Solomon's building of temples for the gods of his foreign wives (1 Kgs 11:4–8) set a precedent that sanctioned worship of other gods. The priesthood in the capital could not police these illicit practices, which apparently continued throughout the history of Judah (1 Kgs 14:22–24). Recent drawings and an inscription found at Kuntillet Ajrud, in the northern Sinai desert, add fuel to the argument that Yahweh worship was blended with that of the Canaanite fertility gods Baal and Asherah.

The division of the kingdom further weakened local worship of Yahweh. In the northern kingdom of Israel, popular religion was given free rein by Jeroboam and his successors, who only demanded the people's political loyalties. Local "high places" were promoted by the kings as a way to curry favor and build support for their rule (1 Kgs 12:31). Worship of one deity did not preclude devotion to another (see 1 Kgs 16:31; 22:1–8). While Yahweh was worshiped on Mount Carmel in Jezreel (1 Kgs 18:19–45), Ahab erected a temple to Baal in Samaria (1 Kgs 16:32–33). Israel's royal shrines, like Bethel, were staffed by priests loyal to the regime, and served as rallying points for major festivals (see Amos 7:13). Prophets active in the north often pointed to these local and political shrines as justification for the destruction of Israel (Amos 7:9 and Hos 10:8).

Standing stones (*massebot*) were erected on the high places as well as in the temple of Baal in Samaria (1 Kgs 16:32–33). The slabs of stone marked the entrance to sacred precincts, or represented the presence of the deity. They were so closely associated with Canaanite worship that Josiah of Judah singled them out for destruction, along with the sacred posts (*asherim*), in his seventh-century reform movement that began in the southern kingdom of Judah and spread to portions of the northern kingdom (2 Kgs 23:14–15).

While less is known about religious practice in the southern kingdom of Judah, Jerusalem remained a major cultic center. Local shrines did exist in Judah, but some kings attempted to suppress their use. Archaeologists have found a horned altar from the shrine at Beer-sheba which dates to Hezekiah's time (ca. 701 B.C.). Unlike the horned altars that Moses built for the tabernacle during the wilderness period (Exod 27:1–2) and David constructed for the tent of the Lord in Jerusalem (1 Kgs 1:50–51), the altar at Beer-sheba was re-used as fill for a wall, evidencing a royal attempt to eliminate the high place at this site (2 Kgs 18:22; on tabernacle, see p. 71).

Josiah's seventh-century reform (2 Kgs 23:4–24) actually provides a long list of Canaanite religious practices engaged in by the people of Judah. Idols and their priests were removed from the temple, along with all sacred vessels and incense burners associated with their cult. The Asherah, a sacred wooden pillar set up in the temple, was taken out and burned, with its ashes scattered over a "potter's field" graveyard (v. 6). Cult prostitutes were banished and the "high places" were defiled and abolished from one end of the land to the other (vv. 7–8). In addition to these efforts to purify Yahweh worship in Judah, Josiah also eliminated religious practices and icons associated with neighboring peoples. He destroyed a shrine in the valley of Hinnom that was being used for the sacrifice of children to the god Molech (2 Kgs 23:10). He removed the images of horses and chariots from the temple precincts, a vestige of Assyrian sun worship possibly introduced in Judah by his grandfather Manasseh (v. 11). Altars that had been built to foreign gods by previous kings were pulled down and destroyed (vv. 12–15), and the graves (vv. 16–20) of Baal priests at Bethel (one of the sites in which Jeroboam had placed a golden calf, 1 Kgs 12:28–29) were defiled. The final expression of his clean sweep comes in v. 24 with the outlawing of mediums, wizards, *teraphim*, idols, "and all the abominations that were seen in the land of Judah and in Jerusalem." Josiah's efforts did not extend far beyond the boundaries of his own country, and much of what he attempted to accomplish ended with his death at the battle of Megiddo in 609 B.C.

Role of the Prophets

The office of prophet, present in cultures throughout the Near East, developed early in Israel's history. King Abimelech of Gerar understood Abraham to be a prophet (Gen 20:7). Moses and his brother and sister were called prophets (Deut 34:10; Exod 7:1; 15:20). During the period of the judges, when "the word of the LORD was rare" and "visions were not widespread" (1 Sam 3:1), Samuel served as a prophet (vv. 2–21), judge (7:17), and priest (7:3–17; 9:13–14). When he appointed his corrupt sons as successors (8:1–3), the elders demanded that Samuel ask Yahweh for a king to rule over Israel (1 Sam 8:4–5).

Israel's prophets received word from God regarding who was to be chosen as king and who was to be rejected (1 Sam 9:16; 15:10–11, 22–23; 16:1). They anointed Israel's kings (10:1; 16:13; 1 Kgs 1:34, 45; 2 Kgs 9:1–13) and, at times, the kings of other nations as a prophetic sign (1 Kgs 19:15–16). During a king's rule, prophets advised the king in military matters (1 Kgs 22:5–6; Isa 1:1–17), and questions of royal succession (2 Kgs 20:1). Some of the prophets active just before the fall of Israel (722 B.C.), and the later fall of Judah (587/586 B.C.), warned kings of the dangers of yielding to their enemies (Isa 37:5–7, 30–35). Other prophets encouraged surrender, and stated that God would fight on behalf of the conquerors as punishment for Israel's, and then Judah's, disobedience (Jer 21:9).

The biblical picture of the relationship between prophets and their audiences usually depicts conflict. Before a monarchy is even established, Samuel warns the people against kings and the power they wield (1 Sam 8:11–18). The court prophet Nathan berates David, Israel's most fondly remembered king, for stealing Bathsheba from her husband (2 Sam 12). After the monarchy divides, the narrative declares that the most "evil" northern king (1 Kgs 16:30) Ahab "hates" the prophet Micaiah for consistently speaking against Ahab's military actions. Rather than listen to Micaiah's warnings, Ahab surrounds himself with prophets who tell him what he wants to hear (1 Kgs 22:5–28). According to the biblical record, the king dies in a battle Micaiah has warned him against (vv. 29–40). Results of these conflicts prove deadly for others besides the kings. Jezebel, Ahab's queen, systematically kills those prophets who claim loyalty to Yahweh instead of to her preferred deity, Baal (1 Kgs 18:4).

Throughout the monarchic period, prophets active in Israel and Judah deliver two messages: worship only Yahweh and, as part of that worship, treat others justly. The eighth-century northern prophet Hosea likens Israel's worship of other deities to adultery (Hos 2:2–13). As a **prophetic sign act** symbolizing Israel's sins, the prophet himself takes a "wife of whoredom" and fathers "children of whoredom" whose names—"God sows," "No pity," and "Not my people"—represent the consequences of Israel's adulterous worship of other gods (1:1–8). Later prophets echo Hosea's warning against idolatry, reminding Israel and Judah of their deliverance from Egypt and their covenant agreement to follow God's law (Hos 11:1–2; Amos 2:10; Micah 6:4; Jer 2:6–7; 11:1–8; Ezek 20:1–21).

In order to follow this law, the prophets

Now this man used to go up year by year from his town to worship and to sacrifice to the LORD of hosts at Shiloh, where the two sons of Eli, Hophni and Phinehas, were priests of the LORD.
—1 Sam 1:3

warn, the people of Israel and Judah must stop unjust economic practices like rushing the end of the Sabbath in order to begin business, and using false weights to cheat trading partners (Amos 8:4–5; see Hos 12:7; Isa 10:2). The eighth-century southern prophet Isaiah asks on behalf of God, "What do you mean by crushing my people, by grinding the face of the poor?" (Isa 3:15). The prophet Amos concludes that as a result of Israel's oppression of the poor, the houses Israelites build and the vineyards they plant will be lived in and cultivated by foreigners, after they are exiled as punishment for their iniquities (Amos 5:11).

Temple Worship and the Yahweh Cult

There were several temples and shrines scattered throughout Canaan during the premonarchic period. These included the ones at Shechem (Josh 24:25–26), Shiloh (1 Sam 1:3), and Dan (Judg 18:27–31), and the three corners of Samuel's circuit as a judge: Bethel (1 Sam 10:3), Gilgal, and Mizpah (1 Sam 7:16). Archaeological investigations indicate that after the Philistines captured the ark of the covenant (1 Sam 4:10–11), Shiloh and the temple, which had housed the ark, were destroyed. Shiloh's prominence probably ended at that point, and the ark went into obscurity in the village of Kiriath-jearim (1 Sam 7:1–2). The priestly group that had served at Shiloh transferred their operations to the city of Nob (1 Sam 21:1–9). This was not, however, the only priestly community operating in Canaan at that time. David was also associated with the cult center in

> They brought in the ark of the LORD, and set it in its place, inside the tent that David had pitched for it; and David offered burnt offerings and offerings of well-being before the Lord.
>
> —2 Sam 6:17

Hebron (2 Sam 15:7), and his family worshiped in Bethlehem (1 Sam 20:6).

Jerusalem Temple

The temple most associated with the Davidic monarchy in Judah was the one built by Solomon in Jerusalem. Its site, like Jerusalem itself, was on politically neutral ground—the threshing floor of Araunah the Jebusite (2 Sam 24:18–25 and 2 Chr 3:1). Suggestions of previous cultic usage were supplanted by a Yahweh theophany, which ends the plague punishment for David's illegal census-taking and establishes the site as hallowed ground, and by David's sacrifice on the spot. Through David's mediation, the priestly community of Yahweh was given exclusive rights to the site. King David's purchase of the threshing floors (a place associated with justice in the older village culture) and King Solomon's construction of the temple at this site provided royal sanction for the Yahweh cult.

The key which associated this site with Yahweh was the ark of the covenant. David had it brought to his new capital with great fanfare and ceremony after he became the king of all the tribes (2 Sam 6:1–19). The ark was housed in a tent, a parallel to the wilderness tabernacle (Exod 40:1–8), and the sacrificial routine was initiated with David making burnt offerings and peace offerings before the tent (2 Sam 6:17).

The next logical step for David would have been to construct a formal temple for Yahweh worship. However, the text offers a variety of reasons why David did not build a temple to house the ark. According to 2 Sam 7, the need for a temple was replaced by the need to create a ruling house. First Kings 5:3 excuses David from this task because of the press of military campaigns to protect the nation. But 1 Chr 28, despite giving David credit for establishing the priestly bureaucracy that would supervise temple worship, says that he was denied the right to build the temple because he is "a warrior and has shed blood" (v. 3).

Plan of Solomon's temple

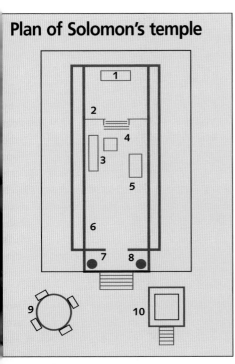

Jerusalem in the time of David and Solomon

Temple
?Mount Moriah
Palace
Valley Gate
Ophel
Tyropoeon Valley
Kidron Valley
Gihon Spring
Gate
City of David
Kidron Brook
Hinnom Valley
N

——— Suggested extension of Jerusalem during Solomon's reign
===== Suggested line of city wall
N. B. It is difficult to be sure about the northern part of the city at this time.

Key to Plan

1 Ark of the covenant
2 Holiest place
3 Seven–branched golden lampstand
4 Altar of incense
5 Table of showbread
6 The holy place
7 Jachin
8 Boaz
9 Laver
10 Altar of Sacrifice

Solomon's temple

As a result, it was David's successor Solomon who had the leisure time and resources to build the temple to Yahweh in Jerusalem (1 Kgs 5:4–6). Even the shaping of the stones at the quarry, rather than on site, eliminated the war-like noises of iron tools and signaled that this was a time of peace (1 Kgs 6:7). In Solomon's dedication of the completed temple, he followed David's example, initiating sacrifices of various kinds (peace offerings, burnt offerings, cereal offerings), followed by a seven-day feast for all the people (1 Kgs 8:62–66). From the beginning, then, David set the precedent: the king officiated at sacrifices and initiated national worship festivals (note that much later, Josiah re-initiated the Passover, 2 Kgs 23:21–23). Some of David's sons are even described as being priests (2 Sam 8:18).

Role of the Priestly Community

While David was credited with establishing the temple priesthood (1 Chr 15:1-24), and Solomon was recognized as significantly reorganizing it (1 Kgs 2:35), the Levitical priesthood eventually disputed the idea of the king as both political and religious leader. Over time, the Levites gained more complete control of the sacrificial rituals; and the king, while still an advocate for the people with God, took a secondary role. For example, whereas Solomon functions in a priestly role by offering sacrifices, prayers, and blessings at the dedication of the temple (1 Kgs 8), generations later, Hezekiah offers only a brief prayer on behalf of the people, as the priests and Levites offer sacrifices during the reinstatement of the Passover (2 Chr 30:13-27).

> The people of Israel who were present at Jerusalem kept the festival of unleavened bread seven days with great gladness; and the Levites and the priests praised the LORD day by day, accompanied by loud instruments for the LORD.
> —2 Chr 30:21

Starting with Solomon (1 Kgs 11:6–8) and Jeroboam (1 Kgs 12:28–33), several kings built altars to foreign gods and promoted non-Levitical priests to lead their worship (1 Kgs 13:33). The result in the biblical text was to portray kings as either evil idolaters, like Manasseh (2 Kgs 21:2–9), or as reformers who looked to the prophets and priests to help them cleanse the temple and renew the worship of the people (Joash, 2 Chr 24:2–14, Josiah, 2 Kgs 22:3—23:25). The biblical account does not take into consideration the internal political pressures that were placed on the kings, who ruled over both strict Yahweh worshipers and those who conformed to Canaanite religions. The latter of these groups would have welcomed many of the religious changes made by kings like Manasseh.

Similarly, the text does not explore the external political pressures put upon kings by their Assyrian and Babylonian masters. Neither the Assyrians nor the Babylonians forced those they conquered to convert to their national religion, but the pressures to remain loyal to their overlords dictated the actions of Judah's kings. Manasseh, who ruled for forty years as a loyal vassal of the Assyrians, had a long reign that might well be attributed to his success in conforming to their rules.

With kings fighting for their own survival, the priests became the protectors and interpreters of the law. Josiah's reform, by centralizing worship in the Jerusalem temple, reinforced the priests' position and strengthened their control over popular religion. The Deuteronomic Code in chapters 12–26 provides a blueprint for the religious activities in Judah's villages and towns. As a revision of earlier law codes (on this see p. 118), the Deuteronomic Code updated Israel's laws for a new generation, while at the same time solidifying the theological thinking behind Josiah's reforms. Dietary laws (14:3–8), the proper

> *If the offering is a sacrifice of well-being,*
> *if you offer an animal of the herd, whether*
> *male or female, you shall offer one without*
> *blemish before the LORD.*
> —*Lev 3:1*

place and means of slaughtering animals (12:15–27), the religious calendar (16:1–17), the referral of difficult legal cases to the Levitical priests (17:8–13), and more were covered by the Deuteronomic Code.

In Jerusalem itself, the actual routine of sacrifice and temple worship was left in priestly hands. Extremely elaborate ritual and sacrificial instructions are described in the book of Leviticus (on types of sacrifice, see pp. 72–74). In particular, the Holiness Code in Leviticus stresses the role of the priests to teach the people to "distinguish between the holy and the common, and between the unclean and the clean" (Lev 10:10). Among the statutes is a list of which animals were to be used for particular sacrifices (Lev 1:3–17), what portion of the

animal was reserved for God (3:16), the use of the sacrificial blood (4:6–7), and the offerings that were acceptable from a man who could not afford the normal sacrificial animal (5:11).

Matters such as ritual purity, interpretation of the law, and the treatment of disease (Lev 13–14) are also found here as the exclusive province of the Levitical priests. This code was most likely an ideal one. It may not have been strictly enforced until the postexilic period, when the monarchy had ended and the priests were the principal leaders of the people.

> *This is the list of the people of Israel, the*
> *heads of families, the commanders of the*
> *thousands and the hundreds, and their*
> *officers who served the king in all matters*
> *concerning the divisions that came and*
> *went, month after month throughout the*
> *year, each division numbering twenty-four*
> *thousand: . . .*
> —*1 Chr 27:1*

Assyrian relief from Nineveh depicting Assyrians capturing a fortress in Egypt.

> *David took from him one thousand seven hundred horsemen, and twenty thousand foot soldiers. David hamstrung all the chariot horses, but left enough for a hundred chariots.*
> —2 Sam 8:4

WEAPONS AND WARFARE

At the beginning of the monarchic period, the most important element in warfare was establishing military parity between the Israelites and their neighbors. David's mercenary years with the Philistines almost certainly gave him an intimate knowledge of their battle tactics and their skill in the use of weapons. While it is unlikely that iron weapons were the predominant item in the Philistine arsenal, learning about the enemy from the "inside" must have contributed to the eventual Israelite victory over the Philistines and other neighboring peoples.

The establishment of the monarchy itself was another important factor in the war against the Philistines. With the tribal groups united under a single leader, they were a much more powerful and effective force. From his capital at Jerusalem, David led his armies (2 Sam 8), or entrusted them to Joab's leadership to protect the villages and towns of his kingdom from invaders (2 Sam 10). As the area of his effective control grew, the valley of Succoth grew in strategic importance. It guarded the fords leading into Transjordan from the invading armies of Ammon or Syria. Under Solomon, the area of Mahanaim was incorporated as one of the twelve administrative provinces of the kingdom (1 Kgs 4:7–19).

Organization of the Army

One innovation of the united kingdom of Israel was the organization of the army into two different units: the regular army, and local militia. Naturally, most strategy was based around the professional soldiers of the regular army. Like Uriah the Hittite, many of these "Mighty Men" were foreign mercenaries whose loyalty was to the crown, and who were expected to possess the military experience needed in the wars against the Ammonites and Syrian princes. Others, at least at the beginning of David's reign, were from his family or the group of outlaws he had led before the death of Saul (2 Sam 23:8–39). They served as an elite shock force that could be reinforced as needed by the less experienced village militia (2 Sam 12:26–29). First Chronicles 27:1–15 provides a somewhat idealized description of the command structure and size of the militia. Each formation is said to consist of 24,000 warriors, a number somewhat high for the Davidic period. It is likely that a portion of this force was kept on alert, in case the king needed to call them into service quickly.

Weaponry

One sign that the Israelite monarchs were achieving military parity with their neighbors was the incorporation of chariotry into their armed forces. In the settlement and judges period, chariots had been a weapon of the Philistines and Canaanites, not the people of Israel (Josh 11:4–9 and Judg 1:19). David's and Solomon's enhanced political status and military success can be gauged, however, by their acquisition of chariots (1 Sam 8:11; 2 Sam 8:3–4) and their building of stables to house the horses (1 Kgs 4:26). Their successors in both Israel and Judah use chariots as a matter of course in every military campaign (2 Kgs 3:7; 8:21). For instance, in the annals of the Assyrian king Shalmaneser III (858–824 B.C.), King Ahab of Israel contributes 2,000 chariots and 10,000 soldiers to a coalition army (OTPar, 169). The commander of chariot forces becomes one of the major military officers in Israel, but also a potential threat to kings who cannot control them (1 Kgs 16:9).

The Siloam Tunnel in Jerusalem, which may have been constructed prior to the Assyrian siege.

In the armies of Israel and Judah, as well as those of their enemies, infantry was separated into fighting units and equipped with three basic weapons—spear, bow, and sling. Assyrian reliefs from the period of the divided monarchy (ca. 900–721 B.C.) depict spearmen in mailed coats carrying a shield in one hand and equipped with a sword, either strapped to the back or thrust into the belt (1 Chr 12:8; 2 Chr 14:8). With weapons designed for close infighting, the spearmen formed the first wave of attack. Depending on the terrain, chariots and cavalry were used both on the flanks and in formation. Chariots were also used to conduct commanders (1 Kgs 22:31–34; 2 Kgs 9:21) and messengers around the field, while the entire force was supported by the missiles of bowmen and slingers (1 Chr 12:2; 2 Chr 26:14; Isa 13:18).

Siege Strategies

Open field tactics, terrain considerations, and strategies based on the number of chariots and soldiers on the field are found in a number of biblical passages (1 Kgs 20:23–30; 22:29–36). However, a major challenge to military strategists in the monarchy period was the capture of a walled city. The strong points of the city (walls, glacis, moat, and gate complex) had to be overcome. Again, it was the Assyrians who perfected strategies to offset each of these challenges. Their reliefs and royal annals (COS, 303) depict Assyrian armies employing assault ramps, wheeled tanks attached with battering rams, sappers tunneling under walls, infantrymen with inflated goatskins crossing rivers and moats, and mobile towers bristling with archers thrust up against the city wall. These methods and structures were probably used in the Assyrian capture of Samaria (2 Kgs 17:5–6) and the Babylonian capture of Jerusalem (2 Kgs 25:1–4).

While the people of the city rained down stones and arrows on their attackers (2 Sam 11:24), the strategy of the besieging army was to spread the defenders as thinly as possible along the walls. During lulls in the fighting, psychological ploys were sometimes exercised. In 2 Kgs 18:19–35, the Rabshakeh, the Assyrian spokesman, called to the people of Jerusalem to surrender and to overthrow King Hezekiah. His pleas were not answered, but Hezekiah's negotiators were clearly worried, since they asked him to speak in Aramaic rather than Hebrew so that the people would not understand him (v. 26).

Famine also worked in favor of a besieging army. They could obtain food and other items from the surrounding countryside and from

Then the king of Assyria invaded all the land and came to Samaria; for three years he besieged it.
—2 Kgs 17:5

> *In the ninth year of Hoshea the king of Assyria captured Samaria; he carried the Israelites away to Assyria. He placed them in Halah, on the Habor, the river of Gozan, and in the cities of the Medes.*
> —2 Kgs 17:6

supply columns. However, if the siege lasted too long, the price of goods rose precipitously for the defenders (2 Kgs 6:25), and they sometimes resorted to cannibalism (2 Kgs 6:26–29). Water supplies were a constant matter of concern. Cisterns were dug around the city (Jer 38:6) and built into the roofs of many homes to catch rainwater. In times of war, the entrance to springs outside the city walls were concealed (2 Chr 32:4), and a water tunnel was cut from inside the city to the spring. Hezekiah may have constructed the Siloam Tunnel to divert the waters of the Spring of Gihon prior to the Assyrian siege of Jerusalem (2 Kgs 20:20). According to the inscription found in the tunnel, two teams of workmen, working from opposite directions, cut through over 1,700 feet of solid rock until "[there was heard] the voice of a man calling to his fellow" (*ANET*, 321; Sir 48:17–19). In some places this tunnel is over 155 feet below the ground. Water was stored in the tunnel and was channeled into a pool inside the city. Sometimes these tunnels were also a weak point for the city, as David's men demonstrated when they traversed the tunnel into Jerusalem to surprise and capture the city (2 Sam 5:8).

During the fighting, forces of slingers (2 Kgs 3:25) and archers harried the defenders with flights of missiles, masking the approach of towers or reserve forces. Eventually, an attack was made at a particular spot to breach the wall and enter the city (2 Kgs 25:4). The text indicates that breaching the wall was usually followed by a general pillaging and burning, as the attacking force took out their built-up frustrations on the defenders (2 Kgs 14:12–14

and 25:9–11 are two examples of this). The Assyrian king Sennacherib describes how his army captured Babylon in 689 B.C., filling the city squares with corpses, smashing its idols, tearing down houses and city walls, and seizing the wealth of the city (COS, 305).

Policy of Deportation

The ultimate punishment for peoples who continued to revolt against the Assyrians and Babylonians was deportation. Many cities were destroyed and their inhabitants slain or enslaved during these military campaigns. The Assyrians in particular relished the brutal slaughter and mutilation of their victims. King Ashurnasirpal records in his annals that his troops killed 3,000 soldiers, and disfigured many of the captives, cutting off arms, hands, noses, and ears, and gouging out the eyes of others. The heads of the slain were hung in trees around the fallen city. When such terror tactics were not enough and vassal kingdoms continued to revolt, the answer was to deport the troublemakers to some other portion of the empire where they would have less reason to revolt. Into the empty space created by this deportation, the kings of Assyria transported subjects from elsewhere in their realm.

Despite the fall of Samaria to the forces of Shalmaneser V in 722 B.C., Israel took advantage of that king's death and joined a league of other states lead by Hamath (Syria) and Gaza (Philistia). This generated another Assyrian campaign in 720 B.C., headed by the new Assyrian king, Sargon II. When he recaptured Samaria, Sargon deported 27,290 people. Second Kings 17:6 states that they were "placed in Halah, on the Habor, the river of Gozan, and in the cities of the Medes." This ended the monarchy in the northern kingdom and led to the creation of a new people in that area. Sargon records that he "brought into it [Samaria] people from countries conquered by my hands" (COS, 296). The Samaritans, who are later identified as living in what had been the northern kingdom of Israel (Ezra 4:17; Neh 4:2), may have descended from these people imported by Assyria.

The other major example of deportation is Nebuchadnezzar's transport of large groups of people from Judah and Jerusalem to Babylonia. This was done twice, in 597 and again in 587 B.C., following revolts by Jehoiakim (2 Kgs 24:1–16) and Zedekiah (2 Kgs 25:1–11), respectively. Unlike the Assyrian deportation of the people of Israel, however, descendants of Judah's exiles did return to Jerusalem after 538 B.C. The Persian king Cyrus made this possible when he captured Babylon. He issued a decree, recorded on the Cyrus Cylinder, that allowed captive peoples to return to their countries, and even provided funds for them to rebuild their temples (Isa 45:1).

Monarchy Period Review

1. How were city walls built in the monarchy period?
2. What were the characteristics of monarchy period gates?
3. How was Solomon's temple laid out and furnished?
4. Describe the social changes that Israelites experienced in the monarchy period.
5. What sorts of clothes and personal adornments did Israelites wear during the monarchy period?
6. How did Israelites of this period entertain themselves?
7. How did monarchy era Israelites think about death and the afterlife?
8. Describe monarchy period mourning and burial customs.
9. What impact did royal authority have on the practice of legal customs in Israel?
10. How did local and centralized worship in Israel differ?
11. What was the role of the priesthood during the monarchy period?
12. How did the prophets influence local and national policies and practices?
13. Describe weapons and systems of defense during the monarchy.
14. What methods of warfare and conquest characterized the monarchy period?

4. Exile and Return

HISTORICAL INTRODUCTION

The period from the Babylonian exile, beginning in 597 B.C., until the conquest of the Persian Empire by Alexander the Great of Macedon in 332 B.C. brought drastic changes to the Jewish community at home and in exile. During this period of their history, the people of Judah only had minimal control over their own affairs. The power vacuum left by the elimination of the monarchy gave the priests a new position as the arbitrators for the nation. In order to survive as a people, the Jews left behind in Judah, and those in the exilic communities, accepted some things that they could not control, while clinging to those aspects of their culture that set them apart. Among these were their story of the exodus, the covenant at Sinai, Sabbath observance, and the developing canon of law and history. Even more drastic changes took place later on during the **Hellenistic** (Greek) and Roman periods, but these will be dealt with more fully in the next chapter.

Written sources for this period of Israel's history are incomplete and sometimes difficult to fit together. For example, Ezra's praise of the "wall in Judea and Jerusalem" suggests that upon his arrival in Jerusalem as early as 458 B.C., he found the walls already under reconstruction (Ezra 9:9). Other texts indicate they were rebuilt later by Nehemiah around 445 B.C. (Neh 2:1-6). While Ezra's return to Jerusalem is traditionally thought to have preceded Nehemiah's, it is possible that Ezra should be dated later to the reign of Persian King Artaxerxes the *second* (404-358 B.C.). In addition to the biblical narratives in Ezra and Nehemiah, some information can also be drawn from Haggai, Zechariah, and Malachi.

The Book of Daniel, while perhaps useful in getting impressions of court life in the Babylonian and Persian periods, has some problems chronologically, and may have been written much later than the events it records (note that chs. 2-7 are written in Aramaic, the principal spoken language of the postexilic era). The Book of Esther has similar chronological problems, although portions of the book seem to date to the late Persian period and offer some insight into life during this time. The apocryphal book of 1 Esdras provides a slightly different, Greek version of the narrative from 2 Chr 35, through Ezra, to Neh 7:73—8:12. In 1 Esdras, there are some additions (see especially 1 Esd 3:1—5:6) and omissions from the biblical narrative, which probably reflect the changed concerns of the Maccabean community that compiled the book.

Extra-biblical sources include Babylonian court records, official decrees of the Persian government (including the "Cyrus Cylinder," *ANET*, 315-316), and a variety of legal and business documents from Mesopotamia. There are also letters from the Jewish military colony at Elephantine in Egypt, which tell of life during the Persian regime of the fifth century B.C. **Josephus,** the Jewish historian of the first century A.D., records some of the events of the

The Cyrus Cylinder, one of the Persian official decrees that are a valuable source for this period.

return from exile in the eleventh book of his *Antiquities*. Generally, his chronicle is based on tradition as well as written sources, and thus must be treated carefully by historians.

Exile Period

The traumatic effects of the deportations and the end of the monarchy, plus the destruction of Jerusalem and the temple, forced some drastic shifts in the cultural practices of the peoples of Judah and the various areas of the exile. One of the most fundamental changes that came to Judah in the wake of the Assyrian and Babylonian conquests of that region was an end to political independence. The northern kingdom of Israel ceased to exist after 720 B.C. A large percentage of the upper and middle class population was deported and was replaced by non-Israelites, resulting in a mixed population, some of whom would later be called the Samaritans. They were ruled as an Assyrian province by a succession of foreign masters, and had a strictly limited autonomy in deciding local issues. Provincial boundaries apparently remained the same from the Assyrian through the Persian period. The position of governor, however, appears to have become hereditary in the fifth century, with five generations of rulers coming from the Sanballat family.

Judah remained an Assyrian vassal state for another century. The fall of the northern kingdom lead to an influx of northern refugees into Judah. In 701 B.C., Sennacherib ravaged the Judean countryside and deported a portion of the population (2 Kgs 18:13; *ANET,* 287–88). Gradually, however, Assyria's power in the south began to decline. The result was a loosening of controls, which set the stage for Josiah's Deuteronomic reform movement (640–609 B.C.) with its emphasis on religious and political centralization (2 Kgs 23). More than ever, Jerusalem and Solomon's temple were identified as the site of Yahweh's presence. The royal theology of God's everlasting covenant with the Davidic house of kings (see 2 Sam 7:8–17) seemed once again to be vindicated.

During the wave of reform enthusiasm, Josiah attempted to expand his political control and religious reform even to Bethel in the north (2 Kgs 23:4, 8, 15, 19). Eventually, Josiah's kingdom also succumbed to the superpower struggles for control of the area. He was killed at Megiddo in 609 B.C. in an aborted attempt to prevent the Egyptian pharaoh Necho II from joining forces with the Assyrians in northern Syria (2 Kgs 23:29–30). Subsequently, Judah became a province first of Egypt, and then of Babylon.

> *In the twenty-third year of Nebuch-*
> *adrezzar, Nebuzaradan the captain of the*
> *guard took into exile of the Judeans seven*
> *hundred forty-five persons; all the persons*
> *were four thousand six hundred.*
> *—Jer 52:30*

This period ended with revolts by kings Jehoiakim and Zedekiah. In reprisal, Jerusalem was sacked twice and the temple destroyed in 587 B.C. Babylon took a fairly large proportion of the ruling class, including King Jehoiachin, into exile in 597, and deported two additional groups in 587 and 582 (Jer 52:30). The displaced persons were settled throughout the Babylonian empire, some perhaps set to the task of rebuilding ruined city sites. For example, the name Tel-abib (Ezek 3:15) means "city mound of the flood," suggesting that the site had been damaged by flood waters. Other groups were established near administrative centers such as Calah, Nineveh, Babylon, and Nippur.

Some refugees who fled during the Babylonian conquest went to Egypt, while others scattered into the Transjordanian kingdoms (Jer 40:11–12) and the Judean wilderness (Ezek 33:24–27). Even with the deaths of many due to war, famine, and disease (Jer 21:9), and the removal of a portion of the population to Mesopotamia, the land would not have been emptied to the degree that is described in 2 Chronicles 36:20–21. It is possible that the compiler of Chronicles wished to minimize the importance, or even existence, of a Judean remnant left in the land during the exile. This is reflected in the later disputes between the returning exiles and the Samaritans, and other "peoples of the land."

Excavations have shown that the towns and villages in the eastern, southern, and western sections of Judah, including Jericho, Lachish, and Beth-shemesh, have massive destruction levels and periods of abandonment after 587 B.C. However, the territory of Benjamin, north of Jerusalem, was left relatively untouched by the Babylonian armies. The people who dwelt there were able to plant and harvest their fields and continue commerce as before. With the seat of government moved to Mizpah, they would have also benefited from the maintenance of order supplied first by Gedaliah's administration, and then, after his assassination, by a Babylonian appointee. Babylonian provincial governance, following the assassination of Gedaliah, was probably exercised from Samaria (Jer 52:30). It is quite likely that this political arrangement was also adopted by Persians; but once the exiles began to return to Jerusalem in larger numbers, and the province of **Yehud** (Judea) was established, then that province would have been separated from Samaria and become an autonomous unit reporting directly to the **satrap** (or provincial governor) and the emperor.

One sign that the general makeup of the population of this region remained virtually the same is found in the ceramic record and other evidence of the material culture. Surveys demonstrate that seventy to eighty percent of the pottery forms that had previously been used in Judah continued to be used. Those that remained behind in Judah were ruled by Babylonian-appointed governors, and were expected to pay tribute from their harvests (Lam 5:1–6). For Judah to be able to pay this tribute, however, attempts were made to stabilize the economy by redistributing farmlands

> *Ishmael son of Nethaniah and the ten*
> *men with him got up and struck down*
> *Gedaliah son of Ahikam son of Shaphan*
> *with the sword and killed him, because the*
> *king of Babylon had appointed him*
> *governor in the land.*
> *—Jer 41:2*

to the poor (Jer 39:10). Those whose towns were destroyed during the Babylonian conquest, as well as those Judeans who had been living in Moab and Ammon, were resettled in the few remaining city sites (Gibeah, Gibeon, Mizpah; see Jer 40:10). Jerusalem was not rebuilt. Other than the temple complex that was restored in 515, the rest remained in ruins until the time of Nehemiah, in the mid-fifth century.

An indication of the indignation that the people of Judah felt for their foreign masters was the assassination of the Babylonian-appointed governor, Gedaliah. Although he was a member of the prominent family of Shaphan, which was previously involved in government affairs (2 Kgs 22:3, 12; Jer 36:10–12), apparently the people were angered because he was not a member of the Davidic royal house. His movement of the political capital from ruined Jerusalem to Mizpah also may have increased their antagonism. As a result, a faction headed by Ishmael, son of Nethaniah, and other members of the royal family took out their frustrations by killing Gedaliah (2 Kgs 25:22–26; Jer 41:1–3). Although most of the rebels apparently escaped to Egypt, taking the prophet Jeremiah with them (Jer 43:5–7), this act became the justification for the third deportation (2 Kgs 25:26).

The biblical text passes over the historical events during most of the remainder of the exilic period. Babylon went into a swift decline after the death of Nebuchadnezzar in 562. His immediate successor, Amel-Marduk ("man" or "servant" of Marduk = Evil Merodach of Jer 52:31; 562–560 B.C.), is mentioned in 2 Kgs 25:27–30, when he frees King Jehoiachin from house arrest. Jehoiachin, as a ruler in exile, sat at court in a place of honor. As noted in the Babylonian Chronicle (*ANET*, 308), he and his sons ate from the king's table, and he was granted a pension from the royal treasury.

However, this Babylonian king was assassinated two years later, and his two successors

> *I returned the images of their gods to their sanctuaries which had been in ruins for a long period of time. I now established for them permanent sanctuaries. I also gathered all the former inhabitants of these places and returned them to their homes.*
>
> *Furthermore, upon the command of Marduk, I resettled all the Gods of Sumer and Akkad, which Nabonidus had moved to Babylon, unharmed in their former places to make them happy . . . and I endeavored to repair their dwelling places.*
> —Cyrus Cylinder

ruled only five years between them. A palace revolt then placed Nabonidus, a son of a priestess of the moon god Sin, on the throne. The polemical Verse Account of Nabonidus (*ANET*, 312–15), which dates to the period from 555–539, is filled with references to his neglected duties as the chief officiant at national religious festivals. This may have been due to his allegiance to family gods, especially the moon god Sin. Failure to support the chief gods of the pantheon angered the powerful Marduk priesthood in Babylon, and contributed to his overthrow.

Nabonidus made the situation even worse by his long absences from the capital. He spent ten years fighting the Arab tribes for a portion of the spice trade, and engaged in archaeological projects from his base at Tema in northern Arabia. During this time his son Belshazzar ruled as his co-regent. As a result, opposition grew among the Babylonian priesthood, as well as the general population. The Verse Account of Nabonidus records complaints that the king entrusted Babylon to his son, in effect "letting everything go" in order to "start out for a long journey . . . to a distant region" (*ANET*, 313). If Cyrus's claims in his victory inscription (Cyrus Cylinder) are to be believed, the priesthood and people of Babylon actually welcomed the Persian king in 539, turning the city and the empire over to his rule with only a minimal amount of fighting.

Postexilic Period

Technically, the Babylonian exile ended in 539 B.C., when Cyrus issued a decree allowing all captive peoples to return to their homelands. However, there does not appear to have been a mass exodus of people from Mesopotamia. Initially (Ezra 2:64–65) only a small group returned to Jerusalem with Sheshbazzar, the new Persian governor of Yehud. One tradition suggests that he was one of Jehoiachin's sons, if he is the "Shenazzar" mentioned in 1 Chr 3:18. However, it is just as possible that he was a non-Judean Persian appointee. He is credited with laying the foundations for the new temple and returning the sacred vessels taken by Nebuchadnezzar when he sacked the temple in 587 (Ezra 5:14–15).

A few years later, a second and larger group of exiles returned to Jerusalem under the leadership of Jehoiachin's grandson, Zerubbabel, and the priest Joshua (Hag 1:1). They also experienced some trouble in rebuilding the temple and the ruined portions of the city. The Samaritan governor was suspicious of the returnees, feeling that they might be a threat to his authority. The Samaritans were further angered when Zerubbabel rebuffed their request to help with the rebuilding process (Ezra 4:3). Tattenai, governor of the province "Beyond the River," and his associates sent letters to the Persian king, trying to delay or end further construction in Jerusalem (Ezra 5:6–17). These tactics worked during the confusing period after the death of Cyrus (530) and the reign of his son Cambyses (530–522), but eventually the returned exiles received official sanction from the new Persian king, Darius, and completed construction of the temple in 515.

Once the temple was completed, Zerubbabel disappears from the text, despite the royal titles given him by the prophets Haggai

> *Speak to Zerubbabel, governor of Judah, saying, I am about to shake the heavens and the earth, . . .*
> —Hag 2:21

("signet ring," 2:23), and Zechariah ("the branch," 6:12). He may, in fact have, died or been recalled by the Persian government. However, it is also possible that the biblical writers considered his mission fulfilled with the rebuilding of the temple. As a result, his narrative ends, and the next stage in the restoration process, rebuilding the walls of Jerusalem, is then addressed.

One conclusion that might be drawn from this is that political events are of less concern to the biblical authors than religious matters. The revival of the Davidic monarchy takes second place in the narrative to the rebuilding of the temple and the priestly community. A further sign of this shift in priorities is found in the book of Malachi, which may be dated to the period immediately after the rebuilding of the temple. Attention is given by the prophet to improper sacrifices (1:6–14) and unlawful mixed marriages among the people (2:10–12). However, no real picture of political events can be reconstructed from this book.

Even more frustrating to historians is the fact that the biblical narrative tells us very little about the period from 515 to 445 B.C. Reference is made to a succession of governors (Neh 5:15), but no details of the administration of this long period of time are found until the appointment of Nehemiah as Persian governor of Judea by Artaxerxes I (ca. 445 B.C.). The archaeological record is also scanty, yielding only a few ring seals, clay **bullae** (hardened seal impressions), and stamped jar handles that contain the names of provincial governors. No chronological scheme can be determined using this evidence, although it is interesting to note that some of these governors do have Jewish names (Elnathan, Yehoezer, Ahzai).

During the intervening years of the sixth and fifth centuries, the Persian government concentrated its efforts on an attempted conquest of Greece. The energies of the empire were also required to suppress revolts in Egypt and in Babylonia (486–484). Darius and Xerxes, his successor, spent huge sums of money raising and equipping armies for these enterprises. This left little time to consider minor political matters in outlying provinces. Jerusalem's problems were virtually ignored until the war with the Greeks was over. Only then did it become possible to obtain the king's attention for local concerns.

Perhaps taking advantage of this emerging concern for matters within the empire, Nehemiah sought the support of the king to stabilize the situation in Jerusalem personally (Neh 2:1–8). He had received word of its ruined walls, and used his rank within Artaxerxes I's court to obtain permission to rebuild them. Nehemiah is described as the "cup-bearer" of the king (Neh 1:11). This was a title given to a trusted and generally high-ranking official responsible for tasting the king's food and drink to guard him against assassination by poisoning. It is also probably a ceremonial title, since Nehemiah himself most likely delegated the actual testing to others.

The fact that Nehemiah, a Jew, was in such a high position, demonstrates the degree of social mobility within the empire. Apparently, those who chose to remain in exile could find opportunities to advance to even the highest levels of government (see Dan 6:1; Esth 8:2). The Persian king also showed good sense by sending a representative to Jerusalem whose cultural and ethnic background was the same as that of the people he was to investigate.

Upon arrival, Nehemiah made a personal inspection of Jerusalem's walls before meeting with the political representatives of the provinces of Judea and Samaria (Neh 2:11–16). Despite the threats of Sanballat the Samaritan governor, Tobiah the Ammonite official, and

Bulla dating from eighth century B.C. showing a warrior leading a captive with tied hands and inscribed in ancient Hebrew "lmlk"—belonging to the king.

Geshem the Arab tribal leader, the decision was made to rebuild the walls. Nehemiah brushed aside their opposition, saying, "you have no share or claim or historic right in Jerusalem" (Neh 2:20). This may be his assertion of the full independence of the province and of the governor of Judah, as well as an attempt to separate the religiously suspect Samaritans and other "foreigners" from connection with Jerusalem and the temple.

Sanballat and his allies continued to plot against Nehemiah and the construction in Jerusalem (Neh 4:7–8). Their plans to attack the city and the workers were not idle threats. Excavations at several sites in central Judea have revealed destruction levels dating to the period around 480 B.C. This evidence may reflect the clashes between Persia and Egypt. It could also indicate abandonment of indefensible

> *So the wall was finished on the twenty-fifth day of the month Elul, in fifty-two days.*
> —Neh 6:15

sites, suggesting that some places in Judea were not safe from lawlessness or attack. Persia's conquests of Egypt in 525 and 343 B.C., and the constant skirmishes in between, left few resources for mediation between the returnees and the Samaritans. In any case, Nehemiah was able to complete the project and prevent an attack by the Samaritans by arming his workers and posting guards on the walls at night (Neh 4:10–23).

After fifty-two days, the citadel's walls were completed, and the inner city of Jerusalem (the old City of David) was thus secured against attack (Neh 6:15). Sanballat and Tobiah attempted on several occasions to lure Nehemiah into a trap or to discredit him (Neh 6:1–13), but he was able to survive them all (see his statement of honest administration in Neh 5:14–19). Nehemiah then secured his position by appointing Hanani, his brother, and Hananiah, the governor of the citadel, as administrators in Jerusalem (Neh 7:2). Because of the need to resettle the city and provide enough men to defend it (Neh 7:4), a census was taken and lots were cast to determine the one in ten who would live within the newly-constructed walls (Neh 11:1).

The remainder of Nehemiah's administration, divided over two terms as Persian governor under Artaxerxes I (Neh 13:6–7), concentrated on civil and religious reforms. A general remission of debts and mortgages was granted to alleviate pressures on the people who had been working on the walls (Neh 5:1–13). Levites were appointed to oversee temple worship, officials were designated to gather taxes and tithes (Neh 12:44), and the Sabbath was enforced by closing the gates of the city so business could not be transacted during the holiday (Neh 13:15–21). A further sign of Judah establishing itself as a separate and unique province within the empire was a purge of foreign influence in Jerusalem. For example, Tobiah the Ammonite was expelled from his furnished room within the temple (Neh 13:7–9), and one of the grandsons of Eliashib the high priest was exiled for marrying the daughter of Sanballat (Neh 13:28). In addition, Nehemiah forbade all marriages between Jews and non-Jews (Neh 13:23–27).

The final stage of postexilic history chronicled in the biblical text is the career of Ezra the scribe. Ezra, along with a group of priests, Levites, temple singers, gatekeepers, and servants, came to Jerusalem to "study the law of the LORD, and to do it, and to teach the statutes and ordinances in Israel" (Ezra 7:10). In order to accomplish this, Ezra emphasized the religious and social reforms set forth by Nehemiah, and brought about the impetus to formulate the **canon** of Scripture. Ezra's purpose in coming to Jerusalem may have been tied to Persia's desire to control Judea in the face of growing unrest in Egypt. By establishing a consistent legal system and a strong internal power structure based on the Persian governor and the priests of Yahweh, Artaxerxes may have hoped to ensure the loyalty of the Jews. The Persian government had previously ordered the codification of law in Egypt to prevent disputes over land. Ezra's role in codifying Jewish law could have fit into this administrative practice.

Whatever the reason for his coming, Ezra was given extraordinary powers to administer

> *And I contended with them and cursed them and beat some of them and pulled out their hair; and I made them take an oath in the name of God, saying, "You shall not give your daughters to their sons, or take their daughters for your sons or for yourselves."*
> —Neh 13:25

the province. His letter (Ezra 7:12–26) from the king instructed him to: (a) take with him any Jews who wished to return to Jerusalem; (b) "make inquiries about Judah and Jerusalem according to the law of your God, which is in your hand"; and (c) carry with him a great sum of gold and silver with which to purchase animals for sacrifice and for the general fund of the temple. Additional funds, up to a specified limit, could also be obtained from the provincial treasurers for the maintenance of the temple and the cult, and Levites and priests were now to be exempted from the payment of tolls, customs, and other duties (Ezra 7:21–24).

Each of these royal commands was designed to give Ezra a free hand when he arrived in Jerusalem. The large numbers of returnees (over 5,000, as the list of heads of families in 8:1–14 suggests) made an impressive entourage, and the wealth Ezra brought to the temple demonstrated the backing of the Persian government and the regard that Persia had for the religions of its subject peoples (Xerxes, 485–465 B.C., is an exception; see *ANET*, 317). Such regard served the Persian government well in that it allowed Persian kings to claim the backing of a subject people's gods (Ezra 1:2-4; 2 Chr 36:22-23). One last stipulation in the letter gave Ezra the power to "appoint magistrates and judges who may judge all the people in the province Beyond the River who know the laws of your God; and you shall teach those who do not know them" (Ezra 7:25). Those who chose not to obey Ezra and his judges were subject to punishments ranging from the death penalty to imprisonment, exile, or the confiscation of goods (7:26).

Having received his orders, Ezra gathered the group of exiles who would return with him to Jerusalem. After taking a census of these people, it was discovered that there were no Levites among them (Ezra 8:15). A special effort was then made to recruit priests and temple servants "for the house of our God" (8:16–17). Once these men were gathered, they were given charge of the gold and silver donated by the king to the temple treasury. The narrative states that they arrived without incident, having escaped ambushes and enemies along the way (8:31). After taking three days to recover from the trip, Ezra publicly placed the contributions in the temple treasury and delivered the king's commission to the provincial officials. Sacrifices of thanksgiving and sin offerings were then made by the newly-arrived exiles (8:33–36).

Once these initial steps were taken, Ezra set about investigating the situation in Judah. He heard testimony from officials that mixed marriages between Jews and non-Jews were still occurring (Ezra 9:1–2). Citing the prohibition of these types of marriages as a corruption of the people (Deut 7:3), Ezra demanded that the priests and Levites take an oath to put away wives and children of improper marriages (Ezra 9:12—10:5; on Ezra's actions against intermarriage, see pp. 150-151).

The continuation of Ezra's actions in reforming the religious and social character of the people is found in Neh 8. Using the Sinai tradition of a "new beginning," Ezra staged a covenant renewal ceremony. This involved a public reading of the law and an oath taken by all of the people that they would henceforth adhere to that law (Neh 8:1-6). In conjunction with the reading, however, interpreters of the law helped to give the people "the sense, so that the people understood the reading" (v. 8). This was probably due to the fact that Aramaic was the spoken tongue of that day, but the law read by Ezra was in Hebrew.

For they have taken some of their daughters as wives for themselves and for their sons. Thus the holy seed has mixed itself with the peoples of the lands, and in this faithlessness the officials and leaders have led the way.
—Ezra 9:2

> *And Ezra opened the book in the sight of*
> *all the people, for he was standing above all*
> *the people; and when he opened it, all the*
> *people stood up.*
> —Neh 8:5

Following the initial reading of the law, the Feast of Tabernacles was celebrated for seven days. There was a reading of the law on each day of the feast (Neh 8:14–18). Another assembly, in which a collective act of penitence was made, then followed their joyful celebration. Prayers were made confessing past sins while the people fasted and wore the sackcloth of mourning (Neh 9:1–37). The scroll of the law was then signed by the priests and Levites (9:38—10:27), while the remainder of the people took an oath to obey its injunctions (10:32–39). Included in this oath was a set of special regulations involving sacrifice and the payment of tithes in support of the Levites and the temple (10:33–39). These stipulations, as much as anything else, point up the enhanced role that the priestly community now played in the shaping of postexilic Judaism.

No further mention of Ezra or his activities is found in the biblical text. Whether he returned to Persia and the service of the king or remained to enforce the covenant is unknown. However, his reform galvanized the priests of the second temple into compiling an authoritative version of the law and the history of the people. By the second century, as seen in the writings of Jesus ben Sirach (Sirach or Ecclesiasticus), this had become, by tradition, the official canon of Hebrew Scriptures.

Starting with the Assyrian conquest and deportation of the people of Israel (721 B.C.), and continuing with the Babylonian destruction of Jerusalem (587 B.C.), a great **Diaspora,** or scattering of the Jews, began. Initially they were spread throughout the Near East, and in later periods, under Greek and Roman rule, they were scattered throughout Mediter-

ranean and European countries. Influences of Persian culture during the postexilic period, and dispersion of the Jews, resulted in the creation of two basic types of Judaism: Judean and Diasporic. While each retained a basic respect for Israelite traditions, the laws (Torah), as well as the sanctity of Jerusalem, language differences and variances in social climate gradually widened the gulf between them. More differences arose because of Hellenistic influences and the politics of the Roman emperors and their administrators. These influences will be discussed in the next chapter.

LIFE IN THE DIASPORA

With the rule of the monarchy ended and the temple in ruins, many people chose, or were forced, to leave. Some were political refugees who fled into temporary exile in the Transjordanian kingdoms. Others founded communities in Egypt (Jer 43:1–7). Many of these people chose to remain in Egypt after the exile ended. These, and other exiles that came in later periods, eventually formed the nucleus of Jewish communities in major cities like Alexandria in Egypt. Some of them even served as mercenaries in the Egyptian and Persian armies. Letters and other documents confirming the existence of these communities (dating to the 5th cent. B.C.) have been found at the Jewish military colony of Elephantine, located on an island in the Nile River near modern Aswan. These documents describe business dealings, contracts, wills, and other aspects of everyday life that suggest the people had settled into their foreign existence.

A similar picture emerges from texts describing life among the exiled Jews in Mesopotamia. They were forced into exile, carrying few possessions (Ezek 12:1–7), and were taken to new settlements. For some, beginning a new life was a difficult task (Ps 137), but the realities of prolonged captivity must have sobered the hope of quick return (Ezek

Jewish history from the Exile to Bar Kochba

DATE	EVENT	RULERS
587 B.C.	Jerusalem destroyed by Babylonians. Exile in Babylon begins.	BABYLONIANS
539 B.C.	Persians invade Babylon. Persian domination begins.	PERSIANS
538 B.C.	Cyrus' decree permits exiles to return to Jerusalem.	
520 B.C.	Temple in Jerusalem rebuilt.	
445/444 B.C.	Walls of Jerusalem rebuilt.	
333 B.C.	Alexander the Great defeats the Persians. Macedonian rule begins.	MACEDONIANS
323 B.C.	Alexander dies. His kingdom is divided among his generals.	PTOLEMIES
198 B.C.	Palestine captured from Egypt by Antiochus III.	SELEUCIDS
167 B.C.	Maccabean Rebellion following Antiochus IV's persecution of Jews. Jews recapture temple in Jerusalem.	HASMONEANS
A.D. 63	Roman general Pompey conquers Jerusalem.	ROMANS
A.D. 66	First Jewish Revolt. Jerusalem destroyed.	
A.D. 132	Second Jewish Revolt (Bar Kochba).	

24:15–24), and sparked the energies necessary to get on with life.

Despite the loss of their former status and the symbols of past glories, the people were given some hope that the exile would eventually end. For instance, the book of Kings (see also Jer 52:31–34) ends its chronicle with the positive note that Jehoiachin was released from house arrest in his thirty-seventh year of exile. He and other members of his family were also given a pension and a place of honor at the table of King Evil Merodach, whose name means "man of [the god] Marduk" (2 Kgs 25:27–30). Confirming this are Babylonian ration lists, uncovered by archaeologists, which state that Jehoiachin and his family received yearly allotments from the king (*ANET*, 308).

As the years went by, many of the exiles became more a part of the land and culture of Mesopotamia. By the second generation, they spoke the Mesopotamian dialect of Aramaic and used Aramaic script in writing. They took Babylonian names (Zerubbabel, Mordecai; see Esth 2:5), and functioned as a normal part of the local economy. In calculating their transactions, they went so far as to adopt the use of the Babylonian month names.

Evidence of the cultural adaptation made by the exiled Jews is found in the Murashu documents, found at the southern Mesopotamian city of Nippur, and dating to the second half of the fifth century B.C. These legal texts provide documentation that life in the exile was not too restrictive for the Jews. Signs that these communities did have some power to manage their own affairs can be seen in Ezra 8:17–20, which indicates that the temple servants had

So Jehoiachin put aside his prison clothes. Every day of his life he dined regularly in the king's presence.
—*2 Kgs 25:29*

> *I gathered them by the river that runs to Ahava, and there we camped three days. As I reviewed the people and the priests, I found there none of the descendants of Levi.*
> —Ezra 8:15

retained their former status as cultic officials. There is no evidence of discrimination against the Jews in matters of business. They paid the same interest rate on loans as everyone else, participated in a wide variety of occupations (including date-grower, fisherman, and goat-herder), and negotiated contracts for the use of land as tenant farmers.

The apparent fullness of life evidenced in these texts may be one explanation for why many of the Jews chose to remain in Mesopotamia after the Persian decree allowed them to return to Judea. The first-century A.D. Jewish historian Josephus suggests that their reluctance to return was based on their "being unwilling to leave their possessions" (*Ant.* 11.8).

To be sure, new groups continued to return throughout the Persian period. However, in recruiting returnees, leaders sometimes found it difficult to obtain a full range of skills and occupations. For instance, when Ezra was gathering the people to return with him to Jerusalem, he found that no Levites had gathered for the trip (Ezra 8:15). As a result, he sent out messengers to various towns to recruit these traditional temple servants.

LIFE AFTER THE RETURN FROM EXILE

Perhaps the first place that describes life after the exile is the census lists of those who returned to Jerusalem. The list of those who followed Zerubbabel, the Persian governor (Hag 1:1), and Jeshua, the chief priest, is found in Ezra 2:1–70 and Neh 7:6–69. This census contains the names of leaders, clan or family members, temple officials, men of mixed or suspect family origin, servants, and animals.

A short appendix to the list is found in Neh 12:1–26, and provides additional information on the priests and Levites who "came up with Zerubbabel." The total number mentioned in the text exceeds the numbers of the groups listed. However, the total probably includes unnamed or undistinguished members of the group of returnees.

Another census list is found in Ezra 8:1–14. It contains the priestly and secular clans (numbering about 1,500) who returned with Ezra. An emphasis on the priestly members of the company indicates their importance to the writer as well as to the postexilic community. Persian governors like Zerubbabel and Nehemiah came and went, but it was priests and scribes like Jeshua (spelled Joshua in Haggai) and Ezra who really shaped postexilic society.

We can only speculate on exactly who returned to Jerusalem after 538 B.C. Certainly, the priests had a vested interest in resuming the cult, and the court employees who accompanied each new governor had a specific job to perform. However, the average individual may have come either out of piety inspired by Isaiah's vision of a glorious procession through the wilderness (40:3–5), or out of a desire to make a new life in a place where land would be easier to obtain and new businesses could flourish.

Political Conditions

Whatever their reason for coming, the former exiles found a ruined capital city and a neglected countryside upon their arrival. They also quickly discovered that Judah was only one small province (*medinah*) within the larger

> *Now these were the people of the province who came from those captive exiles whom King Nebuchadnezzar of Babylon had carried captive to Babylonia; they returned to Jerusalem and Judah, all to their own towns*
> —Ezra 2:1

administrative unit (*satrapy*) of "Beyond the River" (Ezra 4:11). As such, they could not expect the Persian government to have any more interest in them than their neighboring states. They could do nothing about the resettlement of some of Judah's former territory by Edomites and Ammonites, or the control held by the Arab tribes over Gaza and the routes south to Egypt. Neighboring governors watched their every move. The returned exiles represented a potential political threat to their influence over the region. This was especially true for the governor of Samaria. Thus, it is not surprising that for over one hundred years Samaritan governors and their allies attempted to obstruct the rebuilding of Jerusalem as an administrative center (Ezra 4:4–6; Neh 4:1–9).

City Planning

Since the biblical narrative concentrates on rebuilding Jerusalem's temple and walls (Ezra 3:8—6:15; Neh 2–4), little is known about the dwellings of its inhabitants. Babylonian governors probably allowed some small amount of construction on the ruined site, as long as it served no military purpose. There are some indications that Jerusalem may still have served as a destination for religious pilgrims. The passage in Jer 41:4–6, which describes pilgrims coming to Gedaliah's court in Mizpah, at least suggests that worship was planned, whether in Mizpah or Jerusalem.

At the end of the exile, it seems reasonable, although there is no archaeological evidence to support it, that the returning Jews restored some of the buildings in the ruined portions of Jerusalem to provide themselves with housing and business space (Hag 1:4). After a delay of over twenty years, the temple was rebuilt under the direction of Zerubbabel in 515 B.C. (Ezra 6:15). At this point, however, the city walls were not rebuilt, and the majority of people would have lived in nearby villages and farms. The prophets Haggai (1:10–11) and Joel

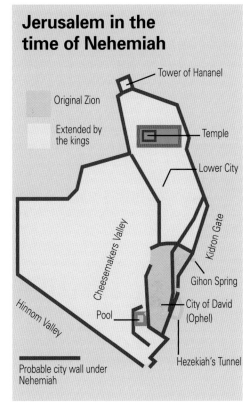

Jerusalem in the time of Nehemiah

Tower of Hananel

Original Zion

Extended by the kings

Temple

Lower City

Cheesemakers Valley

Kidron Gate

Gihon Spring

Hinnom Valley

Pool

City of David (Ophel)

Hezekiah's Tunnel

Probable city wall under Nehemiah

(1:4, 9–12) describe the hardships faced by these farmers, who lost crops to locusts and to drought. Still, no substantial number of people would have been attracted to settling in Jerusalem until its fortifications were repaired, and it stood once again as a symbol of Israelite nationalism.

This important step in rebuilding the pride of the Jewish people was accomplished by the Persian governor Nehemiah. Because of the limited resources and manpower in Judea, Nehemiah confined his construction to the eastern hill of the city, the site of the City of David, and the temple mount. Modern

And this house was finished on the third day of the month of Adar, in the sixth year of the reign of King Darius.
—*Ezra 6:15*

147

excavations in Jerusalem support this conclusion. Material from the Persian period has only been uncovered on the eastern side of the site.

Utilizing a mixed workforce, and assigning each group to rebuild a particular portion of the wall, the new inhabitants completed fortifications and gates of this small area of the total city site in fifty-two days (Neh 3:1—6:15). Again, it seems likely that further construction took place after this, but archaeological evidence is still lacking.

Housing for the *nethinim* (temple servants) and priests, within the newly walled area, was constructed on the ridge of the Ophel, near the sanctuary. Shops for the tradesmen guilds and artisans, such as jewelers, were located to the east and southeast of the walls of the temple mount. Other commercial and industrial districts that supplied the city's needs were probably located outside the city walls (Neh 3:8, 11). Evidence for this is found in Nehemiah's order that the gates of the city be closed on the Sabbath. His action prevented the entrance of Tyrian fishmongers and other merchants on this holy day (Neh 13:15-21).

Most of what is known about city construction and planning outside of Jerusalem in the Persian period comes from excavations in the more heavily settled areas of Galilee and the coastal plain. This information is limited, however, since some of the most important cities (Megiddo and Jericho) were abandoned during this period and became badly eroded as a result. Others that did survive destruction after the fall of Babylon, like Samaria and

> *When it began to be dark at the gates of Jerusalem before the sabbath, I commanded that the doors should be shut and gave orders that they should not be opened until after the sabbath. And I set some of my servants over the gates, to prevent any burden from being brought in on the sabbath day.*
>
> —Neh 13:19

Ashdod, had their Persian era strata badly damaged by construction during the Hellenistic and Roman occupation.

Relatively intact evidence of Persian period occupation has been found at the coastal cities of Tell Megadim and Shiqmona. The Persian period levels at these sites show that some quarters of the city were set out in a standard gridiron pattern. This was an obvious improvement over the narrow, twisting street patterns common to earlier periods. In the gridiron pattern, large tracts of houses were built on either side of a road that was crossed by avenues running perpendicular to it. Similar homogeneous housing patterns have been found in Persian cities in Greece (i.e., Olynthus) and at Sardis in Anatolia. Such finds suggest that many local satraps used a standard pattern of construction. This local pattern of strictly-organized city streets was part of a larger system of roadways built and maintained by the Persian Empire. These highways connected the capitals of the empire to the capitals of the local satraps, and facilitated trade and military movements throughout the empire (Herodotus, *Hist.* 5.52–53).

Those sites in Judah that were rebuilt and fortified by the Persians and the returned exiles were not strengthened to the extent that they had been in the past. Lachish had been abandoned after its destruction by the Babylonians in 587 (see Jer 34:7). The Persians rebuilt it as an administrative center, but did not expend much effort on its defenses. The threshold of its restored gateway was paved with undressed stones. The entranceway was plastered with clay and soft chalk over a gravel base to accommodate the flow of traffic to and from the city. This suggests a role for the city more commercial than defensive.

The excavated portion of Jerusalem's wall dating to the Persian era (summit of eastern hill) also shows signs of being built with less care than in the past. For instance, cracks in the spaces between standing stones were

A section of the "broad wall" of Nehemiah 3:8, which has been uncovered in the Jewish Quarter of the Old City of Jerusalem.

simply filled with smaller stones. Perhaps the haste with which Nehemiah rebuilt the walls (fifty-two days) is one explanation for this style of construction (Neh 4:21–23). It may also reflect a lack of materials or funds, as well as a decision on the part of the Persian government to prevent true refortification of these cities at the edge of the empire.

Domestic Architecture

One domestic architectural form that endured in the postexilic period was the "open court house." Originally introduced to the region by the Assyrians, this structure remained practically unchanged in style throughout the Babylonian and Persian occupations. It consisted of a central open court with rooms on three or four sides. This lack of uniformity may reflect an uneven construction site or the relative affluence of the owner. Also, it may have been based on a pattern found in Mesopotamian cities, in which buildings are linked into units sharing a common partition wall.

The governor's residence at Lachish also contains some Persian architectural innovations. Among these are the use of drum-shaped columns on cut stone bases, which supported the porch and lined the stairways, both of which are found in Persian and Greek palaces, and temples elsewhere. The building also had a vaulted stone roof and arched doorways. Rooms containing storage areas and residential apartments were arranged around a central courtyard. The entire structure, except for the columns, was constructed of stone salvaged from the ruins of earlier buildings.

For those Jews who lived in the farming villages in Judah, housing remained much as it had in earlier periods (on earlier domestic architecture, see pp. 52–53). Depending on the relative wealth of the occupants, the pillar or four-room house, of one or two stories, continued to be the principal style of construction. Excavated levels within these villages from the Persian period contain some new pottery types (some imported from Greece and Cyprus), a few Persian and Greek coins, and the usual array of domestic items common to every Israelite home.

Marriage Customs

If the Book of Esther is any indication, marriage between Jews and non-Jews was not seen as inappropriate in Diaspora communities (Esth 2:1-18; see Jer 29:6). For the exiles who returned, a chief desire was probably to settle quickly and easily into community life in Judea. To achieve this, many of them married into Moabite, Ammonite, and Samaritan families of Judea and Samaria (Ezra 9:1-2). In order to make new family alliances possible, it may have been necessary to divorce Jewish wives (Mal 2:13-16). Intermarriage was apparently quite common from the beginning of the return from exile until Ezra's time at the end of the fifth century B.C. It brought with it social acceptability for the exiles among the people already living in the land, as well as assured title to land that returning exiles would not otherwise have.

On at least two separate occasions, however, a concerted attempt was made by governors of Judea, both of whom came from the stricter religious environment of the Diasporic community, to outlaw these mixed marriages. Nehemiah's ordering of strict endogamy had a variety of social causes (on endogamy, see p. 66). For one thing, these marriage alliances, especially those made between Israelite elders and priests and the noble families of Samaria, threatened the political independence of the province of Judea. If enough of the ruling class from both areas became allied by marriage, a case could be made to the Persian government to unite them under a single ruler. Thus, when Nehemiah learned that the grandson of

> Do not intermarry with them, giving your daughters to their sons or taking their daughters for your sons, . . .
> —Deut 7:3

Eliashib the high priest had become the son-in-law of the Samaritan governor Sanballat, he expelled the young man as a defiler of the priesthood (Neh 13:28-29). Elite marriages were also the main concern for Ezra, whose lists of the intermarried contain a disproportionate number of elders and priests (Ezra 10:16-44).

Another reason given for banning these mixed marriages is offered in both Nehemiah's and Ezra's reform decrees. They bemoaned the fact that children of these marriages no longer spoke the language of Judah. Instead, they were taught the languages of their Moabite, Ammonite, and Ashdodite mothers (Neh 13:23-24). This could cause the social and religious heritage of the returning exiles to get lost quickly in the Persian imperial melting pot (Ezra 9:14). Recognizing this, Nehemiah cited the precedent set by King Solomon, who had married many foreign wives and thus brought idolatry to Israel (Neh 13:26-27). This final argument was his justification for demanding that the people cleanse themselves "from everything foreign" (Neh 13:30).

Ezra took the religious arguments against these marriages a step further by orchestrating a dramatic series of events. In the ninth month (November–December), some eight months after leaving Babylon to return to Yehud, Ezra learned that the "people of Israel, the priests, and the Levites" were intermarrying (Ezra 9:1). In response, he performed acts that are usually associated with mourning: tearing his garments, pulling out his hair, and fasting. He further shamed the Israelites by praying and weeping in public (Ezra 9:3-10:1). The leaders then proposed making a covenant prohibiting intermarriage. Ezra took this under advisement, and decreed that all of the returned exiles assemble within three days to deal with this issue (10:2-8).

The assembly of the people in Jerusalem took place in an open space in front of the temple. In the midst of a rainstorm, Ezra insisted that the entire assemblage separate themselves from the people of the land by divorcing their foreign wives (Ezra 10:9-12). The sheer magnitude of Ezra's request caused the assembly to ask for the appointment of a panel of elders to investigate mixed marriages throughout the province, including those of priests and other temple officials. Within two months, they compiled a list of those men with foreign wives and their children (Ezra 10:17). These men then pledged to divorce their wives, disinherit the children of the marriage, and make a guilt offering (Ezra 10:19). Such a radical solution was deemed necessary in order to purify the people, and especially the priesthood. Only then was a covenant renewal ceremony conducted, and the nation once again proclaimed to be the people of Yahweh (Neh 8-10).

Economic Life

As might be expected, the economy of the province of Judea continued to be based on agricultural production. The initial problems of repairing hillside terraces and reclaiming abandoned fields were dealt with by the first groups of returnees. It was the duty of the governor to aid them in this task, since it was his responsibility to see to it that the province became productive enough to pay its taxes (Neh 5:15). The smaller population of Judea after the return from exile meant a larger concentration of land in the hands of a few families, and a general labor shortage. Those who attempted to work small farms ran into the double problem of paying taxes and farm

The former governors who were before me laid heavy burdens on the people, and took food and wine from them, besides forty shekels of silver. Even their servants lorded it over the people. But I did not do so, because of the fear of God.
—Neh 5:15

debts. When a bad harvest occurred (Hag 1:6), they were forced to either forfeit on their mortgages or sell themselves and their families into slavery to pay off their debts (Neh 5:3-5).

Nehemiah dealt with this problem by bringing charges against the nobles and officials who were demanding interest on loans, and thus driving their fellow Israelites further into debt (Neh 5:6-9). He loaned the destitute farmers money and distributed grain to their families. Furthermore, their creditors were required to return all confiscated lands and interest payments (5:10-13).

Other economic activities practiced in the cities and towns of Judea also benefited from membership in the Persian Empire. Most obvious among these economic benefits was the right to strike its own coinage. This helped standardize commercial transactions, and also contributed to a return of national pride. In the fourth century, coins bearing "Yehud" were circulated within the country and the empire. A sign that these coins were a product of the Persian period, however, was the inclusion of the Athenian owl on one side.

The road system, so important to communication (Esth 3:13; 8:10) and commerce, was maintained and expanded by the government, and caravans were protected by groups of soldiers and horsemen (Ezra 8:22; on the Persian road system, see p. 148). Sea and land merchants throughout the empire, coming to the markets of Judea on a regular basis, transported luxury goods and manufactured items. The traders from Tyre on the Phoenician coast brought all sorts of wares to Jerusalem (Neh 13:16), including dried fish, perfumes and ointments from Arabia, fine pottery and jewelry from Greece and the Persian provinces on Cyprus and in Anatolia, and metal utensils and weapons from Mesopotamia or Egypt.

Craftsmen of various types (Neh 3:31) served the needs of the local population and produced goods which could be exported. A business

Alabaster containers used for storing cosmetics.

district outside the walls of Jerusalem was apparently established where the stalls of these craftsmen and traders were constructed (Neh 13:20). Just as Ahab placed Israelite merchants in the bazaars of Damascus in the ninth century (1 Kgs 20:34), this area near Jerusalem most likely included both Jewish and foreign merchants from throughout the empire. Having access to such a variety of goods would have raised the standard of living in the city, and added to the temptations to adopt foreign customs. This concern was probably on Nehemiah's mind when he ordered the closing of the gates of Jerusalem on the Sabbath to prevent commercial activity on that day sacred to the Jews (Neh 13:19).

Tyrians also, who lived in the city, brought in fish and all kinds of merchandise and sold them on the sabbath to the people of Judah, and in Jerusalem.
—*Neh 13:16*

Burial Customs

Looking at the sixth century, it is difficult to discern any changes in burial customs other than in the grave goods left with the body. Rock-cut or cist tombs, with benches along the walls and a straight entrance, continue to be used. The chief means of identifying a transition into the Persian period is the increased number of metal burial offerings. These include bowls, mirrors, strainers, and bracelets. Imported Egyptian cosmetic jars made of alabaster, and black kohl eye makeup sticks made of crushed galena mixed with gum and water, are also found in these tombs (on eye paint, see p. 114).

In the fifth and fourth centuries there are two main types of tombs in Judea and the surrounding lands: the shaft tomb and the pit grave. The shaft tomb, with either a vertical shaft or sloping steps down to the burial chamber, is found primarily along the coastal plain. These tombs were constructed by wealthy Phoenicians for themselves or for the Persian officials of the area. Tombs of this type have been excavated at Gezer, Lachish, Dor, Gesher ha-Ziv, as well as several other sites.

Pit graves, in which the body is buried in a shallow depression, were common among the less well-to-do. Among the sites so far excavated that contain this grave type are Hazor and Tell el-Hesi. Grave goods in these tombs include Greek pottery, alabaster jars, Phoenician coins, and gold jewelry.

RELIGIOUS PRACTICES

In what had been the northern kingdom of Israel, ties to the Yahwist faith were mixed with the ideas of the new settlers who were brought in by the Assyrians after 720 B.C. These peoples included representatives from the Transjordanian kingdoms as well as Mesopotamia. Eventually, their religious practices began to center on the early history of Israel and its link to Shechem and Mount Gerizim. Their major shrine was built there (*Ant.* 11.321–324) in the time of Alexander the Great (ca. 330 B.C.).

For the exiles and for the people who remained behind after the destruction of Jerusalem, one direct sign of change came in the message of the prophets. They now began to place a greater emphasis on apocalyptic themes featuring the restoration of the nation and the "reign of Yahweh." Ezekiel's visions of the valley of dry bones (37:1–14) and the restored temple (chapters 40–48) are good examples of this theme. In addition, there emerged in exilic communities a greater reliance on the law and the priests who interpreted it. This development came at the expense of the monarchy, an institution that earlier historical events had rendered defunct.

Initially the exiles found it difficult to worship away from the Jerusalem temple (Ps 137). Some would have fallen into the worship of the Mesopotamian gods, or a mixed religion including both Yahweh and the gods of their captors. Others, who wished to remain strict

> *But seek the welfare of the city where I have sent you into exile, and pray to the LORD on its behalf, for in its welfare you will find your welfare.*
> —Jer 29:7

Yahwists, were reassured by Jeremiah's claim that they could worship God in Babylon (29:4–7). When they realized that the return would not occur as soon as they had hoped, they placed greater emphasis on prayer (Dan 6:10; 9:3–19), fasting (Dan 10:2–3; Esth 4:16), and certain aspects of the law which set them apart from their captors (Esth 3:8). These included laws prescribing ritual purity (including dietary habits), Sabbath observance, and circumcision. The prohibition against marriage outside the group was also enforced by leaders of the postexilic community (Ezra 9; 10:10–15), and may have originated among the stricter customs of the Mesopotamia exiles.

It may be that the **synagogue,** or some similar place of non-sacrificial worship, also developed during the Babylonian exile as a response to the loss of the temple in Jerusalem. Although no physical evidence has been found for a synagogue prior to the first century A.D., at some point it would have been necessary for the synagogue to develop as a center of the community's religious life. Synagogues are prominently mentioned in the New Testament period (Matt 4:23; Mark 1:21; Luke 4:16). It is therefore generally agreed that they existed in Mesopotamia, Egypt, and Judea at least two centuries prior to the common era, if not before.

Another factor which suggests the possibility of some sort of worship place being established in the exilic communities is the large numbers of priests and Levites (including Ezekiel) who were taken into the exile. They undoubtedly continued to provide for the religious needs of the people, even though they no longer had a temple to serve as the focal point for their worship activity. A non-sacrificial cult, which emphasized prayer and the study of the law, would have presented little political threat, thus accommodating the Babylonian and Persian governments. That priests and Levites still existed as something more than ceremonial titles when the exile ended suggests they continued to take an active role in worship.

In Egypt, the refugees from Judah established communities that maintained some contact with Jerusalem. Jeremiah spoke to them, condemning their improper rituals, such as burning incense to foreign gods (Jer 44:2–10). During the fifth century, the Jewish colony at Elephantine built a temple to serve the cultic needs of its community. This was a clear violation of the Deuteronomic reform that required all cultic activity to take place in Jerusalem (Deut 12 and 2 Kgs 23:1–25). In this instance, however, the religious needs of the people in the Diaspora may have outweighed this prohibition (see Isa 19:19–22 for the prophecy of an altar in Egypt). In any case, according to the Elephantine papyri, this temple was destroyed by the Egyptians and was never rebuilt, despite pleas for assistance sent by the Elephantine Jews to the leaders in Jerusalem.

The influence of the polytheistic society in which they were living also may have softened the restrictions against the worship of other gods. The letters from Elephantine mention worship of Yahu (= Yahweh) by these Jewish mercenaries. However, they also describe sacrifices being made and oaths being taken in the name of the Canaanite goddess Anat, as well as several other gods.

Postexilic Religious Practices

Following the return from exile, several forces molded postexilic Judaism. Some voices, perhaps encouraged by the Persian aid, advocated a return of all of the people of Israel to Jerusalem, where a rejuvenated Judaism

> *Why do you provoke me to anger with the works of your hands, making offerings to other gods in the land of Egypt where you have come to settle? Will you be cut off and become an object of cursing and ridicule among all the nations of the earth?*
> —Jer 44:8

would provide a framework of worship for all nations (Isa 49:5–6). Universalism, however, was not the theological path chosen by most of the leaders of the returned exiles or those who remained in Mesopotamia. They had worked to protect the cultural identity of the people while they were in exile by emphasizing the covenant made at Mount Sinai. Obedience to the law and maintenance of proper worship practices thus came to represent the unique character of the people of Yahweh. The Torah and these ceremonial practices provided them with a sense of continuity with their past, and kept hope alive that it could be revived.

The Role of the Priesthood

Priests and Levites were considered protectors of the law and officiants at all religious ceremonies (Deut 17:8–13; 18:1–5). As a result, it is not surprising that when the first groups of exiles returned, four families of priests, numbering 4,289, joined the caravan (Neh 7:39–42). What is unusual is that only seventy-four Levites were in the company (Neh 7:43), fewer even than the number of temple servants and singers who made the journey (392; Neh 7:44–60). One explanation for this is that more

> *[The LORD] says, "It is too light a thing that you should be my servant to raise up the tribes of Jacob and to restore the survivors of Israel; I will give you as a light to the nations, that my salvation may reach to the end of the earth."*
> —Isa 49:6

During the exile, most Jewish leaders tried to protect the people's cultural identity by stressing the covenant made at Mount Sinai.

priests were taken into exile than Levites, and these numbers simply represented the ratio of their descendants.

Another argument, however, is based on competition between priestly groups that dates back to David's bringing the ark to Jerusalem and his division of cultic responsibilities between Abiathar, a Levitical priest, and Zadok. Zadok's lineage is traced back both to the priestly line of Eli (2 Sam 8:17) and to the priestly line of Aaron (1 Chr 5:29–34). It is also possible that he is a Jebusite priest, ministering

to those who controlled Jerusalem before David made it his capital (2 Sam 20:25; see 2 Sam 5:6–10). By assigning Abiathar cultic duties, David helped to relieve the strain put on Levitical priests caused by the decline of the central sanctuary at Shiloh (1 Sam 4; see Jer 7:12). When Shiloh deteriorated after the battle in which the Philistines captured the ark of the covenant, the Levitical priests spread themselves across Israel, serving at local shrines. There, the priests survived solely on what worshippers provided for them (Deut 14:29).

> *But their duty shall be to assist the descendants of Aaron for the service of the house of the LORD, having the care of the courts and the chambers, the cleansing of all that is holy, and any work for the service of the house of God; . . .*
> —1 Chr 23:28

The support David gave to the Levites was short-lived, however. While Abiathar and Zadok shared the role of chief priest throughout David's reign, in the transition between David and Solomon, Zadok and his descendants won the chief place in the priestly community. Abiathar, who had supported a rival to Solomon as David's successor (1 Kgs 1:7), was exiled to Anathoth, two miles north of Jerusalem (1 Kgs 2:26, 35).

As a result of this exile, the Levites once again found themselves performing cultic duties at local shrines, rather than at a centralized sanctuary. When they did serve at the Jerusalem sanctuary (and later the temple), they acted as "temple servants," having no claim to the chief priesthood or to the sacrificial functions of the Zadokite priests in Jerusalem. Josiah's reform brought the Levites back to Jerusalem and increased their status, but not to the extent that they were considered to be among the chief priests (2 Kgs 23:9; Ezek 44:10–16). The only change in this posture came after the fall of Jerusalem, when most of the priests were killed (2 Kgs 25:18–21) or taken into exile (2 Kgs 24:14). With no one else to officiate at sacrifices, it is possible that any Levites who remained in the land were pressed into service to maintain cultic practices in Judah (see Ezra 4:2).

When it became possible for the exiled Levites to return to Jerusalem, they may have decided that exile was better than a return to an inferior status in Judea. The Zadokite priests could be expected to resume their position as the chief religious officials.

Descendants of Levites, who had led the people in worship during the exile, may have had other ideas on this subject. However, when the priests arrived in Judea, some compromise must have been made with these Levites, since the text makes no mention of a conflict between them. Feelings between the two groups may have softened during the exile when they had to work together to preserve the law. One sign of this may be the importance Ezra placed on including Levites within his company of returning exiles (Ezra 8:15–20).

A higher regard for the Levites is also found in the accounts of the books of 1 and 2 Chronicles, Ezra, and Nehemiah. This history covers the same time period narrated in the books of Samuel and Kings. But the 1 chronicles—Nehemiah account interprets Israel and Judah's histories as a series of divine punishments and blessing to an even greater extent than does Samuel and Kings. In the former's retelling of God's dealings with Israel and Judah, we see a high regard for David, Solomon, the Jerusalem temple, and the cult that operated there. The Chronicler's respect for the Levites is a reflection of the enhanced role played by the priestly community during the postexilic period.

Other places in the Bible reflect this appreciation for the Jerusalem cult, most notably those concerned with the priestly concerns of proper worship and purity, found throughout the Pentateuch, especially in the books of Leviticus and Numbers. The **Holiness Code** (Lev 17–26), a reworking of the Priestly legislation offers practical descriptions of how to maintain purity.

All of those texts emphasize the importance of the priests who serve as the judicial and religious leaders of the community. Thus, during the postexilic era, Levites took on a much more important role in the worship ceremony. While still subordinate to the "sons of Aaron" (an interchangeable term for Zadokite priests), the Levites took charge of temple administration

> *I also found out that the portions of the Levites had not been given to them; so that the Levites and the singers, who had conducted the service, had gone back to their fields.*
> —Neh 13:10

(2 Chr 24:6, 11). They also had worship-associated duties: cleansing of holy objects and chambers, the preparation of the showbread and cereal offerings, and service as a choir of thanksgiving during burnt offerings (1 Chr 23:25–32).

The enhanced role, portrayed in Chronicles for the priests and Levites, does not fully explain the initial difficulties the clergy had in establishing themselves in Judea. Like the other returnees, they craved acceptance from the authorities already in the land. For instance, Eliashib, the high priest, gave Tobiah the Ammonite a specially furnished chamber within the temple precincts (Neh 13:4–5). This bestowal might have had something to do with the meaning of Tobiah's name: "Yahu (or Yahweh) is my good." While Tobiah is described as an Ammonite, it could be that he had risen to prominence in Jerusalem, and had some devotion to Israel's God. In this case, Eliashib's motives may have included a desire to gain political and financial support from this important official for the Jerusalem priesthood. Whatever the case, Nehemiah, representing the strict Yahwism of the exile, refused to allow a foreigner, even one with a Yahwistic name, access to the temple, and expelled Tobiah the Ammonite (Neh 13:7–9).

Apparently, a great deal of the exiles' energies were taken up with reopening the land to farming and rebuilding the temple and the city fortifications. The payment of tithes to support the work of the priesthood became secondary to these tasks, and was simply not made in some years. Nehemiah found many Levites and singers who had left temple service in order to survive (Neh 13:10). He ordered that the regular tithes of grain, wine, and oil be brought to the temple storehouses. The responsibility for distribution of these commodities was then given to a committee of trustworthy priests and Levites (Neh 13:12–13).

Worship in the Second Temple

Two factors direct much of the worship in the exile and Second Temple period. They are the emphasis on proper action, and the enhanced role of the priesthood in directing this proper action by the people. The Holiness Code set the standard for worship, ensuring ritual purity and orderly religious activities. Under this code of law, all worship was to be conducted with the proper solemnity by the priests. These individuals, in turn, were required to adhere to a strict code of ritual purity to maintain their holiness and thus qualify them to conduct the rituals when sacrifices were made (see Lev 21).

Special care was taken to guarantee that sacred acts were performed at the proper time, using the prescribed sacrificial rituals. For example, the offering of the "**first fruits**," or a portion of the first gleanings from a harvest, was to be brought to the priest, who would ceremonially raise it to God on the first day after the Sabbath (Lev 23:9–11). Animal, grain, and drink offerings were then made (v. 13). Most importantly, eating from the first fruits was forbidden before this set of sacrifices was complete (v. 14). In this and other offerings, strict attention was given to every detail to assure that the ritual in no way resembled that of the idolatrous religions of Canaan or Mesopotamia (Lev 18:1–5).

> *Speak to the people of Israel and say to them: These are the appointed festivals of the LORD that you shall proclaim as holy convocations, my appointed festivals.*
> —Lev 23:2

Sacrifice also served as a link with the past for the returned exiles. By reinstituting the major forms of sacrifice, which had not been performed during the exile, the covenant was renewed and the temple worship of the monarchy period was restored. Those major festivals tied to the religious calendar (Ezra 3:1–6) allowed the priests to reinforce their authority while at the same time strengthen the practice of the Yahweh cult. Individual sacrifices and guilt offerings involved the use of priests, and further established a tie between the community and the priesthood (Lev 27).

Within the laws of the sacrificial cult, proper observance of the Sabbath was of particular importance because it was one of those Jewish religious activities that was unparalleled by any other people of the ancient Near East. It set them apart, just as it set the day apart in recognition of Yahweh's role as the creator. The Sabbath functioned both as a weekly reminder of the covenant with God and as the basis for calculation of all religious festivals (Lev 23).

The major religious festivals were celebrated on the first day of each lunar month. The most important of these were Passover and the Feast of Unleavened Bread in the first month (Lev 23:5–8), the Feast of Trumpets in the seventh month (23:23–25), the Feast of Weeks at the beginning of the wheat harvest (23:15–21), and the Feast of Booths at the end of the harvest (23:34–36, 39–43). They comprised general convocations of the people to mark yearly harvests and to remember major events in the history of the people. The feasts also promoted an ingathering to Jerusalem of the Jews from throughout the region.

During the exilic and postexilic periods, several new feasts were instituted, and others made more elaborate. For instance, Purim was a festival created to celebrate Esther's deliverance of the Jews from destruction in the Persian period (Esth 9:18–32). Another feast included in the religious calendar of this period was the Day of Atonement (Lev 23:26–32). It is not mentioned in any preexilic text or in Nehemiah, but, like other feasts contained in the Priestly legislation of Leviticus, it may have its origin in the settlement period.

There are Near Eastern parallels to the events prescribed for the Day of Atonement. For instance, purification rituals during the Babylonian New Year's festival include the decapitation of a ram, and the wiping of the carcass on the temple precincts. Whatever its origins, the Day of Atonement eventually became one of the most solemn rituals in the Jewish calendar. As described in Lev 16, this yearly ceremony, which included an ancient ritual involving a "scapegoat," was observed on the tenth day of the seventh month. It was designed to atone for the sins of the people in the previous year. Blood from the sacrifice of a bull and a goat were rubbed and sprinkled on the altar and within the Holy of Holies by the high priest. This double expiation restored the ritual purity of the sanctuary and of the nation.

Within the strict system of laws developed in the period after the exile, attention was also given to protecting the individual and the community from all forms of contamination (see Lev 10:10; Hag 2:11–13). Thus, just as the animal or cereal offering had to meet the requirements for sacrifice, business and social associations also had to be scrupulously correct. Every attempt was made to avoid the taint of the unclean and the foreign. In this regard, the genealogical system became extremely important as a means of determining membership in the priesthood (Ezra 2:1–63; Neh 12:1–26), as well as proper or correct lineage for the rest of the people.

According to these statutes, lepers (all those with discolorations or "eruptions of the skin"), their dwellings, and clothing were to be examined by the priests. They were expelled from the community if no signs of healing were noted within seven days (Lev 13–14). Similarly, menstruating women, and men defiled by

The sacred calendar and major feasts of Judaism and Christianity

Jewish Month names	Canaanite Month names	Babylonian Month names	Julian Month names	Jewish Feasts	Christian Counterpart
Nisan	Abib	Nisanu	March–April	Passover (14th)	Easter
				Unleavened Bread (15th, 7 days)	
Iyyar	Ziv	Ayaru	April–May		
Sivan		Simanu	May–June	Feast of Weeks	Pentecost
Tammuz		Du-uzu	June–July		
Ab		Abu	July–August		
Elul		Elulu	August–September		
Tishri	Ethanim	Tehsritu	September–October	Rosh Hashanah (1st)	
				Yom Kippur (10th)	
				Feast of Booths (15th, 7 days)	
Marcheshvan	Bul	Arah-Samma	October–November		
Chislev		Kislimu	November–December	Hanukkah (25th, 8 days)	Christmas
Tebeth		Tebitu	December–January		
Shebat		Shabatu	January–February		
Adar		Adaru	February–March	Feast of Purim (14th, 15th)	

sexual or other body emissions, were to be avoided until they had been cleansed through ritual purification and bathing (Lev 15).

The degree of ritual purity required of individual members of the community was based on their family background and occupation. The high priest was thus required to guard himself against contamination even more strictly than lay members of the community (Lev 21:10–15). As the only member of the nation who could enter the Holy of Holies (Lev 16:2), it was imperative that he stand apart as a symbol of ritual purity. To a lesser degree, the other priests also practiced rites that kept them ritually pure. For instance, bathing of the

When a person has on the skin of his body a swelling or an eruption or a spot, and it turns into a leprous disease on the skin of his body, he shall be brought to Aaron the priest or to one of his sons the priests.
—Lev 13:2

body and clothing were required of priests after performing sacrifices (Num 19:7–8).

To determine those who could freely participate in the ritual activities of the temple, the entire nation was divided according to the pattern set in the genealogical list in Neh 7:6–60. The male population of Judah was therefore made up of the following classifications: priests, Levites, laypersons, converted Jews, men of uncertain descent, eunuchs, and non-Jews. To participate fully in the religious activities of the community, a person had to be able to provide proof of pure lineage. Ezra 2:59–63 describes measures taken to deal with those who could not prove their descent.

The increased influence of the priesthood in the life of the returned exiles is reflected in the amount of religious activity it generated. In addition to the reestablishment of the sacrificial practices, the use of the Psalms became even more formalized in Jewish worship. Part of creating the canon of sacred texts included organizing the Psalter into a songbook of the

> *David and the officers of the army also set apart for the service the sons of Asaph, and of Heman, and of Jeduthun, who should prophesy with lyres, harps, and cymbals. The list of those who did the work and of their duties was: . . .*
> —*1 Chr 25:1*

second temple. Thus the biblical writer's description of the musical guilds established in David's time (1 Chr 25) probably reflects the situation in the period after the exile.

There was also an integration of new cultic practices and religious festivals into the service of worship. Continuity with past practices was a goal, but some changes were inevitable. Many of the new procedures are reflected in the Holiness Code (Lev 17–26), a sixth-century B.C. revision of older Priestly material, that served as an outline for religious practice after the temple was rebuilt in 515 B.C. In general, it can be said that the increased sophistication of temple activities was due to the enhanced role of the priestly class. The role of the priests continued to grow in importance during the Hellenistic and Roman periods. However, they had to cope with the political ambitions of their rulers, as well as competing philosophies and mystery religions introduced by the Greeks.

Exile and Return Review

1. Where did the exiles live, and how did they adapt during the exile from Israel?
2. What were the political conditions under which the exiles returned to the province of Judah?
3. How did the rebuilding of Jerusalem and the temple progress?
4. Describe the economic constraints of postexilic life.
5. How did religious practices change in the postexilic period?
6. Describe worship in the second temple.

5. Intertestamental and New Testament Period

HISTORICAL INTRODUCTION

This final chapter on the manners and customs of Bible times will focus on the transformations in Palestine during the Hellenistic (331–67 B.C.) and Roman (67 B.C.– A.D. 135) periods. Attention will also be given to the origins of the Christian movement within its social context. The primary factors responsible for these events are the introduction of Hellenistic culture after the conquest of the Near East by Alexander the Great of Macedon, who ruled from 336 to 323 B.C., and the emergence of the Roman world empire in the period from about 150 B.C. to A.D. 150 Jewish resistance to these forces briefly allowed for an independent Jewish state to emerge. However, the **Hasmonean (Maccabean)** kingdom soon succumbed to the ambitions of its rulers, and was easily absorbed into the Roman domain.

The Levant had long been the victim of the ambitions of the Near Eastern superpowers. Nevertheless, the Jews were able to maintain a basic continuity of belief and worship despite the syncretistic influences of the Assyrian, Babylonian, and Persian cultures. This can be seen in Daniel 1–7. Although this was written

The Roman city of Jerash.

The Persian empire

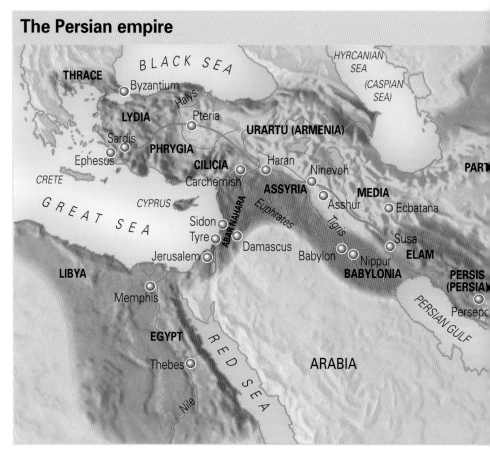

in the time of the Maccabean revolt (167–164 B.C.), the model of courage exemplified by its four young heroes speaks of resistance to oppression in earlier periods as well.

Where earlier civilizations failed, Hellenistic philosophies and Greek urban-based administrative policies succeeded in sparking a new set of priorities in Judaism. The sense of world culture implicit in Hellenism contributed to the creation of a new, Hellenized Judaism in Palestine and throughout the Diaspora. Thus, when the Romans came, the Jews were more ready to deal with the cosmopolitan attitudes of a world empire. They became a part of its commercial and social life and contributed to its blend of many cultures.

The success of the Christian movement can also be attributed to the general social atmos-phere first created by the Greeks and then per-petuated by the Romans. Popular philosophies such as Stoicism and Epicureanism were very attractive in the period from the first century B.C. to the third century A.D. Mystery religions like **Mithraism** were readily adopted by the Roman legionnaires and were spread by soldiers, merchants, and traveling philosophers. In an empire where the only requirement was loyalty to Rome, new ideas could take root with little hindrance. They were particularly attractive to the disenchanted, the disadvantaged, and the seeker of fresh knowledge. Safe and well-constructed travel routes were a final ingredient in the phenomenal growth of Christianity, as well as many other new religions during this time.

BACTRIA

GANDHARA

— Royal Road
▦ Persian homeland
▦ Annexed land of the Medes, 550 B.C.
▦ Annexed land of the Babylonians, 539 B.C.
▦ Maximum extent of the Persian Empire

BACKGROUND TO HELLENISM:
The Persian Period

While they were under the rule of the Persians, the Jews of the Diaspora, as well as those who had returned to Judah, enjoyed nearly two hundred years of relative peace. This allowed returned exiles to rebuild their destroyed cities and reestablish economic stability within their province of Yehud (Judah). Agricultural lands were returned to cultivation and industrial activity resumed after being dormant throughout the Babylonian exile.

A greater emphasis on urbanization also began in the Persian period. With its walls rebuilt and the temple once again functioning as a center of religious activity, Jerusalem provided a focal point for life and a model of urbanism for the other cities and towns of Judah. Persian authority throughout the empire assured a continuous stream of foreign businessmen into Judah, and the creation of a more cosmopolitan culture there. Greater acceptance of the outside world made the eventual transition to Greek domination easier for many Jews.

The second major factor which influenced the development of Jewish culture during the Persian period was the elimination of the civil office of the king. One direct result of this policy was the enhancement of the high priest's position in Jerusalem. He became the titular religious and civic head of the Jewish community, bowing only to the authority of the Persian king and his governor. The high priest's position, like that of the local governor, was confirmed by the Persian government (Hag 1:1), and was solidified by his control of the sacrificial cult in Jerusalem.

According to tradition, the office was held by a member of the Zadokite priestly family, referred to in the postexilic texts as the "sons" or "descendants of Aaron" (Lev 1:7; 2:3; 3:2; Neh 10:38; 12:47). This family tie to preexilic temple worship provided legitimacy and continuity to the position of high priest (Hag 1:12; Zech 3:1-9; 6:11). However, because of the civil influence wielded by this office, it became increasingly secularized. As a result, to serve as high priest, or to be able to choose who would hold that post, became a political prize throughout the Hasmonean rule (165-63 B.C.).

A third important characteristic of the Persian period was the continued canonization of Hebrew Scripture, that probably began in

This Ezra went up from Babylonia. He was a scribe skilled in the law of Moses that the LORD the God of Israel had given; and the king granted him all that he asked, for the hand of the LORD his God was upon him.
–Ezra 7:6

> But Zerubbabel, Jeshua, and the rest of
> the heads of families in Israel said to them,
> "You shall have no part with us in building
> a house to our God; but we alone will build
> to the LORD, the God of Israel, as King Cyrus
> of Persia has commanded us."
> —Ezra 4:3

the monarchic period. Related to the growth in importance of the priestly community during the Persian period, canonization became one of their tasks as they developed a religious and ethnic identity for the people in exile. Its intent was to compile and edit both the oral, as well as the written, traditions of the people of Israel. After the traumatic experience of exile, the priests wanted to be certain that sacrifice and other cultic acts were performed regularly and correctly (Lev 1–7). They hoped to ensure

God's continued goodwill by a strict conformity to the law. Thus the law was written down and canonized into an authoritative document, the Torah, which could be consulted to prevent future mistakes or misunderstandings of what was expected. The result, the Holiness Code (Lev 17–26), served as an updated version of the law for the exiles.

Over the next few centuries, the entire body of traditional writings was edited again into what eventually became the Hebrew Canon. The writings chosen for inclusion in the canon were unlike other works of the time (e.g., the "Book of Jashar"; see p. 12), as they were judged to be divinely inspired. Compilation and editing of the canon also sparked increased study of the text and the development of a group known as scribes, or **rabbis** (teachers). They became authorities on the law and its inter-

Excavations at the Samaritan temple site on Mount Gerizim near Shechem. The temple complex covered one hundred acres, including living quarters for about 1,500 people.

Persepolis

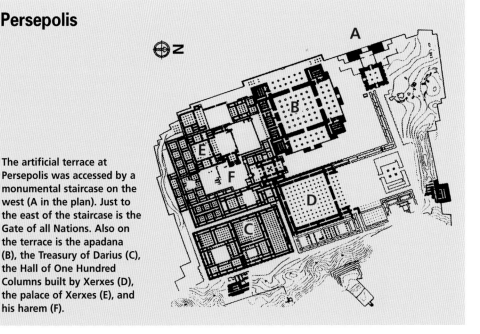

The artificial terrace at Persepolis was accessed by a monumental staircase on the west (A in the plan). Just to the east of the staircase is the Gate of all Nations. Also on the terrace is the apadana (B), the Treasury of Darius (C), the Hall of One Hundred Columns built by Xerxes (D), the palace of Xerxes (E), and his harem (F).

pretation, and were consulted on these matters by the religious community.

A final development that can be ascribed to the Persian period is the separation between the Jews of Judah and the Samaritans. This break has its roots both in the political conflicts between these two Persian provinces, and in their individual religious differences. The returning exiles excluded Samaritans from rebuilding the Jerusalem temple (Ezra 4:1–3). Later, Nehemiah also stood up to Samaritan pressure against the rebuilding of the city's walls, and denied that they had any "claim or historic right in Jerusalem" (Neh 2:20). With the Jews denying them participation in the cult of Jerusalem, and calling them unfit because they had not experienced the exile, and because some were of mixed cultural heritage (on the cultural heritage of the Samaritans, see pp. 134–135), it is no wonder that the Samaritans rejected Jerusalem as the true site of God's presence. Instead, they declared Mount Gerizim near Shechem to be their place of worship (see Gen 12:6–7 and Josh 24 for events justifying their position). The

Samaritans took advantage of Alexander's political goodwill to construct an alternative temple on Mount Gerizim around 330 B.C. (*Ant.* 11.321–324).

THE RISE OF HELLENISM:
Alexander and the Diadochoi

Following a series of campaigns in Greece and Anatolia from 336 to 335 B.C., Alexander of Macedon turned his full attention to the Persian Empire. First, the Greek city states of Asia Minor were freed from Persian control. Then, in order to cripple the Persian navy, Alexander systematically captured Persian strongholds along the Mediterranean coast. In 332 B.C., he entered Egypt unopposed and was crowned pharaoh. Continually pressing the Persian armies, Alexander eventually burned the Persian capital of Persepolis and, in the years from 330 to 323 B.C., completely broke their control over the Near East. His armies campaigned as far east as the Indus delta in western India. The breadth of his conquests set the stage for an entirely new period in that

Alexander the Great

area's history. Alexander believed in the creation of a "world culture" based on Greek philosophy, law, and political administration. He began this dissemination of Greek culture by founding Greek cities throughout the former Persian Empire. Hellenistic, Greek-like culture was eventually formed from the blend of Greek ideas with the customs and traditions of the areas into which it was introduced.

One sign of Alexander's determination to create such a synthesis of cultures can be seen in his inclusion of Greek scholars and scientists in his army. These scholars introduced the use of Greek as the principal language in conquered regions. The scholars also studied local languages and customs, popularizing some of them among the Greeks, and thereby speeding the process of cultural blending. Another, and farther-reaching, contribution to the spread of Greek culture was the establishment of many new cities, such as the Egyptian port city of Alexandria. The Greeks had founded their society upon the **polis,** the political community of the city-state. Because Greek immigrants within the Near East were familiar with the polis, it became the primary vehicle for the transmission of their cultures to the rest of the

ancient world.

The speed with which Alexander conquered the Near East reflected his own genius as a military commander as well as the general discontent with Persian rule. This was especially true in Egypt and the Mediterranean coastal regions north and east of Egypt. Pacification of these conquered areas was made even easier by retention of the old administrative structure. To maintain political stability, Alexander and his successors retained those officials who proved loyal to the new regime. The local economy was then stimulated by the introduction of Greek marketing techniques and fresh operating capital.

Following Alexander's death in 323, his generals divided up his empire among themselves. These *Diadochoi* (the Greek word means "successors") completed the process of pacifying conquered regions and introducing Hellenistic culture. Within the western reaches of the former Persian Empire, two of these generals eventually held sway. Ptolemy ruled Egypt, Syria and Palestine, while Seleucus gained control over the provinces of Asia and Asia Minor. Their successors introduced typical forms of Greek culture: the gymnasium, the theater, and the social associations for professional, cultural, and religious groups. At the same time, these foreign rulers and their Greek subjects acclimated themselves to the patterns and traditions of their new homes, forming a Hellenized culture that would dominate the area until the coming of Islam.

During the early years of Greek rule, Palestine saw no drastic cultural changes. The Ptolemies introduced new coinage and exploited the economic resources of that region, but they did not impose Hellenistic ideas on the Jews. Temple worship continued unhindered, and the office of high priest still exercised great authority in matters of religion. Hellenization was most popular among the generation following the conquest and among those who had contact with Jews in the

The conquests of Alexander the Great

MACEDONIA THRACE BLACK SEA
Aegae Pella
Sestus Zelea
Eleus Dascylium Ancyra CAPPADOCIA
AEGEAN SEA Gordium
MYSIA
Sardis PHRYGIA
Athens LYDIA
Ephesus Sagalassus Cilician Gates Issus
CARIA Perge TAURUS MOUNTAINS
Miletus Tarsus Myriandrus
Sparta Halicarnassus LYCIA Side CILICIA
Phaselis Syrian Gates SYRIA
RHODES
CRETE CYPRUS Aradus
Byblos
MEDITERRANEAN SEA Sidon PHOENICIA
Tyre
Damascus

→ Alexander's route
✕ Battle site

| 0 | 200 | 400 km |
| 0 | 80 160 | 240 miles |

Samaria
Jerusalem
JUDEA
EGYPT

Diaspora, such as the large communities in Antioch and Damascus. There were also obvious advantages for merchants and administrators who adopted Greek language and manners.

Competition between the **Ptolemies** and **Seleucids** for control of the Levant heated up during the mid-third century B.C. Continual intrigue occurred as both sides tried to create or maintain support for their rule. When the high priest Onias II took a pro-Seleucid position, refusing to pay tribute to the Ptolemaic government around 245 B.C., the battle began. Even members of the high priest's family chose sides; his nephew Joseph, the son of Tobias, remained loyal to the Ptolemies and

served as chief tax collector of Syria-Palestine. Josephus (*Ant.* 12.160–195) records that Joseph's economic success caused the Tobiads to become chief advocates of Hellenization as a result.

The Tobiads' political loyalties, however, shifted after 200 B.C., when the Seleucid king Antiochus III won the battle of Panias in northern Galilee and gained control over Palestine and Jerusalem. This battle changed the political balance, leaving the Ptolemies bottled up in Egypt, and requiring a quick transfer of allegiance by the new high priest Simon II to Antiochus' camp. Simon was the leader of the group that advocated strict adherence to Jewish tradition and as little

167

The Ptolemaic and Seleucid empires

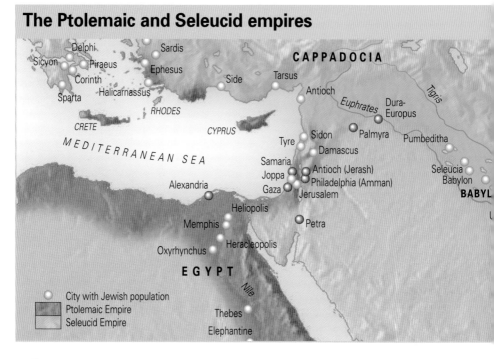

Delphi
Sicyon
Piraeus
Corinth
Sparta
Halicarnassus
RHODES
CRETE
Sardis
Ephesus
Side
Tarsus

CAPPADOCIA

Antioch
Euphrates
Dura-Europus
Tigris

MEDITERRANEAN SEA

CYPRUS

Tyre
Sidon
Palmyra
Pumbeditha
Damascus

Samaria
Joppa
Gaza
Jerusalem
Antioch (Jerash)
Philadelphia (Amman)

Seleucia
Babylon
BABYL

Alexandria

Heliopolis
Petra

Memphis
Heracleopolis
Oxyrhynchus

EGYPT

Nile

○ City with Jewish population
▢ Ptolemaic Empire
▢ Seleucid Empire

Thebes
Elephantine

Hellenization as possible. To obtain its support, Antiochus made a series of concessions to the leaders in Jerusalem. His decree forbade Gentiles from entering the precincts of the Jewish temple. He also made grants of financial assistance to the Jerusalem temple, and authorized an exemption from taxes for members of the priesthood and the council of elders, the **Sanhedrin** (*Ant.* 12.138–146).

These concessions and promises of religious freedom quickly evaporated as Antiochus became embroiled in the international disputes of the Romans, coming to the aid of the embattled Greeks of Asia Minor. Roman territorial ambitions and military prowess were too much for both the Greeks and Antiochus. He was forced to sign a treaty in 188 B.C. ceding his territories in Asia Minor and sending twenty hostages to Rome. Among these hostages was his son, Antiochus IV. The loss of revenues from these areas forced Antiochus III to increase taxes and caused him to seek additional revenues by plundering the temple of Bel in the Persian city of Susa, but he was killed during

this campaign. Thus in 187 B.C., Antiochus III's eldest son, Seleucus IV, succeeded his father. Eventually, Seleucus IV sent his own son, Demetrius, to Rome in exchange for the release of his brother Antiochus IV. When Seleucus was murdered by his own prime minister, Heliodorus, Antiochus IV Epiphanes usurped the throne in 175 B.C.

The power struggle among the Seleucids apparently sparked a new wave of political shifts as various factions attempted to gain control of the position of high priest in Jerusalem. The intrigue begins when Onias III, Simon II's successor as high priest, has an argument with Simon, the "captain of the temple" over the administration of the city market (2 Macc 3:4–8). Simon, in turn, goes to Apollonius, governor of Coelesyria and Phoenicia, and tempts him with stories about the wealth in the Jerusalem treasury. Apollonius then sends his deputy Heliodorus to loot the temple, but according to the account in 2 Macc 3:22–28, Heliodorus is thwarted by the appearance of supernatural beings. On the

this state was the capital of the Seleucid kingdom, Antioch. First Maccabees 1:11–15 disapprovingly describes Jason's role in carrying out Antiochus' policy of Hellenization. The text portrays a group of "lawless men" as **Hellenizers** (Jews who supported the importation of Greek culture), who willingly violated the covenant in order to please the Greek king. Opposition to Hellenism became increasingly vocal when Jason built a Greek-style gymnasium in Jerusalem, and Jews began to "remove the marks of circumcision" in order to participate. Jason's policies are further criticized when temple priests started to attend sporting events rather than offering sacrifices (2 Macc 4:10–15).

When Jason sends Menelaus, the brother of Onias III's old enemy Simon, to Antioch in 172 B.C. with that year's tribute money, Menelaus takes the opportunity to put in his own bid for the high priesthood. He succeeds by offering a bribe of three hundred talents of silver, and Jason is "driven as a fugitive into the land of Ammon" (2 Macc 4:23–26).

This new high priest only made matters worse, embezzling funds and stealing sacred vessels from the temple treasury to pay his debts to Antiochus IV (2 Macc 4:27–32). When Onias III denounced him for doing this, Menelaus conspired with Antiochus IV's deputy, Andronicus, to have Onias murdered (2 Macc 4:27–34). On his return from a campaign in Cilicia, Antiochus IV learns of the murder of Onias III, and executes Andronicus himself (2 Macc 4:35–38). Meanwhile, in Jerusalem, Menelaus and his deputy, Lysimachus, have been committing further outrages.

When Antiochus IV invades Egypt in 168 B.C. and rumors circulate that he has been killed, a struggle ensues for control of the office of high priest between Jason and Menelaus. At one point, Jason captures the city of Jerusalem and drives out the Seleucid officials (2 Macc 5:5–7). On his return from

political level, Simon continues to slander Onias III, and the high priest appeals to Seleucus IV for assistance (2 Macc 4:1–6).

After Seleucus' death, Antiochus IV's attention is attracted by the huge bribe Jason, Onias III's brother, offers in order to secure the high priesthood. Jason, who also indicates his willingness to introduce Greek institutions such as a gymnasium in Jerusalem, is able to purchase the office, and Antiochus ousts Onias in 175 B.C. (2 Macc 4:7–10). Onias apparently flees to Transjordan, where he continued to denounce the leaders in Jerusalem.

As high priest, Jason hoped to further his own political position with Antiochus IV by transforming Jerusalem and the rest of Palestine into a Hellenized state. His model for

Not content with this, Antiochus dared to enter the most holy temple in all the world, guided by Menelaus, who had become a traitor both to the laws and to his country.
—2 Macc 5:15

Egypt, Antiochus IV interprets these chaotic conditions as open rebellion, and he sends in troops to pacify the province. This results in a brutal loss of life (2 Macc 5:1–14). Menelaus curries favor with the king by inviting Antiochus to carry off vessels and treasures from the temple, and the king maintains Menelaus' rule as high priest (2 Macc 5:15–16). However, Antiochus IV also appoints governors to keep a close watch on the territory, and he builds the Akra citadel. This is quickly followed by an anti-Jewish campaign designed, according to 2 Macc 6–7 (compare 1 Macc 1:41–42), to make all of the people of the Seleucid realm "one people," and to cause

them to renounce their old traditions and religion. Continued Roman pressure on Antiochus' kingdom may have increased his anger; however, the stipulations of his decree all suggest that his plan was to completely Hellenize the Jews. Their shrines and altars were defiled, and swine were sacrificed in the temple. Other ritual acts, like circumcision, were no longer allowed (1 Macc 1:45–48).

TEMPORARY INDEPENDENCE
The Hasmonean Kingdom

Antiochus's policies culminated in the construction of an altar to the Greek god Zeus

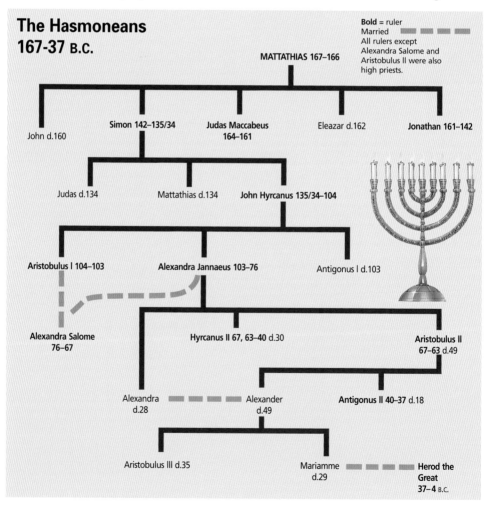

**The Hasmoneans
167-37 B.C.**

Bold = ruler
Married
All rulers except Alexandra Salome and Aristobulus II were also high priests.

MATTATHIAS 167–166

John d.160 — Simon 142–135/34 — Judas Maccabeus 164–161 — Eleazar d.162 — Jonathan 161–142

Judas d.134 — Mattathias d.134 — John Hyrcanus 135/34–104

Aristobulus I 104–103 — Alexandra Jannaeus 103–76 — Antigonus I d.103

Alexandra Salome 76–67 — Hyrcanus II 67, 63–40 d.30 — Aristobulus II 67–63 d.49

Alexandra d.28 — Alexander d.49 — Antigonus II 40–37 d.18

Aristobulus III d.35 — Mariamme d.29 — Herod the Great 37–4 B.C.

Olympios in the Jerusalem temple (Dan 11:31; 1 Macc 1:54; Mark 13:14). This "abomination of desolation," combined with his other anti-Jewish measures, sparked in 167 B.C. a revolt led by the priest Mattathias of the house of Hasmon. Reflecting the more conservative attitudes of the rural areas of Palestine, the revolt began in the village of Modin, northwest of Jerusalem. Mattathias refused to obey the decree to sacrifice to idols, and went so far as to kill the first Jew who attempted to obey this command (1 Macc 2:13–26). His justification for the killing was the precedent set by Aaron's grandson Phinehas, who killed an Israelite for marrying outside the congregation (Num 25:6–8). In both cases, the principle involved obedience to the covenant and the purity of the nation.

Following his act of defiance, Mattathias led his five sons into the hill country where they began to wage a guerrilla war against the Seleucids and their Hellenized supporters. The rebels, joined by the traditionalists called the Hasidim, "holy ones" (2 Macc 2:42), saw this war as both a national struggle and a cultural one. Their adherence to the law, however, led to a massacre when a group of one thousand Jews refused to defend themselves from attack on the Sabbath (1 Macc 2:29–38). This reluctance was eventually overcome, as the idea of holy war made it possible to temporarily set aside legal restraints.

By 164 B.C., Judas, Mattathias's oldest son, had recaptured most of Jerusalem (1 Macc 3:1–9), and justified his title Maccabaeus, "the hammer," by his exploits. This title provided the name for the **Maccabean revolt,** as well as for the rest of Judas's family. The temple was rededicated and restrictions on the practice of Judaism were removed, an event still celebrated today as the feast of Hanukkah (1 Macc 4:41–58; 2 Macc 10:1–8).

Final victory was made possible by disputes within the Seleucid royal house. Since the death of Antiochus IV in 164 B.C., rival

> *Then his son Judas, who was called Maccabeus, took command in his place. All his brothers and all who had joined his father helped him; they gladly fought for Israel.*
>
> —1 Macc 3:1–2

claimants to the Seleucid throne had attempted to outbid each other for the support of provincial leaders. One of these claimants was none other than Demetrius I Soter, who had been traded to the Romans by his own father, Seleucus IV, in order to secure the release of his father's brother, Antiochus IV (on this see p. 168). After Antiochus IV dies, the army commander Lysais seizes Antiochus's young son Antiochus V from his foster uncle Philip and claims power. Meanwhile, Demetrius escapes from Rome for Palestine, where he kills Antiochus V and Lysias and usurps the throne (1 Macc 7:1–4; 2 Macc 14:1–2; *Ant.* 12.189—13.79).

Demetrius is approached by at least one Maccabean rival asking to be made high priest (1 Macc 7:16). Judas Maccabeus is killed in the ensuing violence (1 Macc 9:11–21). Demetrius's own rule (162–150 B.C.) falters when Alexander Balas, claiming to be a son of Antiochus IV, changes his name to Alexander I Epiphanes, and establishes a rival kingship in the Seleucid-controlled city Ptolemais. When Demetrius tries to affirm his power by allying himself with Jonathan Maccabeus, he finds that Alexander has already done so. To underscore the legitimacy of his position as a secular leader, Alexander appoints Jonathan high priest in 152 B.C. (1 Macc 10:20).

After Jonathan's death, the people proclaimed his brother Simon to be "their leader and high priest forever, until a faithful prophet should arise" (1 Macc 14:41; *Ant.* 13.213). This appointment was particularly important since Simon was not of the Zadokite line and thus was not, according to tradition, entitled to hold the office of high priest. Josephus (*Ant.* 16.163)

> *The Jews and their priests have resolved that Simon should be their leader and high priest forever, until a trustworthy prophet should arise.*
>
> *–1 Macc 14:41*

describes John Hyrcanus, the successor of Simon, as the high priest of "God Most High." The implication is that the Maccabees were attempting to justify their position as priest and civil leader through a comparison with the Old Testament figure of Melchizedek, who was described as a king of Salem and priest of "God Most High" (Gen 14:18).

Political developments, and a shift in the people's expectations of a return of prophetic direction, made Simon's appointment possible; the **Hasmoneans,** as they now called themselves, took full advantage of the situation. Indications are, however, that significant numbers dissented against the Maccabean claims to high priesthood. Documents associated with the **Essene** community (the *Manual of Discipline* and the so-called *Damascus Document* from the Cairo Geniza) indicate that during this period, the Essenes' support for the Hasmoneans ceased, and a separatist nature developed in this group instead. The *Testament of Moses* (6:1–4), a document probably dating to the early first century A.D., also contains a statement of discontent with the Hasmonean claims to both civil and religious authority.

Simon and his son, John Hyrcanus, continued to use the unsettled political situation in the Seleucid Empire to their advantage. In 141 B.C., Simon captured the Akra, the Seleucid fortress just south of the Temple Mount, a bastion of Seleucid control and a "thorn in the side" of the Maccabees (*Ant.* 12.252–253; 1 Macc 13:49–51). It was then totally demolished to prevent it from standing higher than the temple, and to guarantee that it could never be used against the people (*Ant.* 13.215–217). To add a further dimension of support, Simon, like his older brother Judas (1 Macc 8:17–32),

turned to Rome, and obtained official recognition of his position from the Roman Senate in 138 B.C. (1 Macc 15:15–21). The Seleucids did attempt to reassert their power at the beginning of Hyrcanus' reign. However, according to Josephus (*Ant.* 7.393), when Antiochus VII besieged Jerusalem, Hyrcanus bribed him to leave with spoil from David's tomb. During his long reign (134–104), Hyrcanus expanded his area of control. Moving north, he conquered Samaria and destroyed the temple on Mount Gerizim (*Ant.* 13.275–281). In the south, he forced the Idumeans, living in the area once known as Edom, to convert to Judaism and to be circumcised (*Ant.* 13.257–258).

Despite these accomplishments, Hyrcanus was not popular with all segments of his people. His Hellenized court and lifestyle were offensive to the stricter elements of Jewish society. One group, known as the **Pharisees,** demanded that he renounce the office of high priest, and in one instance, accused him of uncertain parentage, saying his mother had been a captive of Antiochus IV (*Ant.* 13.288–292). This did not prove to be a particularly damaging accusation, however, since Hyrcanus was able to rely on the support of the wealthier landowners and merchants. This group, known as the **Sadducees,** also controlled membership in the priesthood (*Ant.* 13.293–296). Both of these groups eventually emerged as important elements in the political and religious history of the nation (on Pharisees and Sadducees, see pp. 228–229).

> *Now when their father Hyrcanus was dead, the eldest son Aristobulus, intending to change the government into a kingdom, for so he resolved to do, first of all put a diadem on his head, four hundred and eighty-one years and three months after the people had been delivered from the Babylonish slavery, and were returned to their own country again.*
>
> *—Josephus, Ant. 13.301*

Palestine under the Hasmoneans

Independent Judea after Jonathan's campaigns, 142 B.C.
Land conquered by Simon, 142-135 B.C.
John Hyrcanus I, 128-104 B.C.
Aristobulus I, 104-103 B.C.
Alexander Jannaeus, 103-76 B.C.
Boundary of Hasmonean kingdom, 76 B.C.
○ Hellenistic city

MEDITERRANEAN SEA

PHOENICIA

Tyre

Antiochia

Gischala

Seleucia

Ptolemais

Gabara

Sea of Galilee

Hippos

Dium

Sepphoris

Geba

Mount Tabor △

Philoteria

Abila

Gadara

Dora

GALILEE

GILEAD

Strato's Tower

Scythopolis

Pella

SAMARIA

Jordan

Samaria

Gerasa

Shechem

Apollonia

Mount Gerizim

Joppa

Arimathea

PEREA

Lydda

Philadelphia

JUDEA

Jamnia

Emmaus

Jericho

Samaga

Azotus

Jerusalem

Medeba

Ascalon

Beth-zur

Anthedon

Marisa

Hebron

Dead Sea

Gaza

IDUMEA

En-gedi

Orda

Gerar

MOAB

Raphia

Beer-sheba

Malatha

Rinocorura

NABATEA

Zoar

0   25   50 km
0   10   20   30 miles

Hyrcanus's son, Aristobulus I, was the first to bear the title of king of Judea (*Ant.* 13.301). He continued his father's expansion policies in the north, but died after only one year of rule, in 103 B.C. He was succeeded by his brother Alexander Jannaeus. This particularly ambitious and cruel ruler used the support of the Sadducees and a company of mercenary troops to impose his rule on the people. The Pharisees, however, were ardently opposed to his position as high priest, ridiculing him as he officiated at sacrifices (*Ant.* 13.372), and allying themselves with the Seleucid king Demetrius III in an effort to depose him (*Ant.* 13.376; for Pharisees and Sadducees, see pp. 228–229). Jannaeus managed to gain his revenge after withstanding the Seleucid invasion. He systematically exterminated the leading Pharisee families, crucifying eight hundred of them and killing their wives and children during a banquet for his supporters (*Ant.* 13.380).

The potential problems of continuing this internal struggle against his own people took their toll on Jannaeus. On his deathbed, he advised his wife and successor, Alexandra Salome (76–67 B.C.), to make peace with the Pharisees. Alexandra appointed her older son, Hyrcanus II, as the new high priest, and she herself ruled as queen. However, her more energetic younger son, Aristobulus II, was not satisfied with this arrangement, and precipitated a civil war in 67 B.C. after Alexandra died.

During this period of political chaos, two new elements began to impact Judean politics. The first was Antipater of Idumea. Seizing the opportunity to gain influence in Judean affairs, he advised Hyrcanus II to seek refuge with the Nabatean ruler Aretas III in Petra, while he sought help in his struggle against Aristobulus II. The other new influence, and the decisive element in the dispute between the brothers, was an escalating civil war in Rome, and the arrival in Jerusalem of the Roman general Pompey. The Roman Senate had made an alliance with the leaders of Judah

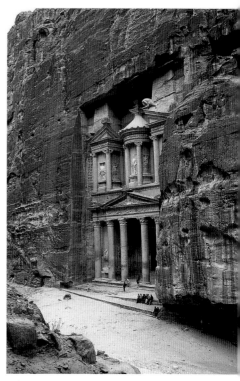

"The Treasury," a rock-cut structure at Petra.

as far back as the time of Judas Maccabaeus (1 Macc 8:17–32). Eventually, their interests in the Near East brought them into conflict with the Armenian king Mithridates. In 66 B.C., Pompey was sent to unseat him and protect the new Roman province of Syria. His success in this mission made Rome the emerging power in the area.

Thus, when Pompey arrived in Damascus, he was met by representatives of many of the small kingdoms of the Near East, including both Hyrcanus II and Aristobulus II of Judea. Pompey sided with Hyrcanus. Aristobulus then fortified the temple mount, and his followers held out against the assaults of the Roman forces for three months. When their position was finally overrun, a general slaughter, luridly described by Josephus, took place. Aristobulus was saved so that he could be taken as a captive to Rome as part of Pompey's triumphal procession (*Ant.* 14.69–79). Jewish

For Pompey went into it, and not a few of those that were with him also, and saw all that which it was unlawful for any other men to see, but only for the high priests. There were in that temple the golden table, the holy candlestick, and the pouring vessels, and a great quantity of spices; and besides these there were among the treasures two thousand talents of sacred money; yet did Pompey touch nothing of all this, on account of his regard to religion; and in this point also he acted in a manner that was worthy of his virtue.
—Josephus, Ant. 14.72

reaction to these events may be found in the Pharisaic document, the *Psalms of Solomon* 2:26–32 (dating to about 40–30 B.C.), which is apparently referring to Pompey when it triumphantly describes the death in Egypt of one who placed himself before God. What may be implied here is Pompey's reported desecration of the temple by entering the Holy of Holies (*Ant.* 14.72).

As a result of Pompey's intervention, Judea was added to the Roman province of Syria, and was administered by Pompey's chief lieutenant Gabinius. The country itself was divided into five districts, each centered on a major population center: Jerusalem, Jericho, Gazara (Gezer), Amathus (east of the Jordan River), and Sepphoris in Galilee (*Ant.* 14.91). The Romans also claimed all the cities in the north and in Transjordan which had been ruled by the Hasmoneans, but which did not have large Jewish populations. Hyrcanus was reappointed as high priest, but with no claims of civil authority (*Ant.* 14.73–76).

For the next twenty years, Judea was plagued by popular uprisings led by Aristobulus, who escaped from Rome in 56 B.C. (*Ant.* 14.92), or by his sons. Hyrcanus and his Idumean adviser, Antipater, managed to survive these threats to their authority, while playing a dangerous game of shifting allegiances with the Roman generals. This was complicated by the bloody civil war that was taking place between these Roman commanders. In 55 or 54 B.C., Hyrcanus' lack of real power was demonstrated when Rome's proconsul for Syria, Marcus Licinius Crassus, plundered the temple treasury (*Ant.* 14.105–109). By campaigning against the Parthians (successors of the Persians), Crassus was hoping to show that his abilities as a general matched those of his fellow triumvirate members, Julius Caesar and Pompey. His theft of sacred items from the temple helped fund this expedition, but all he accomplished was a major defeat, and his own death.

Crassus's death increased the tensions between Caesar and Pompey that eventually led to the climax of the Roman civil war. Antipater, governor of Idumea under Alexander Jannaeus, and Hyrcanus II supported Caesar. After Pompey's murder in Egypt, they helped marshal support for Caesar among the Jews in Egypt. As a reward, Hyrcanus was appointed in 47 B.C. as ethnarch of Judea, becoming, for the first time, a civil as well as a religious leader. In addition, Caesar permitted the rebuilding of the walls of Jerusalem, and promised the Jews free exercise of their religion. Antipater received Roman citizenship and was named procurator of Judea by the Roman Senate.

Antipater's and Hyrcanus's good fortune was once again upset when Caesar was murdered in 44 B.C. Seizing this as an opportunity for more independence, they supported one of the conspirators, Cassius, and helped him gather an army and funds by extorting new taxes from the people. During this time, Antipater's son Herod emerged as a leader. Antipater appointed his eldest son, Phasael, governor of Jerusalem, and he appointed Herod to administer Galilee (*Ant.* 14.158). Herod became the head of the family after 42 B.C., when his father was murdered.

The rise of Mark Anthony as the new Roman power in the east and his triumph over Cassius simply meant a change of masters for Herod and his brother Phasael. They were appointed tetrarchs of Judea by Mark Anthony in 41 B.C. (*Ant.* 14.326). Hyrcanus, however, was placed under the civil authority of a Roman-appointed governor of Coelesyria, and restricted to the role of high priest (*Ant.* 14.73–74). Even with these changes, maneuvering for control in the Levant did not cease. The Parthians now took advantage of Anthony's prolonged stay in Egypt and invaded Syria, installing Antigonus, the son of Aristobulus II, on the throne in Jerusalem. They also captured both Phasael and Hyrcanus II. Phasael committed suicide while in prison, and Hyrcanus II was mutilated (his ears were cut off) so that he could no longer serve as high priest (according to the proscriptions of Lev 21:16–23).

Herod escaped by fleeing with his family to the fortress of Masada in the Judean desert. He

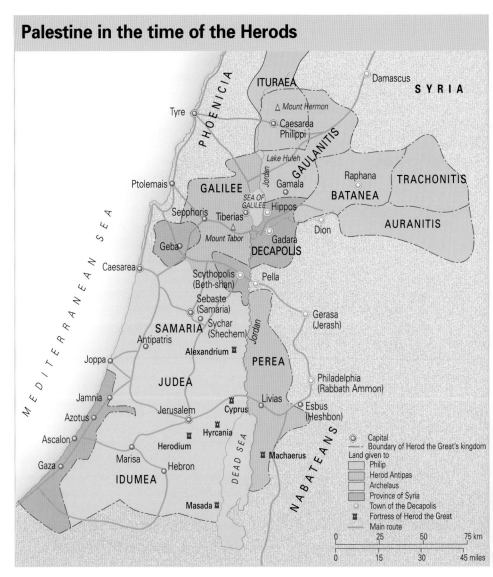

Palestine in the time of the Herods

Damascus
SYRIA
ITURAEA
PHOENICIA
Tyre
△ Mount Hermon
Caesarea Philippi
Lake Huleh
GAULANITIS
Ptolemais
GALILEE
Jordan
Gamala
Raphana
TRACHONITIS
BATANEA
SEA OF GALILEE
Hippos
Sepphoris
Tiberias
AURANITIS
MEDITERRANEAN SEA
Mount Tabor
Gadara
Dion
Geba
DECAPOLIS
Caesarea
Scythopolis (Beth-shan)
Pella
Sebaste (Samaria)
Gerasa (Jerash)
SAMARIA
Sychar (Shechem)
Antipatris
Alexandrium
Joppa
PEREA
Jordan
Philadelphia (Rabbath Ammon)
JUDEA
Livias
Esbus (Heshbon)
Jamnia
Jerusalem
Cyprus
Azotus
Hyrcania
Ascalon
Herodium
Machaerus
Marisa
Gaza
Hebron
NABATEANS
IDUMEA
DEAD SEA
Masada

○ Capital
---- Boundary of Herod the Great's kingdom
Land given to
☐ Philip
☐ Herod Antipas
☐ Archelaus
☐ Province of Syria
○ Town of the Decapolis
⌘ Fortress of Herod the Great
— Main route

| 0 | 25 | 50 | 75 km |
| 0 | 15 | 30 | 45 miles |

Herod the Great and his family

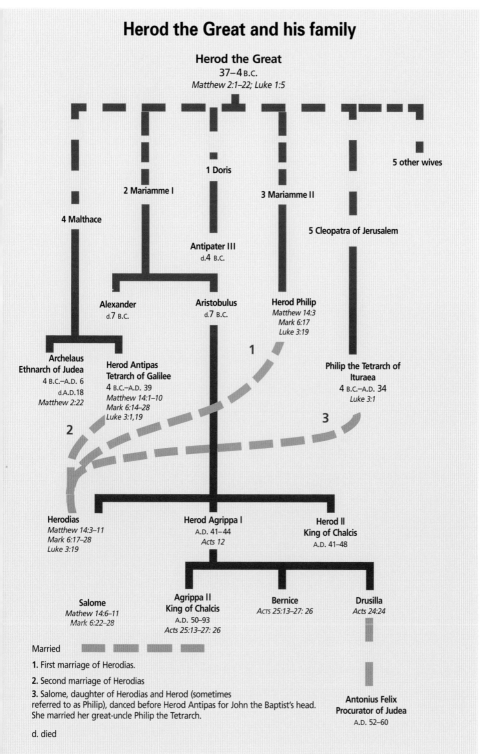

Herod the Great
37–4 B.C.
Matthew 2:1–22; Luke 1:5

1 Doris

2 Mariamme I

3 Mariamme II

4 Malthace

5 Cleopatra of Jerusalem

5 other wives

Antipater III
d.4 B.C.

Alexander
d.7 B.C.

Aristobulus
d.7 B.C.

Herod Philip
Matthew 14:3
Mark 6:17
Luke 3:19

Archelaus
Ethnarch of Judea
4 B.C.–A.D. 6
d.A.D.18
Matthew 2:22

Herod Antipas
Tetrarch of Galilee
4 B.C.–A.D. 39
Matthew 14:1–10
Mark 6:14–28
Luke 3:1,19

Philip the Tetrarch of
Ituraea
4 B.C.–A.D. 34
Luke 3:1

Herodias
Matthew 14:3–11
Mark 6:17–28
Luke 3:19

Herod Agrippa I
A.D. 41–44
Acts 12

Herod II
King of Chalcis
A.D. 41–48

Salome
Mathew 14:6–11
Mark 6:22–28

Agrippa II
King of Chalcis
A.D. 50–93
Acts 25:13–27: 26

Bernice
Acts 25:13–27: 26

Drusilla
Acts 24:24

Antonius Felix
Procurator of Judea
A.D. 52–60

Married

1. First marriage of Herodias.

2. Second marriage of Herodias

3. Salome, daughter of Herodias and Herod (sometimes referred to as Philip), danced before Herod Antipas for John the Baptist's head. She married her great-uncle Philip the Tetrarch.

d. died

> *Speak to Aaron and say: No one of your offspring throughout their generations who has a blemish may approach to offer the food of his God.*
> —Lev 21:17

then went to Rome, where his arguments and his bribes convinced the Roman Senate to declare him king of Judea in 40 B.C. It would take three years of fighting and another Roman siege of Jerusalem before Antigonus and his Parthian supporters could be defeated, and Herod could begin his reign in 37 B.C. At Herod's request, the Roman general Sosius in Antioch beheaded Antigonus, effectively ending the Hasmonean line, and opening the door for Herod's new ruling dynasty.

LAST GLIMPSES OF POWER:
The Herods

Having obtained the rulership of Judea, Herod now plotted to legitimize his position and obtain the support of the people. This would not be easy since he was an Idumean, and his family had converted to Judaism at sword's point. Herod's first step was to tie himself to the Hasmoneans. Like David (1 Sam 18:22–27; 2 Sam 3:13–16), he allied himself to the family of the previous ruler, marrying Mariamme, the granddaughter of Aristobulus II. He also appointed her 17-year-old brother Aristobulus III as high priest; but when the young man's popularity began to grow, Herod quickly found it necessary to arrange his drowning in 35 B.C., thus eliminating the last of the Hasmonean line (*Ant.* 15.31–56). Herod's paranoia also claimed the life of Hyrcanus, now in his 80s.

Violent acts such as these characterized Herod's entire reign (37–4 B.C.). Despite the continued good will of the Roman emperors and the expansion of his kingdom, the rule of terror spread. When he received word that a messiah-figure had been born in Bethlehem, Herod ordered the killing of all male children under the age of two (Matt 2:16–18) in order to stamp out any threat to his rule. Eventually, Herod's violent paranoia claimed the lives of several of his wives and sons, and many others whom he suspected of plotting against him (*Ant.* 15.80–87, 222–239). The executions were so many that, upon signing the death warrant for one of Herod's sons, Augustus Caesar remarked that it was better to be Herod's pig than his son (Macrobius, *Sat.* 2:4:11). Despite the tragedy of his personal life, Herod achieved real diplomatic triumphs, including Augustus's support for his rule, and reacquiring territory around Jericho and in Transjordan that had been lost to Cleopatra and Mark Anthony.

Herod's lasting accomplishments came in his building program. He styled himself as a Hellenistic prince, obligated by his position to rule as benefactor to his people. With this in mind, he constructed Judea's first port (Caesarea Maritima), and restored old cities (Samaria, renamed Sebaste, the Greek equivalent of "Augustus") with all the items considered necessary in a Hellenistic urban center: temples, theaters, and stadia. While he flattered Augustus Caesar with the names of these cities, Herod strengthened his own position by reequipping the strategic hilltop fortresses of Masada, thirty-five miles south of Jerusalem in

> *For that Herod was ill-natured, and severe in his punishments, and had no mercy on them that he hated; and everyone perceived that he was more friendly to the Greeks than to the Jews; for he adorned foreign cities with large presents in money; with building them baths and theatres besides: nay, in some of those places, he erected temples, and porticoes in others; but he did not vouchsafe to raise one of the least edifices in any Jewish city, or make them any donation that was worth mentioning.*
> —Josephus, Ant. 19.329

Herod's fortress of Herodium, with its artificially constructed summit, viewed from his palace at the foot of the hill.

The interior of the fortress at Herodium.

The pool of the palace, Herodium, viewed from the fortress.

The Roman amphitheater at Sebaste, constructed by Herod the Great.

the rugged area west of the Dead Sea, and constructing an elaborate palace-fortress complex at Herodium, seven miles south of Jerusalem, on the edge of the Judean desert.

The crowning architectural achievement of Herod's career was the rebuilding of the temple in Jerusalem (*Ant.* 15.380–425). Its gold inlaid columns and massive construction (using blocks of stone weighing over 450 tons in the supporting platform of the temple complex) were designed to impress the Jews, but it never won their affection. He destroyed any credibility he might have had as a pious Jew by erecting temples to the Roman gods and by staging athletic games in Caesar's honor (*Ant.* 19.329; 15.268).

On Herod's death, riots erupted throughout Judea that had to be suppressed by the Roman legate of Syria, Varus. Herod's will divided the kingdom among three of his sons, Archelaus, Antipas, and Philip. The Roman Senate ratified Herod's will and named Archelaus ethnarch (not king) of Judea, Samaria, and Idumea, while his brothers were appointed tetrarchs of Galilee and Perea, respectively. Archelaus ruled ten years, relying on Varus's backing to control the office of high priest and to continue his father's building projects. In A.D 6., a delegation sent by both Jews and Samaritans convinced Augustus to exile Archelaus to Gaul (France), and Judea was annexed to the Roman province of Syria. A procurator was then appointed to serve as local administrator.

From 6 until A.D. 41, six Roman governors, or procurators, ruled Judea. Their administrative offices were in Caesarea Maritima on the coast, but they were required to attend major festivals in Jerusalem when the influx of pilgrims created a dangerous situation for the Romans. The first of these procurators was P. Sulpicius Quirinius. He began his administration by ordering a census (*Ant.* 18.1; Luke 2:1–2), an action which led to armed rebellion throughout the province by people fearing higher taxes and labor service. He and his

Aerial view of the theater at Caesarea Maritima, constructed by Herod the Great and named for the emperor.

> Then Pilate asked him, "Are you the king of the Jews?" He answered, "You say so."
> —Luke 23:3

> For, in the first place, he [Herod] appointed solemn games to be celebrated every fifth year, in honor of Caesar, and built a theater at Jerusalem, as also a very great amphitheater in the plain. Both of them were indeed costly works, but opposite to the Jewish customs; for we have had no such shows delivered down to us as fit to be used or exhibited by us.
> —Josephus, Ant. 15.268

successors also controlled the appointment of the high priest. Quirinius placed Ananus (Annas in Luke 3:2) in the office, while his successor Valerius Gratus deposed Ananus in A.D. 15, and later appointed and deposed three other high priests.

The best known of the procurators was Pontius Pilate, who succeeded Gratus in A.D. 26 Like his predecessors, he gave little attention to the traditions of the people he was ruling (Luke 13:1). Josephus mentions two examples of this lack of respect for the Jews. Early in his reign, Pilate ordered the Roman legionary standards brought into Jerusalem. These standards, and an accompanying bust of Caesar (Ant. 18.55–59), represented the military occupation of the country, and were also extremely offensive to the Jews, who forbade the worship of images. Some Jews demonstrated their disgust for what Pilate had done by laying down with their necks bared before the soldiers. They challenged the Romans to kill them, since they would rather die than live in a city defiled by the presence of the standards (J.W. 2.169–174).

Perhaps in the hopes of restoring the people's confidence in his rule, Pilate proposed to build an aqueduct that would transport water to the growing population of Jerusalem.

Inscription bearing the name of the Roman procurator Pontius Pilate, from Caesarea Maritima.

Remains of the Roman harbor warehouses, Caesarea Maritima.

Roman aqueduct north of Acre (Akko) on the Mediterranean coast.

This backfired when he financed the aqueduct with funds (*qorban*) from the temple treasury that were restricted to religious projects (*J.W.* 2.175–177).

His dealing with the case of Jesus (Luke 23:1–25) played into the hands of the Sanhedrin council, but also failed to gain him any more respect with the Jews. For instance, his placement of the inscription over the crucified Jesus, "This is the King of the Jews" (Luke 23:38), was an obvious attempt to humiliate them, rather than Jesus. He was eventually ousted from his position in A.D. 36 after massacring a crowd assembled to hear a Samaritan prophet speak (*Ant.* 18.88–89).

While these events were occurring in Judea, Herod Antipas continued to rule in Galilee. He had strengthened his position by marrying the daughter of Aretas IV, the king of the Nabateans. He later divorced her in order to marry Herodias, the wife of his deceased half-brother Philip (Mark 6:17). John the Baptist was one of the many voices raised against this illegal marriage (see Lev 20:21). It was Antipas's fear of John's popularity (*Ant.* 18.118) and his desire to silence the voice of dissent that led to John's eventual execution (Mark 6:18–28). Antipas also showed his disdain for his Jewish subjects by constructing his new capital city of Tiberias on the site of an ancient cemetery, at the southern end of the Sea of Galilee. This violated the Jewish law against contact with the dead and the burial of the dead within city walls (Num 19:11; Jerusalem Talmud *Sheb'it* 9.1; *Ant.* 18.36–38).

A change came in the Judean political situation in A.D. 39, when the mentally unstable Roman emperor, Caligula, exiled Herod Antipas to Gaul. Caligula had given Philip's lands to Herod Agrippa (a grandson of Herod I). When Antipas asked for the title of king, he was exiled, and Herod Agrippa was awarded his lands. Emperor Claudius (*Ant.* 19.274–275) also gave him Judea in A.D. 41 Thus, he controlled all the lands that his grandfather had ruled forty-five years earlier.

Hot springs at the Roman baths at Tiberias on the Sea of Galilee.

The town of Tiberias viewed from the south along the shore of the Sea of Galilee.

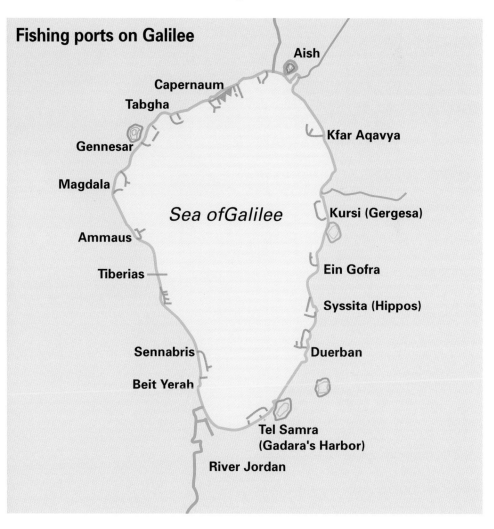

Fishing ports on Galilee

Aish

Capernaum

Tabgha

Kfar Aqavya

Gennesar

Magdala

Sea of Galilee

Kursi (Gergesa)

Ammaus

Tiberias

Ein Gofra

Syssita (Hippos)

Sennabris

Duerban

Beit Yerah

Tel Samra
(Gadara's Harbor)

River Jordan

Herod Agrippa attempted to build support for his rule through strict adherence to the Torah. He also gave several gifts to the temple treasury, including the golden chain he had worn while a prisoner in Rome. Perhaps as another way of currying favor with the Pharisees, Agrippa persecuted the disciples of Jesus. James the brother of John was executed, and Peter was imprisoned (Acts 12:1–3). Shortly after this, the king was stricken with an illness. Tradition suggests that this was a result of his being proclaimed a god. He subsequently died while officiating at games held in the emperor's honor at Caesarea in A.D. 44 (Acts 12:21–23; *Ant.* 19.343–350).

ROMAN RULE AND JEWISH PROTEST:
The First Jewish Revolt

Following Agrippa's death, the Emperor Claudius once again placed Judea under the rule of a Roman procurator. Agrippa's son, Agrippa II, was given the rule over Galilee, but he was thoroughly loyal to the Romans and became one more source of irritation for dissatisfied Jews. Each of the men who held the position of procurator between A.D. 44 and 66 faced a difficult administrative task. They were continually required to quell small rebellions and put down street riots caused by the people's desire to end Roman rule and presence in Judea. Periodic famines, the provocative and insensitive actions of some Roman soldiers, and the teachings of a series of messiah figures who offered the people hope of independence and restored greatness all worsened the volatile situation (*Ant.* 20.97–112; Acts 21:38).

One of the principal measures used by the procurators was to encourage the Jews to fight among themselves. Divided, they were unable to provide a common front against the Romans. In one case described by Josephus, Felix (procurator A.D. 52–60) arranged the murder of the high priest Jonathan, hiring assassins (**sicarii,** so named for the short,

And immediately, because he had not given the glory to God, an angel of the Lord struck him down, and he was eaten by worms and died.
—Acts 12:23

curved sword they carried) to mingle with the crowd during worship and kill him (*Ant.* 20.162–165). This provocative act was followed by an even more dangerous situation; an

BRITANNIA

ATLANTIC
OCEAN

LUGDUNENSIS BEL

AQUITANIA

NARBONENSIS

LUSITANIA   TARRACONENSIS   ALPES COTTIA

BAETICA

MAURETANIA

A

- Roman Empire in A.D.14
- Client state
- - - Boundary of province
- Roman Empire at its greatest extent in A.D.116
- Major road

0   250   500 km
0   100   200   300 miles

Egyptian prophet called for rebellion, and promised to arrange the miraculous destruction of the walls of Jerusalem (*Ant.* 20.169–172).

These insurrections brought a swift and bloody reprisal on the Jews. They also painted every other noninstitutional speaker with the brush of sedition, as the apostle Paul discovered (Acts 21:38). He was subsequently brought before Felix by the Jewish high priest Ananias, but Felix suspended the trial (Acts 24). Paul was not sent to Rome for his hearing before Caesar until after Felix was succeeded by Festus in A.D. 60 (Acts 25:1–12). The narrator of Acts 25:3, 9 suggests that Festus conspired to have Paul assassinated on the way to Jerusalem as a part of the political maneuvering of a procurator who wished "to do the Jews a favor."

Festus died while in office in 62 B.C. His death and the delayed arrival of his replacement, Albinus, led to an anarchic period in which the

The Roman Empire in the first century A.D.

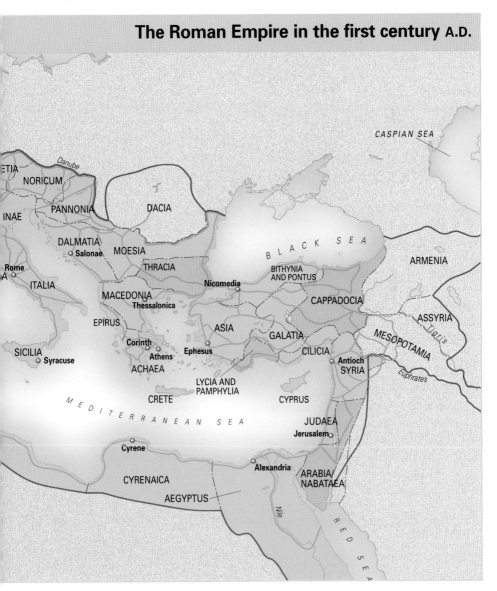

187

high priest Ananus (probably an alternate spelling of Ananias) executed several of his political and religious enemies. Among his victims was James, the brother of Jesus and the head of the Christian community in Jerusalem (*Ant.* 20.200–201). Matters did not improve substantially when Albinus arrived. In exchange for bribes, he allowed the tithes of food from the threshing floor that were earmarked for the priests to be stolen. Albinus was also forced to submit to extortion by the *sicarii*, who kidnapped his servants and then demanded the release of their imprisoned fellows in exchange (*Ant.* 20.204–210).

Gessius Florus succeeded Albinus in A.D. 64. He acquired this position as a result of his wife Cleopatra's friendship with Nero's wife (*Ant.* 20.252). Desiring to make the most financial gain he could from the procuratorship, Florus allowed the plundering of whole villages and took bribes from his political favorites (*J.W.* 2.278–279). Feeding upon the political climate of discontent that Florus had created, religious riots broke out in Caesarea over the obstruction of the entrance of the local synagogue, due to the construction of workshops on an adjoining piece of land (*J.W.* 2.284–292). When it became clear that justice could not be obtained from Florus, and that Nero had no intention of sending a replacement for him, revolt became inevitable.

The First Jewish Revolt began in A.D. 66, with two acts of defiance by those hoping to oust the Romans from Judea. Eleazar, the son of Ananias the high priest, called on the sacrificial priests to refuse gifts or offerings from foreigners. This effectively ended the practice of sacrificing in honor of the emperor (*J.W.* 2.409). Many of the chief priests and Pharisees argued against this action (*J.W.* 2.410–416), fearing Roman reprisals toward the temple and the people. The inflammatory actions of both Florus and Eleazar's radical followers helped initiate the final confrontation with Rome.

The other act which precipitated the war

When, therefore, Ananus was of this disposition, he thought he had now a proper opportunity [to exercise his authority]. Festus was now dead, and Albinus was but upon the road; so he assembled the sanhedrin of judges, and brought before them the brother of Jesus, who was called Christ, whose name was James, and some others [or, some of his companions]; and when he had formed an accusation against them as breakers of the law, he delivered them to be stoned; but as for those who seemed the most equitable of the citizens, and such as were the most uneasy at the breach of the laws, they disliked what was done; they also sent to the king [Agrippa], desiring him to send to Ananus that he should act so no more, for that what he had already done was not to be justified.

—*Josephus, Ant.* 20.200–201

was the capture of the Masada fortress by the rebel leader Menahem ben Hezekiah. The Roman garrison was massacred, and arms were distributed to the people with a call for a general insurrection (*J.W.* 2.433–434). What occurred, however, was not a united effort to throw off Roman rule, but rather a confused period in which debtors rushed to burn contracts (*J.W.* 2.426–427). In the midst of the chaos, various Jewish factions claimed the leadership. There were also some massacres of the Jewish populations of predominantly Gentile cities like Caesarea, Scythopolis, and the Decapolis cities in Transjordan (*J.W.* 2.457–480).

After the Roman forces under Cestius experienced some initial reverses, Nero appointed Vespasian and his son Titus to quell the Jewish

Right: Aerial view of the ancient fortress of Masada, where 960 Jews reportedly committed suicide rather than fall into the hands of their Roman enemies. The stronghold is constructed atop a precipitous natural outcrop.

Qumran and region

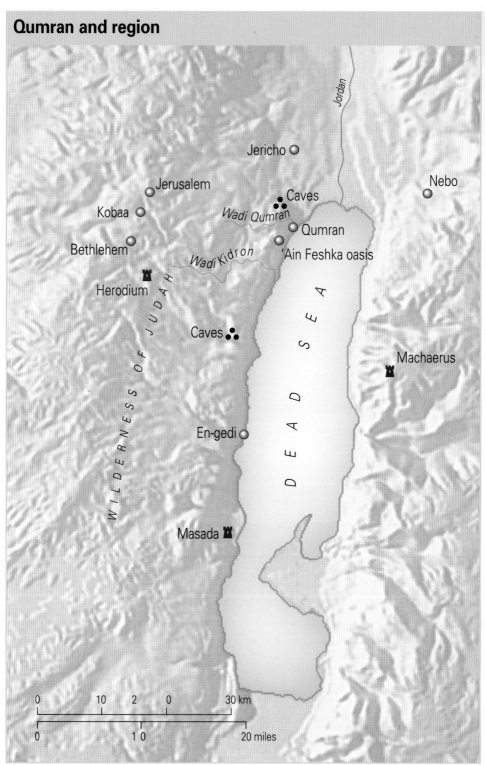

Jordan

Jericho

Nebo

Jerusalem

Caves

Kobaa

Wadi Qumran

Qumran

Bethlehem

Wadi Kidron

'Ain Feshka oasis

Herodium

W I L D E R N E S S   O F   J U D A H

Caves

Machaerus

D E A D   S E A

En-gedi

Masada

| 0 | 10 | 2 | 0 | 30 km |
| 0 | | 1 | 0 | 20 miles |

Top left: cistern at Qumran. Top right: The cave where the first scrolls were discovered. Middle: Watchtower at the Qumran settlement. Bottom: The scrolls were discovered in caves in these cliffs.

revolt. Their more organized efforts led to the surrender of several towns; although some, like Jotapata, were besieged, and most of their defenders were killed (*J.W.* 3.127–339). Josephus himself was one of the Jewish commanders at Jotapata. He escaped the final fall of the city, but was subsequently captured and became an advisor and seer for the Roman generals (*J.W.* 3.341–354).

Gradually, all of the Judean countryside and the rebel fortresses (Tiberias, Gamala, and Gischala) fell to the Romans. Tradition holds that one group of Jews, led by Rabbi Johanan ben Zakkai, made a separate peace with the Romans in A.D. 68 and moved to the town of Jamnia. There they are said to have established a scholarly and commercial community that served as a center of revived Judaism after the

Part of one of the Dead Sea Scrolls on display at the Shrine of the Book, Jerusalem.

revolt. Others, like the Essenes of the desert community of **Qumran,** were scattered, and their villages were destroyed. They did manage to hide their sacred books in mountain caves near their settlement. These "**Dead Sea Scrolls**" were discovered in 1947, and serve as one of the most important modern tools for studying the biblical text.

Jerusalem, overcrowded with refugees from all over Judea and divided into warring factions, finally came under siege in A.D. 70 Vespasian had returned to Rome to become emperor after Nero's death, which left his son Titus to complete the war. His efforts were facilitated by the fighting between the Jewish leaders John of Gischala, Simon bar Giora, and Eleazar (*J.W.* 5.248–274, 527–540). Five months of fighting and starvation gradually wore down the defenders. The end of the fighting came in September, A.D. 70 (*J.W.* 6.435). Herod's temple, as well as large portions of the city and its defenses, was torn down at Titus's command, and a great slaughter of the population followed the siege. An encampment was constructed for the occupying Tenth Roman

legion, but the city itself ceased to be a major Jewish population center (*J.W.* 7.1–12). All that remained of the revolt were some hilltop fortresses; and the last of these, Masada, fell in A.D. 73 after the 960 defenders committed mass suicide, rather than be captured by the Romans (*J.W.* 7.252–406).

A FINAL CHAPTER:
Bar Kochba and Diaspora

The fall of Jerusalem and the destruction of the temple ended the power of the Sanhedrin and the high priesthood (*Ant.* 20.224–251). Never again would the temple community dominate Jewish religion and thought.

Separate centers of learning and worship, such as that established at Jamnia, represented post-A.D. 70 Judaism: a nonsacrificial cult, devoted to study of the law and the development of community religious standards. The Roman emperors attempted to encourage this more peaceful form of Judaism, while doing everything they could to destroy nationalism and messiah figures. An indication of their efforts is found in the writings of the early

Roman emperor Hadrian.

> *I see him, but not now; I behold him, but not near – a star shall come out of Jacob, and a scepter shall rise out of Israel; it shall crush the borderlands of Moab, and the territory of all the Shethites.*
> —Num 24:17

A further step in this policy of preventing nationalism from recurring among the Jews was the rebuilding of Jerusalem by the emperor Hadrian in A.D. 130 He constructed a Roman-style city and renamed it **Aelia Capitolina.** Other construction projects were also ordered at Caesarea and Sepphoris (later renamed Diocaesarea). Instead of quieting the Jews, however, this attempt to extinguish the traditional religious and political heritage of Jerusalem sparked the Second Jewish Revolt in A.D. 132 Sources for this revolt and its primary causes are fragmentary, but they all seem to indicate that Jerusalem and Jewish traditions, including circumcision, were still rallying points for rebellion.

church historian Eusebius (*Eccl. hist.* 3.12, 19–20), who describes attempts by Vespasian and Domitian to hunt down members of the house of David.

The leader of the revolt was a messianic figure named Simon bar Kochba, who appears in rabbinic sources as Bar Kochba, "son of the star" (*j. Ta'an.* iv 68d–69d; Num 24:17–19). He

Coins from the Bar Kochba period uncovered during excavations at Tel Bareket.

drew support from those, like the famous Rabbi Akiba, who believed that Yahweh would use this man to rid their land of the hated Romans. For a brief time, the rebels were successful. They reoccupied Jerusalem, set up a bureaucracy to govern the affairs of state, and reestablished the religious calendar of festivals. Coins minted during this period by the revolutionary government bear inscriptions such as "Year One of the Redemption of Israel," and "Year Two for the Freedom of Israel."

Such high hopes were soon dashed as Rome marshaled distant legions to put down yet another Jewish war. Coins found in excavations dated to this period come from as far away as Britain and Germany, where the legionnaires were paid before they were shipped to the Near East. The Roman general Sextus Julius Severus recaptured Jerusalem in A.D. 134, and drove the rebels into the mountainous areas of the Judean wilderness. Guerrilla warfare continued for another year until the fall of the last rebel stronghold of Bethar in 135.

Rabbinic tradition contends that Jerusalem fell on the same day, the ninth of Ab, in both the first and second revolt. True or not, this became the traditional day for ritually mourning these events. Jews were expelled from the restored Aelia Capitolina and from Judea in general. The expulsions also applied to Jewish Christians, thus leaving the Gentile population to lead the church in that area. Hadrian continued his rebuilding of Aelia Capitolina and the other cities of the province, now renamed **Syria Palestina** ("land of the Philistines"). His plans included the construction of a temple to his personal god Jupiter over the site of Solomon's temple, as well as on the site of the Samaritan shrine on Mount Gerizim.

With the exile of a large portion of the Jews from Palestine came a shift in the history to Diaspora Judaism. Jews were scattered throughout the Roman Empire. Their synagogues became focal points for worship and for the development of **Rabbinic Judaism,** with its study of the Hebrew canon of Scriptures, as

The North Palace, Masada.

Coin of the Bar Kochba rebellion, depicting the Temple and the Ark of the Covenant inside.

well as the Jewish commentaries on Scripture that developed in succeeding centuries, such as the second-century A.D. **Mishnah.** Communities in Antioch, Corinth, and throughout Asia Minor proved to be both fertile ground for converts and a source of contention for Paul and the other missionaries of the Christian faith (Acts 14:1–2; 17:1–8; 18:1–4).

SOCIAL LIFE

Alexander's conquest brought a new and vibrant culture to the Near East. Gradually it mixed with local customs and traditions, creating a Hellenistic culture. In general, this synthesis was beneficial for both. For the Jews, however, the introduction of Hellenism became a major source of controversy, dividing the people between the Hellenizers and the traditionalists. The resulting cultural conflict spilled over into economic, political, and religious areas. Explored below are those developments in everyday life that changed, or became more focused, as a result of the introduction of Hellenistic culture.

Cities and City Planning

At the center of Greek culture was the city state. When Alexander's armies conquered the Near East, they established many new cities

and rebuilt others. In part, this was a way of consolidating their control over the conquered areas, but it also fulfilled Greek immigrants' expectations. Urban centers with gymnasia, theaters, and the **agora** (marketplace) were the basis of life wherever Greeks settled. A further sense of order was created in Hellenistic cities by the imposition, where possible, of the gridiron pattern of streets and buildings. The agora then served as the heart of the business district of the city, with a variety of buildings and shops located on all four sides of a public square. Sometimes another agora was constructed within a quieter district of the city where temples were the focal point. This arrangement was not always possible in the older cities like Jerusalem, but where destruction or mass rebuilding had taken place (as in Herod's Sebaste/Samaria), the new pattern was employed.

In new cities, such as Herod's administrative center and port, Caesarea Maritima (built between 22 and 10 B.C.), the full range of Hellenistic construction and civic planning took place. The port, a vital strategic and economic link for shipping-poor Palestine, had a breakwater, docks, and quarters for sailors on leave. To satisfy his Hellenistic tastes and to please his Roman masters, Herod built a temple to the deified Caesar in the unwalled city, as well as a theater and amphitheater. Some of the sanitation needs of the people were handled by an underground sewage system, and transportation was facilitated by an arrangement of parallel streets (*Ant.* 15.331–341).

Other than the palaces of kings and Roman officials, and the homes of the wealthy, the majority of housing within the cities of Palestine was overcrowded and not well constructed. Evidence at Capernaum, for example, suggests that private houses, set in blocks of four around a central courtyard, often consisted of one story, with a staircase on the outside wall leading up to a living area on the roof.

> *The same thing occurred in Iconium, where Paul and Barnabas went into the Jewish synagogue and spoke in such a way that a great number of both Jews and Greeks became believers.*
> —Acts 14:1

They were crudely constructed of uneven blocks of basalt and mortar. Because of a lack of large wooden beams, the rooms tended to be less than eighteen feet wide, and the ceilings were quite low. There were small windows overlooking the courtyard, allowing some ventilation and providing a relatively cool dwelling in the often hot and humid climate of the Upper Galilee region. The floor was made of uneven basalt slabs, which could easily cause a stumble or the loss of some item, like a coin, between its cracks (Luke 15:8).

These new and expanded urban centers were designed to accommodate relatively large populations (perhaps as many as 80,000 during the Roman period). Such a large number of people (swelling dramatically during festivals like Passover) meant increased demands for water and food supplies. To meet the former need, Herod initiated public works projects to construct new water channels and to stimulate a periodically stagnant economy. Pontius Pilate went a step further, constructing an aqueduct capable of providing a continuous supply of fresh water to Jerusalem's inhabitants. Even with these measures, however, it was standard for every home to have one or more rain-catching cisterns or pools.

The agricultural villages that ringed the urban centers supplied the food and other farm products, which the people of the cities consumed. Concentric circles of smaller communities that produced the grains, meat, and oil that were the staple of the Jewish diet surrounded Jerusalem. There was continuous

> *A man was there named Zacchaeus; he was a chief tax collector and was rich.*
> —Luke 19:2

Part of the site of the biblical town of Capernaum.

Remains of basalt houses at Chorazin, near the Sea of Galilee.

contact between these two population areas, but there were some very large differences between them.

Urban-Based Bureaucracy

Helping to administer both the cities and the surrounding villages was a new group of court employees whose positions were owed to the rulers of Palestine. Thus their loyalties belonged to the dominating Greek and Roman culture. In like manner, the Hasmoneans and the Herods also employed a civil service to collect taxes and enforce order. This service gave many Jews the opportunity to move up socially, and in some cases they became quite wealthy and powerful. For instance, Zacchaeus, the chief tax official in the Jericho region, is said to have been very rich (Luke 19:2). He, like John, the port official at Caesarea, mentioned in Josephus (*J.W.* 2.287), had taken advantage of the Roman system of tax farming. Under this system, the tax collec-

tor was assigned a certain amount to collect, and then was allowed to collect as much more as he could to cover administrative expenses.

In fact, by Jesus' time, nearly all tax collectors, civil officials, and local judges in Palestine were Jews. Like the stewards who manipulated the day laborers and tenant farmers (Luke 16:1–8), these middle and lower level government employees considered themselves socially above the masses, and were despised for this (Luke 19:7; Matt 11:19). Tensions between these officials, who were necessarily loyal to Rome, and other Jews were very real. The Pharisees especially are depicted several times in Luke's gospel as openly disparaging those, like tax collectors, who work for the Romans (Luke 5:30; 7:34; 15:1). In contrast, Jesus preached nonviolence, as when he defused the question of whether to pay tribute to Caesar in Luke 20:22–25, and instructed his listeners to love their enemies in Matt 5:44–45.

Village Life

Despite the growth of urban centers and the incentives offered by jobs and occasionally better housing (see Herod Antipas's inducements to new settlers in Tiberias, *Ant.* 18.36–38), the majority of Palestinian Jews in Jesus' time still lived in small towns and villages. Josephus wrote of the many villages in Galilee that were aided by the richness of the region's soil (*J.W.* 3.43). A conservative estimate of 200 villages with populations of about 500 each would total 100,000 peasant villagers inhabiting that area. The effects of Hellenism were less pronounced here than in the cities. Councils of elders continued to decide local matters, although tax collectors and other government officials would have added another level of authority to their lives. Aramaic remained the common language in the villages, while Greek was the principal tongue in the cities. The basic conservatism of the peasants in these small settlements meant a retention of older traditions and values that tied them more closely to pre-Hellenistic eras.

Those social activities which existed in the rural areas centered on family ties and seasonal religious festivals. Marriages were celebrated with a wedding feast. The ritual included the groomsman escorting the bride to the wedding (John 3:29), while the bridesmaids accompanied the bridegroom to the celebration (Matt 25:1–12). A steward was placed in charge of the arrangements for the feast, orchestrating the festivities and parceling out

> *He who has the bride is the bridegroom. The friend of the bridegroom, who stands and hears him, rejoices greatly at the bridegroom's voice. For this reason my joy has been fulfilled.*
> —*John 3:29*

The Roman aqueduct, which carried water to the port of Caesarea Maritima.

Model of Jerusalem in the time of Christ, showing how the temple (top left) dominated the city.

the wine and other refreshments (John 2:8–10). To separate these activities from other gatherings, a special wedding garment was required for admission to the feast (Matt 22:11–13).

Pilgrimages to Jerusalem to attend the Passover (Luke 2:41), the Feast of Tabernacles (John 7:2), and other major religious events (John 10:22, Hanukkah celebration) were the social highlight of the villagers' year. Religious obligations could be fulfilled while leaving enough time to shop, to see family and old friends, and to pass on to the young the importance of their cultural heritage. After the destruction of the temple in A.D. 70, the law of the Torah and the synagogue took the place of the Jerusalem cult community. Villagers retained the memory and image of that holy

Now every year his parents went to Jerusalem for the festival of the Passover.
—*Luke 2:41*

place, but had to content themselves with local celebrations and an occasional trip to a nearby market center to break the monotony of village life.

Leisure

Leisure was a major pursuit in the urban centers. The Greeks, and later the Romans, demanded the opportunities and pleasures of the gymnasium and stadium. In the gymnasium, a person could engage in a private workout and then bathe, either to begin or to end a workday. This facility also provided a place to make social contacts, conduct club meetings, or participate in the activities of professional or private associations. This latter activity was another innovation of the Greek culture, which was very dependent on the development of social relationships. Businessmen, skilled workers, and even the poor formed these associations of social equals to aid each other in commercial activity, as a social outlet, and even to provide funds to ensure proper burial.

The stadium provided facilities for public

199

A wide-angle lens view of the Roman amphitheater at Beit Shean (Scythopolis).

athletic contests. For instance, the multi-purpose amphitheater (50.35 m. wide and 265 m. long), constructed by Herod in Caesarea, also could function as a hippodrome, accommodating horse and chariot races (*Ant.* 15.341; 16.137). Josephus describes plays, athletic and wrestling matches, chariot races, and battles between condemned convicts and animals in the Jerusalem theater-amphitheater, in which the winners of these contests received rich prizes and public recognition (*Ant.* 15.268-274). However, no trace of this facility has yet come to light.

There are frequent references in Josephus (*Ant.* 12.241 and 19.343-345) and in the intertestamental literature to the use of public facilities by the Hellenizers (1 Macc 1:14). For instance, the high priest Jason created a "gymnasium and *ephebeion*" (a municipal "finishing school" for young men) in Jerusalem as a mark of his commitment to Hellenism (2 Macc 4:9, 12). The Hellenizers, who wished to adopt Greek culture and practice, were stronger in the cities. They freely attended dramatic events and participated in games such as foot races, wrestling, and other Olympian events. By the New Testament period, Paul could describe his ministry using the analogy of running a race in 1 Cor 9:24-27, or comparing it to fighting "the good fight" in 2 Tim 4:7. In these passages, however, he is speaking primarily to Gentiles and Hellenized Jewish Christians. Jews in Judea were still offended by the excesses of Herod in staging Greek games in Jerusalem. The naked performers and the gold and silver statuettes given to the winners caused a great uproar (*Ant.* 15.277-283).

Drama combined the study of Greek literature with live entertainment to enhance cultural life in the Hellenistic city. Regular performances of the Greek playwrights were held in the theaters, like that at Sepphoris, in

So they built a gymnasium in Jerusalem, according to Gentile custom, . . .
–1 Macc 1:14

the cities of the Decapolis, and all over the Near East, further educating the people in Greek values and philosophy. Paul's use of quotations from Greek plays reflects the great familiarity these dramas had in the Hellenized cities. Examples of this are found in 1 Cor 15:33, "Bad company ruins good morals" (a phrase from Menander), and Titus 1:12, "Cretans are always liars, vicious brutes, lazy gluttons" (quoted from Epimenides).

Public baths were also constructed to provide city dwellers with a familiar place to socialize, transact business informally, and engage in the hygienic pleasures of alternating hot and cold baths (*Ant.* 19.329). The recently excavated baths at Capernaum include large pools, as well as smaller rooms where private parties could converse within the cleansing steam. Also uncovered there were separate bath facilities for the Roman garrison. Despite the mixed population of this site on the Sea of Galilee, it was probably best to separate Roman troops from the local inhabitants.

Separate bathing facilities (*miqva'ot*) for Jewish ritual cleansing (Lev 15:5–11) have also been discovered in Jerusalem and at Qumran. These, however, were not designed for social gatherings, but for purifying the body before entering the temple, or after it had been made impure by sexual activity or contact with the dead (Lev 15:18; 17:15).

Education and Scholarship

Throughout the period from 350 B.C. to 70 A.D., traditional Jewish education in Hebrew and Aramaic continued to be conducted in the home, in the temple at Jerusalem (Luke 2:46), and in the local synagogues. Jewish tradition states that local schools for young children were created by the high priest in the first century A.D. (*b. B. Bat.* 21a). There is no scriptural evidence of this, however, except Jesus' demonstrated knowledge of the law (Luke 2:41–51) and his ability to read Hebrew, even though he was only the son of a carpenter (Luke 4:16–17).

In the Diaspora, education for some Jews

Site of the Roman hippodrome at Caesarea Maritima.

and for most of the Greek residents of Hellenistic cities took place in the gymnasium. The gymnasium not only included areas for physical education, but also housed lecture halls where students studied Greek language and literature. They used the same handbooks on rhetorical style and writing exercises that were employed all over the Greco-Roman world. Lessons at the gymnasium were part of the *ephebeion,* an institution of higher education open only to wealthy future aristocrats. There were Greeks who, after secondary school, went on to train in medicine or the law, but for those whose families held high social standing, the *ephebeion* was the proper place to pursue a leisurely education and form the social ties that would ensure success in Hellenistic society. Nevertheless, when the high priest Jason built a gymnasium and *ephebeion* in Jerusalem, where Jews performed exercises in the nude and were educated in the ways of Hellenism, 2 Maccabees labeled him "ungodly," claiming that he was "no true high priest" (2 Macc 4:9, 12–13).

As the writings of **Philo of Alexandria** reflect, the mixture of Greek literature with the study of the Hebrew Scriptures during the first century A.D. produced some new schools of thought on Jewish traditions. For instance, Philo was heavily influenced by Platonism and Stoic philosophy, as is evident in his *Exposition of the Laws of Moses.* His discussion of *Logos* ("the Word") in relation to God's mental activity while in the act of creation can serve as a background (see *Opif.* 15–25; *Pirqe R. El.* 3), or at least a comparative study, for the use of *Logos* in John 1:1–14.

During this period, priests and scholars in Palestine and the Diaspora gradually came to a consensus on those books that were considered Scripture. This process can be seen in the "Prologue" to Sirach, an apocryphal book written by Jesus ben Sirach about 180 B.C., which lists the traditional division of the canon into Law, the Prophets, and the Writings.

Eventually, it became conventional to close the canon of prophetic speech with the time of Ezra. However, new books continued to be authored as late as the second century A.D. One group of fifteen books from this period formed the additional set of writings known as the **Apocrypha** or **Deuterocanon.** Some of these manuscripts were written during the Hellenistic period, and dealt with the events surrounding the Maccabean revolt, or provided traditional material related to books already included in the canon, such as the Additions to Esther and 1–2 Esdras.

Long before the fall of the temple, the communities of the Diaspora accommodated Hellenistic culture by producing the first translation of the Hebrew text of the Bible. The **Septuagint** (abbreviated LXX), a Greek version of the Old Testament books, was completed in Alexandria, Egypt some time after 200 B.C. This was necessitated when Greek became the common language of Diaspora Jews. Being a product of Hellenistic culture, the Septuagint, unlike the Hebrew canon, incorporated some contemporary literature into its collection of writings. Thus the fifteen Deuterocanonical books of the Apocrypha were included in the finalized Alexandrian canon of the Septuagint. By the first century A.D., the Septuagint was the Bible version used by most of the New Testament writers.

After the destruction of the temple in A.D. 70, the development of the Hebrew canon becomes obscured by the tradition that the burden of Jewish education and the preservation of the canon fell to a community of scholars who met at **Jamnia** (Yavneh). According to this tradition, they and their successors set a tone of instruction and study of the Scriptures in synagogues wherever Jews lived. Supposedly, the Jamnia rabbis deliberated throughout the period immediately following A.D. 75, and at least until the end of the Bar Kochba Revolt in 135. They are said to have compiled manuscripts, and in an exhaustive

A visitor studies one of the Dead Sea Scrolls on display at the Shrine of the Book, Jerusalem.

process of debate, to have determined which books should be included in the canon of Scripture. While there is no historical basis for this picture of an academy discussing the canon, certainly some process did take place creating the text that would later be formalized after 500 A.D. through the efforts of another group of scholars known as the **Masoretes.** It should be noted, however, that the Dead Sea Scrolls found at Qumran demonstrate that the Masoretic text of the Hebrew Bible was nearly set by the end of the first century A.D.

Second Esdras 14:37–48 describes the recreation of the traditional canon of twenty-four books, and an additional seventy volumes of apocryphal wisdom. However, the rabbis did not ratify the books of the Apocrypha as part of the Hebrew canon for a variety of reasons, including the fact that they post-dated the period of Ezra, and reflected Hellenistic ideas. Another body of literature known as the **Pseudepigrapha** was also denied a place in the canon, in large part because much of it was fictional commentary on biblical works and contained theological ideas not acceptable to the Jewish community. These sixty-five books, many produced during this time of Hellenistic synthesis, date well into the Roman era, and the early Christian community influenced some of these writings (Testaments of the Twelve Patriarchs). They contain folk stories, additions to canonical books, and the meditations of scholars and scribes in Palestine and the Diaspora. Examples of these works include 1 Enoch, Jubilees, and the Testament of Job. Their worth was considered secondary to the text of the original body of Scripture. Their authorship was often uncertain, and, significantly, most were written in Greek.

Eventually, a dispute arose among the Jews over the importance of these writings in relation to the canonical material. Religious parties arose as a consequence of this issue. The pious Pharisees advocated the free use of the interpretive material, such as the oral Torah and the Mishnah, as the equal of the canonical works. In contrast, the Sadducees argued for strict and exclusive use of the canonical books of the Torah to answer religious questions.

After A.D. 200, the rabbis placed more emphasis on the study and reiteration of the legal pronouncements in the Scriptures. Local communities of scholars taught young men the Torah and expounded on its meaning. This resulted in the compilation of the Mishnah under the direction of Rabbi Judah the Prince. It consists of sixty-three tractates or treatises comprising the consensus of rabbinic opinion on how the laws of the Pentateuch related to aspects of everyday life (agriculture, marriage, and ritual purity) in their time. Additional commentary on these legal treatises is contained in the **Babylonian** and **Palestinian Talmuds,** dating to the period of the mid-fourth through mid-sixth centuries A.D. Commentary, or **Midrash,** on non-legal material, including legendary narratives of the lives of the major biblical figures in the Hebrew canon, is also contained in the Talmud.

Law and the Administration of Justice

There were several shifts of authority in the enforcement of the law during the Hellenistic and Roman periods. During portions of this era, foreign governments and their representatives imposed order, imprisoning offenders and carrying out capital punishment. At other times, the Hasmonean government and the Sanhedrin council took primary responsibility for the administration of justice. In many cases there was little distinction made between civil and religious law, since the Torah imposed penalties for crimes against persons (theft, murder, adultery) as well as crimes against God (blasphemy, pagan worship).

There were several levels of judicial authority. Whether appointed by the Greeks, the

> *While Peter and John were speaking to the people, the priests, the captain of the temple, and the Sadducees came to them, much annoyed because they were teaching the people and proclaiming that in Jesus there is the resurrection of the dead.*
> —*Acts 4:1–2*

Hasmoneans, the Herodians, or the Romans, local courts handled local civil and criminal cases. In situations in which there was a dispute over land or property ownership, the services of a scribe or lawyer (Matt 22:35; Luke 10:25) might be employed to record and argue the case (Luke 11:42; 1 Cor 1:20). Jesus' various legal hearings before Caiaphas the high priest (Matt 26:57–68) and before Pilate (Matt 27:11–14) demonstrate that capital crimes and cases of treason or civil unrest brought the higher authorities based in Jerusalem or Caesarea to bear on the problem. Clear-cut religious crimes were handled by the leaders of the local synagogue or by the high priest and the Sanhedrin. For instance, some Saducean members of the Sanhedrin had Peter and John arrested and tried for preaching the resurrection of the dead in Jesus' name (Acts 4:1–22).

Roman officials throughout the empire had jurisdiction to overrule local courts or to intervene in any case in which they were interested. Thus, when the members of the Sanhedrin and their followers nearly came to blows over Paul's case, the Roman tribune took him to the local army barracks for safekeeping (Acts 23:6–10). Roman citizenship, which had been acquired by some of the people of the provinces, also figured in the process of justice. As a Roman citizen of Cilicia, Paul successfully avoided further prosecution by the Jewish leadership by appealing his case to Caesar. Despite his desire to do a favor for the Jews, Festus, the Roman procurator, was obliged by law to grant Paul's request (Acts 25:9–12).

Clothing and Personal Adornment

The wealthy and those involved in the government during the Persian period and on through the Roman era commonly adopted foreign clothing styles. Among those items of Persian clothing most often adopted were riding trousers with boots and leggings and a high felt cap. The prophet Zephaniah's admonitions (1:8) against the wearing of "foreign attire" suggest that these fashions had become fairly widespread. With the coming of the Greeks, Persian garb was displaced.

At first there was some resistance among the Jews to Hellenistic fashions. For instance, one charge made against Jason, the high priest in the time of Antiochus IV, was that he forced the nobility of Jerusalem to wear a broad-brimmed hat associated with the cult of the Greek god Hermes (2 Macc 4:12). It was not until the mid-Hasmonean period that Greek costume became common among the general

> *And on the day of the LORD's sacrifice I will punish the officials and the king's sons and all who dress themselves in foreign attire.*
> —Zeph 1:8

population. Rejection of the new fashions was less common in the Diasporic communities like Alexandria. There the Jews quickly adopted the Greek styles of dress.

By the time of Jesus, there was no stigma attached to wearing the *colobium*, a long seamless tunic (John 19:23) with a cloak (*pallium*, Matt 27:31) and tassels (*tsitsith*) on the four corners of the hem (Matt 9:20; Mark 6:56). There were often decorative bands on the *colobium* that ran from the shoulder to the hem. Foot coverings included the sandal, as well as the Roman *calceus*, a shoe that covered the entire foot. During this period there was no formal headgear for men, except for the embroidered

Stone relief from Hierapolis, Asia Minor, showing contemporary Roman costume.

A woman's makeup panel from Greece.

caps of the priests (*Ant.* 3.157–158). The fashion of women being required to cover their long hair with a veil is raised in 1 Cor 11:4–7. It is unlikely that Paul is instructing the Corinthian church to adopt a Jewish tradition (see 3 Macc 4:6; *Ant.* 3.270 for this custom). Greek and Roman women also regularly covered their heads with a veil (Tertullian, *Cor.* 4; Plutarch, *Quaest. rom.* 267a).

While specific items of jewelry are seldom mentioned in the New Testament, archaeological discoveries have shown that the jeweler's art continued to flourish. Gold bracelets and clothes clasps encrusted with jewels, colored glass, and pearls have been uncovered, adding credence to the description of the woman in

> The woman was clothed in purple and scarlet, and adorned with gold and jewels and pearls, holding in her hand a golden cup full of abominations and the impurities of her fornication; . . .
> —*Rev 17:4*

Rev 17:4. Greek and Roman styles of jewelry were also borrowed, along with female hairstyles. First Timothy 2:9 contains Paul's admonition that women in the Christian community not adopt unseemly apparel, which he describes as "hair braided, or with gold, pearls, or expensive clothes" (see Juvenal, *Sat.* 6; *T. Reu.* 5:1–5). Inscribed seals and rings, used to stamp documents or possessions or to adorn fingers and toes, are also common finds in the excavation of Roman occupation levels.

Although not specifically for adornment purposes, *tephillim* (meaning "prayers") or **phylacteries** were commonly worn by devout men in the time of Jesus. Found in the excavations of the Qumran community, they were black leather boxes, each containing four passages of Scripture: Exod 13:1–10, 11–16; Deut 6:4–9; 11:13–21. Based on injunctions in Exod 13:9 and Deut 6:8 to keep the law constantly in the mind and heart, they were attached to the forehead and the left arm by leather straps. The phylacteries also became a source of excessive pride, according to Matt 23:5, for some literally wore their religion on their sleeves.

Weapons and Warfare

The methods of warfare continued to become more sophisticated during the Hellenistic and Roman eras. This was due in large part to the introduction of new weapons (catapults, ballistae, and siege engines) by the Greek and Roman armies that conquered the area (*J.W.* 3.80). Acquiring skill with these new weapons and methods took time for the Jews. Their basic lack of military expertise permitted a terrible massacre during the early part of the Maccabean revolt. Being attacked on the Sabbath and refusing to break the Sabbath law, over one thousand were killed (*Ant.* 12.274–275). Subsequently, they set aside this law temporarily in times of national crisis.

Open warfare against Antiochus IV's army of experienced soldiers, horsemen, and elephants (*J.W.* 1.41) was clearly impossible for the under-equipped Jews. It was the guerrilla tactics of Judas Maccabaeus and his brothers Jonathan and Simon that finally outlasted the Seleucid forces. Even after the Greek armies were expelled from most of Palestine, the Jews'

A Jewish man wearing a phylactery.

Replica of a Roman siege engine, such as the legionaries would have used to assault Jerusalem.

> *So this Antiochus got together fifty thousand footmen, and five thousand horsemen, and fourscore elephants, and marched through Judea into the mountainous parts. He then took Bethsura which was a small city; but at a place called Bethzacharias, where the passage was narrow, Judas met him with his army.*
> —Josephus, J.W. *1.41*

lack of skills in siege warfare meant that the Seleucid citadel in Jerusalem, the Akra, was not captured until 141 B.C. (1 Macc 13:49–52; *Ant.* 13.215–217).

In the Roman period there were numerous Jewish uprisings, in addition to the two principal revolts of 66–70 and 132–135 A.D. Weaponry for infantry in these conflicts generally consisted of the Greek or Roman short sword and javelin, a breastplate, shield, and helmet (Eph 6:13–17; *J.W.* 3.94–95). Daggers or short swords were often concealed under the

Relief of a Roman infantryman.

garments of rebels and those, like the *sicarii,* who sought to instigate civil unrest (*J.W.* 7.409–412; *Ant.* 20.164–165; Matt 26:51). The Roman cavalry carried pikes, shields, and a quiver of throwing darts. Their horses were

Relief of a Roman swordsman.

Replica of a Roman *ballista*.

also partially armored (*J.W.* 3.96–97).

Throughout the New Testament period, the Romans were the unprecedented masters of warfare. The effects of their unparalleled organizational skills and expertise in siege warfare could only be delayed, not overcome (*J.W.* 3.70–101). Josephus's description of the siege of Jerusalem is a case in point. The Jews managed to burn the Roman siege works and battering rams. However, famine and loss of life during the many skirmishes eventually led to the fall of the city (*J.W.* 5.466–490).

Disease and Medical Treatment

Ben Sira, during the early second century B.C., described the physician as a partner with Yahweh in the healing process. He was to be given "his place," because his skill came from God. The patient was to pray to God, but "there is a time when success lies in the hands of physicians, for they too pray to the Lord" to aid with the diagnosis (Sir 38:12–14). In contrast, the New Testament does not give such a positive endorsement of physicians or the practice of medicine (Luke 4:23 and 5:31 mention them proverbially), because of its emphasis on the healing character of God's Spirit. Luke is the most prominently mentioned physician (Col 4:14), but of course he is a Greek.

Jewish physicians might well have had the same training as Luke, but it is likely that most of their medical knowledge had Egyptian origin. The Egyptians were the most advanced physicians in the ancient Near East. They performed intricate surgeries including trepanning, boring through a skull to relieve the pressure of fluid built up after a concussion or as a result of a tumor, and the lancing of boils. Their medical treatises display a general knowledge of herbal medicines for the relief of certain ailments such as indigestion, constipation, and sleeplessness. Many times these cures, as Ben Sira notes (Sir 38:1–15), were also accompanied by sacrifices, prayers, and incantations to invoke God's aid.

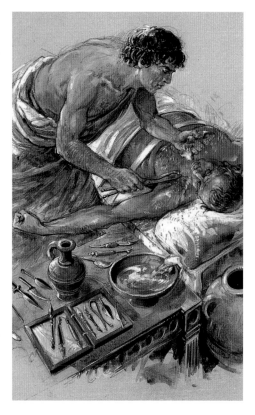

Artist's impression of a Roman surgeon.

There were patients that doctors could not heal. The primitive (by modern medical standards) instruments they used to diagnose and treat illness simply could not cope with many diseases. This is graphically illustrated in Mark 5:25–26 (paralleled in Luke 8:43–44), which tells of a woman who had suffered from a chronic form of hemorrhaging for twelve years and had spent all her savings on physicians, paying for useless cures. With hope and resources waning, she sought out Jesus, whose reputation as a healer had grown throughout the country. This sort of desperation to find a cure is of course still a part of the medical scene today, with people traveling great distances in hopes of a wonder drug or a miracle at the hands of a faith healer.

It had also been standard procedure since the earliest periods of Jewish history to consult

> *He said to him, "Doubtless you will quote to me this proverb, 'Doctor, cure yourself!' And you will say, 'Do here also in your hometown the things that we have heard you did at Capernaum.'"*
> —Luke 4:23

Remains of the pool of Bethesda, Jerusalem

priests (Lev 13:2–8) or prophets (1 Kgs 14:1–3; 2 Kgs 5:3), who would diagnose and cure disease. Although Jesus was not a priest, his stature as a prophet was accepted by many (Matt 16:13–14), and this attracted those looking for the traditional curative abilities of the man of God (Luke 9:37–40; Acts 5:16).

This seems to be especially the case in instances of demon possession. These individuals were afflicted with both physical (blindness, Matt 12:22; epilepsy, Luke 9:39) and severe mental disorders (Mark 5:2–5), and thus were beyond the abilities of normal medical practitioners. The dialogue Jesus has with the possessing spirits in Mark 5:7–10 provides recognition by these beings of his power, just as Jesus' explanation in Matt 12:25–32 differentiates his actions and his realm from that of Satan. There is no modern explanation for Jesus' casting out of demons. The mental distress these people manifested in the Gospels may have been purely psychological, or it may represent the Gospel writers' attempt to emphasize the messianic qualities of Jesus.

The other major source of cures, in areas lucky enough to have it, was water. For instance, hot springs, such as those near Tiberias, were pilgrimage sites for the ill and infirm. Herod is said to have sought a cure at the warm baths at Callirrhoe, near the Jordan River (*Ant.* 17.169–176). Similarly, a pool of water could become a place where the afflicted congregated and dipped themselves, hoping for a cure (see also Na'aman's cleansing in the Jordan River in 2 Kgs 5:10–14). Among the best known of these pools were those at Siloam, that Nehemiah had repaired after the return from exile (Neh 3:15; see p. 147), and at Bethesda (or Bethzatha), near the Sheep Gate in Jerusalem. In John 5:2–7, the latter was said to be surrounded by the sick and the crippled, who believed that the first to enter the water when its surface became troubled would be instantly cured. The movement of the water was probably due to the actions of an intermittent spring, but in antiquity this was attributed to the touch of an angel or other divine being.

Modern scholars have attempted to identify Bethesda through excavation as well as the use

> *Now there was a woman who had been suffering from hemorrhages for twelve years, She had endured much under many physicians, and had spent all that she had; and she was no better, but rather grew worse.*
> —Mark 5:25–26

The Pool of Siloam, outside Jerusalem.

of ancient literary sources. The Copper Scroll from the Qumran community mentions a pool at Bethesda (3Q15.xi.12), and Eusebius mentions two rain-fed pools frequented by the sick. Although the number of ancient churches and other structures built over this area prevent a full tracing of the cisterns in question, it seems likely that those uncovered just north of the temple are the pools of Bethesda.

Burial Customs

The poor and the stranger were buried in unmarked, shallow graves (Luke 11:44) or in a field (Matt 27:3–8). The remains of these burials have long since disappeared. Therefore, our knowledge of burial customs in the Hellenistic and Roman periods is primarily based on the tombs of the more affluent or those who belonged to associations that provided proper burial for their members. Most of these individuals were interred in caves (John 11:38) or rock-cut tombs located outside the city walls,

such as those in the Kidron Valley on the western slope of the Mount of Olives.

After death, the body was washed, its eyes were closed, and its mouth and other orifices were bound shut (John 11:44). A mixture of spices was applied to the body, perhaps as a preservative, or perhaps to ward off the smell of decomposition for those who visited the tomb later (John 11:39; 19:39–40). It was then dressed in its own clothes or placed in a linen shroud (Matt 27:59). Next, a procession, including musicians, family, and (if the family could afford it) professional mourners followed the corpse to the tomb (Eccl 12:5; Matt 9:23). It was customary for mourners to continue to visit the tomb for thirty days, to reanoint the body (Mark 16:1), or to check to be sure the person had not been buried prematurely (John 11:31).

Tombs varied in size and design, reflecting the wealth and influence of the family. The very elaborate tomb of Jason in Jerusalem, dated to the first century B.C., contains four outer chambers separated by stone doors, and a burial chamber with ten radiating loculi (individual interment chambers). There is also a communal charnel chamber, designed as a secondary burial repository for the bones of earlier burials that had been displaced by more recent ones (on primary and secondary burials, see p. 32). This single-family tomb was fronted by a porch area and decorated with a pyramid-shaped monument (*nefesh*), which was placed over the gated entrance to the forecourt. The elements of this tomb seem particularly elaborate compared to the description of Joseph of Arimathea's garden, rock-cut tomb, with its sealing stone, in which the body of Jesus was laid (John 19:41; Matt 27:59–60).

Some of the Herodian era and early first-century tombs, such as the recently discovered burial cave and ossuaries (on ossuaries, see pp. 32–33), apparently belonging to the family of the high priest Caiaphas, show the wealth expended in building a tomb. Most contain carved limestone ossuaries in which the bones of several people were placed. The practice of *ossilegium* ("bone-gathering") was employed to make room for new primary burials in the tomb, while retaining a place for secondary burials of the older remains. The conditions of some of the skeletal remains from this period also show the unrest and conflict of the times. Some clearly reveal sword cuts, and one case of death by crucifixion has been discovered in a tomb at Givat ha-Mivtar. In this instance, an iron nail was driven through one of the victim's heel bones and twisted as it struck a knot in the cross.

Among the most spectacular of the Herodian era tombs in the Kidron Valley are those attributed by tradition to Zechariah, dated to the period of the fall of the temple,

> *Then Jesus, again greatly disturbed, came to the tomb. It was a cave, and a stone was lying against it.*
> —John 11:38

and Absalom, dated to the period just before 70 A.D. They both include a *nefesh*, a pyramidal-shaped monument, considered a habitation for the soul of the deceased in Egyptian and other cultures, but simply as a memorial among the Jews (1 Macc 13:27–30). The outsides of these tombs may have been whitewashed to note a recent burial and thus warn Jews from contaminating contact with the dead (Matt 23:27).

"Absalom's Tomb" in the Kidron Valley.

"Zechariah's Tomb" in the Kidron Valley.

The "Tomb of the Herod Family," Jerusalem, with a rolling stone door.

ECONOMIC LIFE

Trade Routes and the Means of Travel

The international character of the Greek and Roman empires required reliable and well-kept travel routes. Since ancient times, regional travel had relied on the Via Maris, the King's Highway, and a system of roads that had expanded with the fortunes of the Israelite monarchy. With the coming of the Greeks and Romans, however, the network of roads throughout the Near East markedly expanded and improved. There were still dangers along these roads from robbers (Luke 10:30), but a real attempt was made by the Romans to keep them open. For instance, Pompey's swift rise to political power and notoriety in Rome came after he rid the Mediterranean Sea of pirates. With travel to distant places becoming more feasible for large numbers of people (Acts 13:13–14; 16:4; 18:2; see the destinations of letters in Revelation), a general upsurge in commercial activity took place. Along with this was an increase in cultural exchange, as eager merchants carrying goods, gossip, and religious beliefs traveled these improved trade routes.

Wherever the Greek, Roman, or Jewish merchant went, he took with him his goods as well as his culture. Thus, in every commercial center (Antioch, Corinth, Ephesus), ethnic communities were established. For the Jews this meant a synagogue with its governing body of elders, a school, and a network of families in whose houses travelers could stay without encountering the dangers of public inns or taverns. Thus, these communities of Jews provided the first stop for Paul and the other early Christian missionaries (Acts 13—14:1).

The means of overland travel included traditional pack animals, the donkey and camel, as well as two- and four-wheel carts. These latter vehicles, pulled by teams of oxen, were used to

Roman bridge at Tarsus.

> *There he found a Jew named Aquila, a native of Pontus, who had recently come from Italy with his wife Priscilla, because Claudius had ordered all Jews to leave Rome. Paul went to see them.*
> —Acts 18:2

The Persians introduced a system of way stations every ten to fifteen miles along roadways throughout their vast empire. Hellenistic and Roman rulers continued this practice to facilitate the needs of travelers as well as the imperial postal system. One way that archaeologists are able to identify ancient roads today is through the discovery of Roman mile markers that were set up by the rulers who ordered the roads to be built or repaired. These markers not only indicate the route but, based on

City gate and Roman road, Asia Minor.

transport grain to market from the farming villages and trade goods throughout the Near East. Wealthy travelers and government officials also used chariots. One example of this is found in Acts 8:26–29, where Philip meets the Ethiopian eunuch, who is riding in his chariot on the desert road between Gaza and Jerusalem.

Wheeled vehicles needed wider paths and broader, paved city gate complexes. In heavy traffic zones, more than one lane was required to facilitate movement and prevent disputes between teamsters. Because these vehicles and traveling officials needed well-kept roads (Prov 15:19), governments and perhaps even local authorities must have regularly sent work gangs along the more traveled routes to clear away stones and other obstructions (Isa 40:3–4; 62:10). Where a river had to be crossed, fords were identified, and in the Roman period, flat stones were laid in the riverbed to smooth the way for wagon wheels.

Roman milestone, Capernaum.

Embarking on a ship of Adramyttium that was about to set sail to the ports along the coast of Asia, we put to sea accompanied by Aristarchus, a Macedonian from Thessalonica.
—Acts 27:2

the name of the Roman emperor in the inscription, when it was constructed. Satellite photos have also provided remarkable images of the network of roads in antiquity, especially in the unpopulated areas of Saudi Arabia.

Travel by sea, although generally occurring only during certain seasons of the year, was also quite common (Acts 13:13; 15:39). Paul's journey, described in Acts 27, provides a great deal of information on the accommodation of prisoners and passengers on commercial

Artist's impression of a Roman
merchant ship

Paul's voyage to Rome

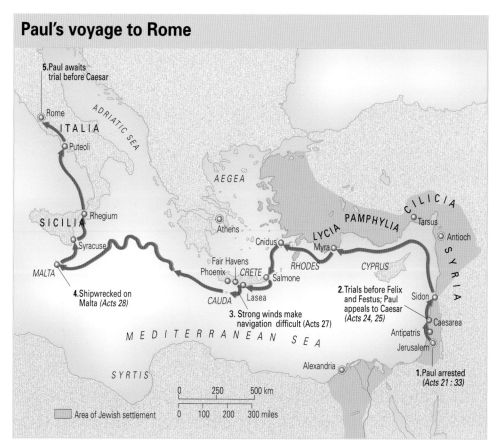

5. Paul awaits
trial before Caesar

Rome

ITALIA

ADRIATIC SEA

Puteoli

AEGEA

Rhegium

SICILIA

Athens

CILICIA

PAMPHYLIA   Tarsus

Syracuse

Cnidus

LYCIA

Myra

Antioch

MALTA

Fair Havens

RHODES

CYPRUS

SYRIA

4. Shipwrecked on
Malta *(Acts 28)*

Phoenix   *CRETE*

Salmone

CAUDA   Lasea

2. Trials before Felix
and Festus; Paul
appeals to Caesar
(Acts 24, 25)

Sidon

3. Strong winds make
navigation difficult (Acts 27)

Caesarea

MEDITERRANEAN SEA

Antipatris

Jerusalem

Alexandria

SYRTIS

1. Paul arrested
(Acts 21 : 33)

0	250	500 km

Area of Jewish settlement

0	100	200	300 miles

The very circuitous route of Paul's ship from Caesarea to Rome was typical of trading vessels. The war galleys of Rome, of course, took a more direct path and had rows of oars to supplement the sails. They were used to support and transport land troops and to carry messages quickly to farther corners of the empires. Paul, whose status as a prisoner did not warrant transport on a galley, had to rely on lesser and slower accommodations (Acts 28:11–13).

Weights and Measures

The commercial advantage of a standardized system of weights and measures was recognized very early in Israelite history. The standard **shekel,** a unit of measurement that weighed 11.4 grams and that originally was a weight used on one side of a scale to balance against portions of a product on the other side, became the primary measuring unit in Israel. The *shekel* was borrowed from the Canaanites, who had borrowed it from Mesopotamia. As trade expanded into Egyptian territory, adjustments were made to provide equivalencies to the Egyptian measurement system. Weights uncovered by archaeologists at eighth- and seventh-century B.C. Israelite sites show this development with Egyptian **hieroglyphics** (pictorial symbols) inscribed on metal balance weights.

Although somewhat cumbersome compared to modern western standards of weights and measures, the *shekel* weight, when used consistently, provided a reasonably sound system for commerce. Multiples or fractions of this weight, for example the *beka,* or half-shekel (Gen 24:22; Exod 38:26), allowed for transference of goods and commodities with a reasonable expectation that a *shekel's* weight in one area would be a *shekel's* weight in another.

Roman oil lamp, depicting a sailing vessel.

ships. Despite ending in shipwreck, their voyage is an excellent portrayal of the difficulties faced by an often-overloaded vessel, whose principal means of forward motion was its sails. Their first ship is described as being one that made calls at the ports of Asia, presumably transporting cargo and making deliveries along the way. At Myra, in Lycia, they transferred to an open sea vessel from Alexandria. During this leg of the voyage, mention is made of sailing leeward of islands to avoid contrary winds; baggage, tackle, and finally cargo (wheat) are thrown overboard to lighten the ship when it had to run before a storm. The cupidity of the ship's owner, captain, and crew are also displayed in their insistence on sailing in the stormy winter season (vv. 9–11), and their attempt to abandon ship during the storm, leaving the passengers to fend for themselves (v. 30).

> *A trader, in whose hands are false balances, he loves to oppress.*
> —Hos 12:7

Discrepancies did occur, of course, since some areas relied on a so-called "heavy" *shekel,* while others used a "light" or "royal standard" *shekel.* Corruption was also a problem, as numerous references to the use of "false balances" show (Hos 12:7; Amos 8:5).

By the New Testament period, units of weight are nearly all expressed in terms of their monetary value rather than their weight on a scale. The "ten thousand talents" owed by the debtor in Matt 18:24 would be equivalent to 60 million *denarii,* or 15 million *shekels.* This incredible sum is equal to nearly 450,000 pounds, or 204 metric tons, of silver. The Roman "pound" (*litra*) weighed approximately 326.4 grams, and when used to refer to ointments or perfumes, reflected both their expense and their actual weight (see John 12:3; 19:39).

Volume measures again varied because of the differences between the Jewish system and the overlapping Greek and Roman systems. According to the terminology of Ezek 45:13–14, it seems the basic unit of dry measure was the *homer,* which was variously equated with 32 to 40 gallons, or 120 to 150 liters. The *cor* was equal to the *homer,* and could be used for liquid measure as well. Its volume varied, with different sources describing it as equal to 60 gallons, or 220 liters. This unit was then broken down, with ten *baths* equal to one *cor.* The *bath,* equal to 6 gallons or 22 liters, was used to determine many smaller measures (1 Kgs 7:26). The *log,* measuring 1/3 quart or 0.3 liters, is the smallest unit mentioned (Lev 14:10). Examining storage jars found at Tell Beit Mirsim that are inscribed with the word *"bath"* helped to demonstrate the approximate nature of this system of measurement. They have the liquid capacity of about 5.5 gallons, or 21 liters.

Roman measures used in the New Testament period include the half-liter (*sextarius*), the liter (*choinix* in Rev 6:6), and the jar (*metrete*), which is the equivalent of 39 Roman liters or 10 gallons. This measure is not to be confused with the "stone jars" of water mentioned in John 2:6 holding "twenty or thirty gallons," which were permanent storage jars, not intended to be transported. The pound of costly ointment that Mary, the sister of Martha, used to anoint Jesus' feet probably weighed 326.4 grams (John 12:3). This was equal in value to the yearly wage of the average worker (John 12:5).

Measurements of distance in Israel were based on the *cubit* (18 inches/0.5 meter, or about the length of one's forearm), the span (about 9 inches/23 centimeters, or about the span of one's hand), and the handbreadth (about 3 inches/8 centimeters, or about the width of one's palm). These units, like all others in antiquity, varied from place to place and over time (see the larger cubit of Ezek 40:5 which equaled 20.6 inches). The Roman *cubit* was approximately 17 inches in length and was used to measure distance (John 21:8) and height (Rev 21:17). A mile (Matt 5:41) in Roman measure equaled about 1480 meters. In Near Eastern usage, the *stadion* (Luke 24:13;

> Now some of the heads of ancestral houses contributed to the work. The govenor gave to the treasury one thousand darics of gold, fifty basins, and five hundred thirty priestly robes.
> —Neh 7:70

Coin of Tiberias depicting the Hellenistic deity Hygeia.

Left: Coin of Pontius Pilate, A.D. 30. Right: Coin of Procurator Felix, A.D. 59.

John 6:19) consisted of 7.5 *stadia*, or 3,263 cubits, for each Roman mile. The fathom, mentioned in Acts 27:28 as a depth guide used by sailors, equaled 6 feet, or 2 meters.

Coins

Since the time of the Persians (6th cent. B.C.), the Near East had become reliant on a money economy (1 Chr 29:7 and Neh 7:70 mention the Persian *daric*). Minted coinage was introduced by the Lydians in the seventh century B.C., and became widespread by the time of Alexander the Great. Standardization of weights and the certification of coinage size and weight with the royal Persian and later Alexandrian seal speeded commerce and facilitated trade between regions.

The fact that the Jews were allowed to coin money during the Persian period (4th cent. B.C.) is attested by the discovery of a number of small silver coins bearing the inscription "Yehud" (Judah). For large transactions and donations to the temple, the *mina* (727 grams) and the *talent* (43,620 grams) continued to be used (Ezra 2:69; 8:26), but the smaller *shekel* weight (11.4 grams) was more common in the marketplace.

The Greek rulers of Palestine restricted the coining of money to their own mints. However, after the Maccabean revolt (as during the Jewish revolts of 70 and 135 A.D.), the Jews once again began minting their own bronze and lead coins to proclaim their independence and to supplement the silver and gold coinage of the Hellenistic kingdoms. Greek inscriptions on these Jewish coins mention the Hasmonean kings Alexander Jannaeus and Jonathan, and contain inscribed anchors and flowers.

Herod's mints in Tiberias and Jerusalem issued dated coins based on the Roman standard weights. Roman procurators used imperial coinage supplemented by locally minted coins, which bore nonreligious symbols to prevent problems with the scrupulously monotheistic Jews. The silver *denarius* from Antioch or Caesarea and the *didrachma* (equal to two *denarii*) of Tyre were commonly used to pay the annual temple tax. One of these was probably the coin mentioned in Mark 12:16, which is said to bear the likeness of Caesar.

By New Testament times, a remarkable variety of Greek, Roman, and foreign coins circulated in Palestine. This was due in part to the longevity of coins and in part to the

> "Show me a denarius. Whose head and whose title does it bear?" They said: "The emperor's."
> —Luke 20:24

introduction of the coins by Roman soldiers, who brought them to the area from all over the empire. Thus the thirty silver shekels given to Judas Iscariot (Matt 26:15; equal to 120 *denarii* or four months' wages) were most likely from Tyre or Antioch. Larger currency contained the image of the reigning emperor who had ordered it to be minted (Mark 12:16; Luke 20:24). These dated coins help archaeologists determine the chronology of levels within their excavations. When they are found embedded in particular levels, they can aid in the determination of when walls were built or floors were laid.

The range of common coinage sizes and types runs from the Greek copper *lepton,* worth half a penny, or 1/64 of a day's wage (the "widow's mite" in Mark 12:42; Matt 5:26), to the *shekel* weight Greek silver *stater* (Matt 17:27) and the Roman silver *denarius* (Matt 22:19). The *denarius* in Matt 20:9, however, was a smaller coin (worth about twenty cents), which apparently was the standard wage for day laborers. There was also a gold shekel worth fifteen silver *shekels,* or sixty days' labor. Larger weight currency included the *mina* (rendered in Luke 19:20 as *pound*), worth a little over three months' wages, and the *talent,* worth more than fifteen years' labor (Matt 25:15). The variations in the origin and value

> *And, because he was of the same trade, he stayed with them, and they worked together – by trade they were tentmakers.*
> —Acts 18:3

of these coins meant that many transactions had to be facilitated by a "money changer," who could be found in the temple precincts (Matt 21:12–13) or the city gate.

Because of the free use of many different currencies, moneychangers performed an essential service exchanging foreign coins for the silver *didrachma* of Tyre that was used to pay the temple tax. A fee of between four and eight percent was charged for this service. They also acted as bankers, paying interest on money left in their charge (Matt 25:27). These commercial transactions and the sale of sacrificial animals within the outer precincts of this holiest of places led the angered Jesus to cleanse the temple (Matt 21:12–13; Mark 11:15–17; Luke 19:45–46).

Urban Industry and Professions

Skilled and service industries dominated the work force in the cities of Palestine and the larger Greco-Roman world. Royal and administrative patrons spent great sums on public works projects, employing large numbers of masons and other workmen. For example, in

Inscription from Corinth with the name "Erastus," probably the city treasurer mentioned in Romans 16:23.

Model of Herod the Great's palace, Jerusalem.

Corinth a Latin inscription of the mid-first century A.D. states, "Erastus laid this pavement at his own expense, in appreciation of his appointment as aedile (an official of the city)." This may be the same man mentioned in Rom 16:23 as city treasurer of Corinth.

The idea of **patronage,** of leaving a permanent monument to one's own service to the people, and the honor to be gained from beautifying a city, motivated many such individual acts by the wealthy and powerful. The Herods were no exception. Herod the Great practically rebuilt Jerusalem, and he endowed temples and other buildings throughout Palestine and the Near East. His sons followed his example, as the monumental structures now emerging in excavations at Caesarea Philippi (Banias) attest. Josephus, taking note of this activity and the desire of the Herods to memorialize their rule, described Herod Agrippa as being:

By nature generous in his gifts, and made it a point of honor to be high-minded towards gentiles; and by expending massive sums he raised himself to high fame. He took pleasure in conferring favors and rejoiced in popularity. (Ant. 19.328)

The Herods did produce a remarkable number of beautiful public buildings. However, the large numbers of workmen attracted to these projects were eventually left without employment when the building boom ended. Their discontent and lack of hope contributed to the passions that exploded in the Jewish revolt of A.D. 70 While cottage industry was the pattern in the villages, in the cities large-scale finishing and manufacturing took place. Woolen thread, spun by village women, was woven into cloth on looms in the garment district of Jerusalem, near the Dung Gate (*J.W.* 5.331). Tailors were also available to cut and sew this cloth into finished garments (Matt 11:8), and fullers could dye or bleach them (Mark 9:3). Pottery, metal utensils, and weapons were all made and sold in the shops of Jerusalem.

221

Then Jesus said to his disciples, "There was a rich man who had a manager, and charges were brought to him that this man was squandering his property."
—Luke 16:1

Leather goods were produced as well, although the tanning process was conducted outside the walls because of the smells and resulting residue. Paul learned the trade of tent making and leather work as a young man in Tarsus, and continued to earn his living at this trade during his missionary journeys (1 Thess 2:9; 1 Cor 9:6). Working gave him recognized status, as well as the opportunity to associate with other urban craftsmen and thus make contacts wherever he went (Acts 18:3).

The grain brought in from the surrounding villages was baked into bread (*Ant.* 15.309–310), and butchers provided freshly-slaughtered meat for the city's inhabitants. The large number of olive trees growing in the vicinity of Jerusalem (Acts 1:12) provided enough oil that it could be exported. Spices and ointments to anoint the body were commonly available (Mark 14:3–5, 16:1), and may have either been refined or prepared in Jerusalem.

Village Economy

Rural life and economic activity were still based on the small family land holding. Jesus frequently drew from simple agricultural activity to make his point in telling parables (e.g., the sower in Matt 13:3–9). John the Baptist speaks of Jesus himself as a winnower in Luke 3:15. Produce from plots of land, often on terraced hillsides, fed the family, the village, and the nearby urban centers. A portion also went for taxes (*Ant.* 14.202–206), thereby impoverishing farmers in bad years. Some villages, like those on the Sea of Galilee around Capernaum, supplemented their income and their diet with fishing (Luke 5:2–11).

Due to economic hardship and political changes, a growing proportion of the better land came into the hands of absentee landlords. On several occasions they gained ownership through the patronage of the Herods (*Ant.* 15.2) or the Romans. They used tenant farmers (Mark 12:1) or day laborers to work the land (Matt 20:1), and employed stewards to manage the affairs of their estates (Luke 16:1). As a result, these landless peasants became discontented with their economic helplessness (Matt 20:1–16; Mark 12:2–9) and formed a portion of the rebel forces during the First Jewish Revolt in A.D. 69–70

Depending upon the size of the village, some goods would have been produced by local craftsmen. Tiny, insignificant Nazareth (John 1:46) was probably pleased to have the services of the carpenter Joseph and his son (Mark 6:3). They probably produced new baskets, chests, and furniture, and repaired old ones. In addition, they would have been responsible for transporting and installing ceiling beams in most of the village homes. Local potters undoubtedly worked in these villages as well, although the finer ware that was imported from Greece and Cappadocia would have been purchased in the cities.

RELIGIOUS LIFE

The rebuilt temple in Jerusalem (515 B.C.) provided Jews with a renewed focus for their religion. Although temple worship and religious life was not perfect (Isa 58:1–9), a symbol of unity was recreated that served communities of Jews throughout the Near East and beyond. Aside from sacrifice, the physical aspect of their devotion to the temple is seen in regular pilgrimages and in the payment of the annual temple tax by all adult males (Matt 17:24). With religious rites and instruction in the hands of the priests, and without a new monarchy, the power of the priesthood grew to

When they reached Capernaum, the collectors of the temple tax came to Peter and said, "Does your teacher not pay the temple tax?"
—Matt 17:24

new heights. However, an increasing number of Jewish sects also grew out of the discontent with the priestly monopoly over the temple and over theological disagreements.

Priests and Temple

Worship in the postexilic temple in Jerusalem was formalized, with the Zadokite priesthood in strict control. Their role during the Second Temple period was one of responsibility and regulation. They were responsible for reinitiating and maintaining the sacrificial cult and the religious calendar of festivals. They probably controlled orchestration of temple music and other lesser rites as well. Levites who returned from the exile, or who had remained in Judah during the Babylonian Captivity, were granted some responsibilities for the maintenance of the temple complex, but were not allowed to participate in sacrificial activities. In addition to performing their cultic duties, the priests also regulated certain aspects of life, such as marriage (Ezra 9–10) and the types of work activities that could be carried out on the Sabbath (Neh 13:15–22).

In the Second Temple period, it once again became customary to make pilgrimages to Jerusalem to attend the three major religious festivals: Passover, the Feast of Weeks, and the Feast of Tabernacles, or Booths. The temple treasury grew with the donations of these pilgrims and the annual temple tax, making it the wealthiest institution in the country. This wealth became an attractive target during the Seleucid period when Antiochus IV plundered the temple (1 Macc 1:20–23; 2 Macc 5:15–21). With so much cash coming into its coffers, the temple must have served as a bank, lending

Artist's impression of a high priest.

out sums to finance business and to stimulate the economy by increasing the amount of money in circulation.

The power and prestige of the temple and the priestly community eventually led to political involvement. The high priest Jason precipitated the Maccabean revolt of 167 B.C. with his introduction of Greek customs and acceptance of Antiochus IV's tribute demands (2 Macc

The Jews then said, "This temple has been under construction for forty-six years, and will you raise it up in three days?"
—John 2:20

Herod's Temple

Photograph of a carefully researched scale
model of the Temple as evidenced by Josephus'
account and other sources.

Right: Great staircase into the Temple: from the same scale model as the main photograph.

> *Thus was the first enclosure. In the midst of which, and not far from it, was the second, to be gone up to by a few steps; this was encompassed by a stone wall for a partition, with an inscription, which forbade any foreigner to go in, under pain of death.*
> —Josephus, Ant. 15.417

4:7–17). Following the revolt, the Hasmoneans gained control of both the office of high priest (1 Macc 14:17) and the secular leadership: "The Jews and their priests have resolved that Simeon should be their leader and high priest forever" (1 Macc 14:41–45). Their control of these offices continued until Herod obtained kingship from the Romans, and thereafter handpicked the high priest (*Ant.* 15.39–41).

Herod's attempt to control the priests and the people also included his construction of a newly-designed and expanded temple over the one built by Zerubbabel. Construction began in Herod's eighteenth year as king, and continued for forty-six years (John 2:20). Josephus, who saw this temple before its destruction, provides a detailed description of its structure and appearance (*Ant.* 15.380–425). A large area was cleared around the temple and a huge, walled platform (approximately 1,440 feet long and 960 feet wide) was constructed as a base for the temple and its adjoining buildings. Massive blocks of limestone enclosed the slope, and the Antonia Tower was founded on the northwest corner to house a Roman garrison and to serve as the residence of the Roman procurator when he was in Jerusalem. Gates were built in all four walls, with a huge staircase leading up to those on the south side.

The older shrine was preserved until the walls of the new building enclosed it. Priests, who had been trained as stone masons, then dismantled it. Although the new sanctuary was patterned after Solomon's temple, its Greco-Roman colonnades and the lavish use of gold-decorated roofs and columns displayed a

Above: Jews at the Western Wall Jerusalem, part of which survives from Herod's Temple.
Right: Model of Antonia Fortress, adjacent to Herod's Temple.

Hellenistic influence. The holy site had been preserved and fortified, but the new temple was as much a testament to Herod's power and wealth as it was to the people's devotion to Yahweh.

Despite Herod's political motives in rebuilding the temple, the Jews accepted the structure itself, and it is described as a central feature in the religious life of the people in the New Testament. Its precincts included several distinct enclosures leading inward to the Holy of Holies. Only priests could enter the inner areas, but ritually pure Jews and their wives could enter the outer temple, or porch. Women, however, were not allowed in the area immediately outside the temple proper where sacrifices were conducted on the altar.

Gentiles were restricted to the outermost part of the temple enclosure. An inscription was set into the wall near the gate leading inward which warned non-Jews, on pain of death, to proceed no further (*Ant.* 15.417). Excavators have discovered such an inscription dating to ca. 20 B.C., written in Greek. It was probably from Solomon's Porch (John 10:23), on the eastern side of this outer zone, that Jesus drove the moneychangers in Matt 21:12.

Jewish Religious Factions

While there were many religious and political factions in Palestine during the period from 200 B.C. until the first century A.D., the four "philosophies" singled out by Josephus as the most influential were the Sadducees, the Pharisees, the Essenes, and the **Zealots.** Drawing most of their support from the wealthy and influential families of the community, Sadducees sat on the Sanhedrin council and generally supported the policies of the Romans as a way of preventing conflict that could further ravage the nation (John 11:49–50). Although they were Hellenized in some of their manners of dress and custom, they rejected the use of anything other than the Pentateuch (Torah) in matters of law, and favored harsher punishments than the other factions (*Ant.* 13.293–295). The Sadducees also rejected the idea of a resurrection of the dead, saying that the soul died with the body and that humans had complete free will to determine their own fate during life (*Ant.* 18.16; Mark 12:18).

Originating as a distinct group during the Hasmonean period, the Pharisees also sat on the Sanhedrin, but they appear to have claimed a broader base of support among the people than the Sadducees. This may have been due to their advocacy for more lenient punishments for crimes (*Ant.* 13.294), their belief in a resurrection of the dead, and their belief in an eternal punishment of the wicked (*Ant.* 18.14–15; John 23:6–8). One indication that this latter idea was fairly widespread among the people may be Martha's statement to Jesus that Lazarus would "rise again in the resurrection on the last day" (John 11:24). Jesus also uses the theme of the resurrection of the dead in a statement dealing with the judgment of the righteous and the unrighteous in John 5:28–29.

The Pharisees also differed philosophically from the Sadducees in their acceptance of both free will and fate as factors influencing human lives (*Ant.* 18.13). Perhaps the most fundamental difference, however, between Pharisee and Sadducee lay in the former's equal acceptance of **oral tradition** and the Torah to interpret the law (*Ant.* 13. 297–298). Jesus seems to take a similar position in Matt 5:21–48, where he quotes several of the commandments from the Sinai code and then expands upon them. Apparently this establishes as legitimate his own oral tradition on the issues of law and personal behavior.

On the other hand, in Mark 7:8, Jesus tells the Pharisees, "You abandon the commandment of God and hold to human tradition." This seems to validate the Sadducean position regarding the sanctity of the Torah as the basis of interpretation of the law. His intent, however, was to point out the ways in which they had overburdened the original purpose of the law by demanding strict adherence to every aspect of ritual.

The Pharisees are generally portrayed as the opponents of Jesus in the New Testament, but Paul continues to identify himself as a Pharisee after his conversion (Acts 23:6). At times, Jesus highlights the positive character of the Pharisees' teachings and strict adherence to the law, and in Matt 23:3 he tells the

> But I say to you, Love your enemies and pray for those who persecute you, . . .
> —*Matt 5:44*

A cistern at Qumran.

disciples and the crowd to "do whatever they teach you and follow it." However, he then notes their hypocritical nature in not practicing what they themselves teach.

The Essenes are not mentioned by name in the New Testament, and thus our chief sources of information on them are Josephus and the scrolls produced by the Essene community at Qumran near the Dead Sea. Founded to protest the usurpation of the high priesthood by Jonathan Maccabaeus in 152 B.C., the Essenes separated themselves from the temple's sacrificial cult. Like the Pharisees, they also believed in the resurrection and in rewards for a righteous life. Some chose to found

Remains of the Qumran settlement buildings. Beyond are the cliffs where many of the Dead Sea Scrolls were discovered.

separate settlements, like the wilderness community at Qumran. According to the scrolls, the "Teacher of Righteousness" led them there so that they might live in the proper way, free from the contaminating influences of the less ritually-pure Jews. This group is said to have lived a strict and regimented life, sharing their wealth with the community and practicing celibacy. The cemetery, however, does attest to the presence of females and children as part of the community. Other groups of Essenes continued to live in cities like Jerusalem, where they engaged in their rituals of purification and performed private sacrifices (*Ant.* 18.18–22).

Josephus's "fourth philosophy," the Zealots, was founded in 6 A.D. by Judas of Galilee (Acts 5:37) in response to the imposition of a census by the Romans (*Ant.* 18:23–25). There were several other rebel groups in Palestine, variously known as Zealots or *sicarii* (*J.W.* 7.262–270), but they had no common agenda and can only be tied to Judas's ideas, not his leadership. It seems that the Zealots were closely affiliated with the Pharisees and their beliefs. However, they were more of an extremist group, violently demonstrating their opposition to Roman taxation and assuring the people that God would come to the aid of his faithful worshippers. Their fanaticism led them to violent acts against the Romans and to the formation of opposition Jewish groups. Eventually their conflict culminated in the ill-fated defense of Masada in A.D.74.

Sanhedrin

In addition to the priestly community and the various religious factions, there was another major religious body that influenced life in Jerusalem. This was the Sanhedrin, a council made up of seventy-one members and chaired by the high priest. This group is described in Mark 15:1 and Luke 19:47 as including "the chief priests, the scribes, and the leaders of the people." It was organized during the

Remains of the synagogue at Gamla, mentioned by Josephus, northern Galilee.

The partially reconstructed synagogue at Capernaum, built on the site of the synagogue where Jesus read the Scriptures.

Hasmonean period and included, at least during the New Testament period, both Sadducees and Pharisees (Acts 23:6). Its duties originally involved hearing criminal cases and imposing the death sentence (*Ant.* 14.167). After Herod became king, however, he killed all but one of its members for putting him on trial for murder, and presumably replaced them with men who could be controlled more easily (*Ant.* 14.175–176).

In the New Testament period, the Sanhedrin's jurisdiction appears to have extended only over religious matters. The members deliberated over what to do about Jesus in John 11:47 and questioned him before turning him over to Pilate for trial in Mark 14:53—15:1. Some within the Sanhedrin arrested Peter and John for preaching in the temple, and the whole council then questioned them, asking, "By what power or by what name did you do this?" (Acts 4:7). Their power to punish the evangelists was limited by popular opinion, since these men had performed con-firmed miraculous healings; thus, they simply warned them not to speak in Jesus' name (Acts 4:18). The Sanhedrin also found it difficult to speak with a united voice against the teachings of the Christians, since some on the council, the Pharisees, believed in the resurrection of the dead, while the Sadducean members did not (Acts 23:7–9; *Ant.* 18.14, 16).

Synagogue Worship and Leadership

During the time that the Jerusalem temple was still in existence, the synagogue served as a secondary place of worship in Palestine. It originated in the Diasporic communities of Egypt and Mesopotamia and spread into Palestine with the establishment of the Hasmonean

> *When he came to Nazareth, where he had been brought up, he went to the synagogue on the sabbath day, as was his custom. He stood up to read, . . .*
> —Luke 4:16

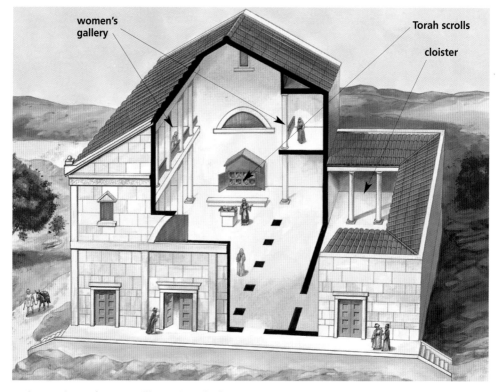

women's gallery

Torah scrolls

cloister

Artist's conjectural cutaway illustration of a first-century synagogue.

kingdom. During the New Testament period, a synagogue was apparently built in every Palestinian village and city of any size.

Jesus began his ministry in the Nazareth synagogue (Luke 4:16–21), and later used the Capernaum synagogue to open his activities in the Galilee region (Mark 1:21–28). Throughout the rest of the ancient world, wherever there was a community of Jews, the synagogue provided a meeting place as well as a seat for the study of Scriptures and for worship. Paul would have received his early Septuagint training in the synagogue in Tarsus before coming to Jerusalem for advanced Hebrew studies with the scholar Gamaliel (Acts 22:3). After his conversion, he first went to the synagogues of the Diaspora before taking his message to the Gentiles (Acts 18:1–6).

Sabbath worship in a synagogue varied from place to place, but generally included the recitation of the **shema'** (confession of faith, Deut 6:4–5), Scripture readings from the Law and the Prophets, prayer, thanksgiving, and individual exhortations (Acts 13:15). Some of the rites associated with temple worship were also transferred to the synagogue after 70 A.D., although not animal sacrifice. These places of worship were open to all people during services, and they did attract some pious Greeks interested in the moral teachings of the Jewish law (*J.W.* 7.45). Some converted to Judaism (Acts 13:43), or were among the group known as the God-fearers (Acts 13:16, 26, 43; 14:1). Many of these same people were later converted to Christianity by Paul and the other apostles (Acts 17:4).

Synagogue leadership was not in the hands of priests. Lay officials and a council of elders (Mark 5:22, *archisynagōgos*) directed synagogue worship, supervised maintenance of the

Extent of Christianity by 100 A.D.

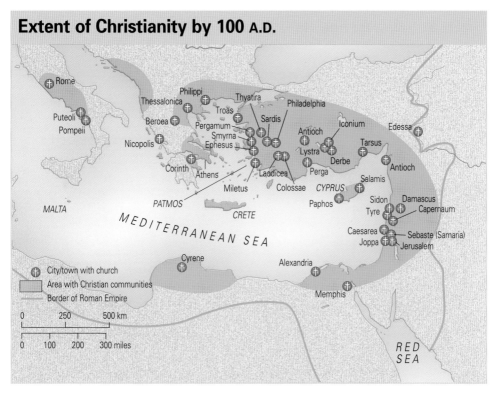

building, and enforced the rules of the congregation. Sometimes an attendant or deputy aided the head of the synagogue (Luke 4:20). It was their responsibility to discipline members who disobeyed some aspect of the law (Luke 13:14). Paul's statement that he had five times received thirty-nine lashes at the hands of the Jews probably refers to synagogue justice (2 Cor 11:24).

Presumably some early converts to Christianity maintained their membership in the local synagogue (Jas 2:2). Being Jews as well as Christians, they may have blended into the life of the congregation, or perhaps shared the building with the Jews. The antagonism of some Jews against Christian converts (Acts 13:45; 14:2; 17:5–9) suggests, however, that this

> *Hear, O Israel: The Lord is our God, the Lord alone.*
> —Deut 6:4

> *For as in one body we have many members, and not all the members have the same function, . . .*
> —Rom 12:4

sort of arrangement could not have lasted long, and Christians were probably forced to meet in private homes and their own churches (Rom 16:5; Acts 20:20).

These early Christian congregations worshipped according to the pattern set in Acts 2:42, "They devoted themselves to the apostles' teaching and fellowship, to the breaking of bread and the prayers." Various talents of the members were used in worship and in the governance of the community (Rom 12:3–8). The letter to Titus describes the qualities needed by elders and other leaders of the church, but all of the adult members were to serve diligently as good examples to each other and to the outside community.

Intertestamental and New Testament Review

1. Describe the characteristics of city planning and administration during the New Testament period.
2. How did Jews in the Greek and Roman period spend their leisure time?
3. What sorts of education did Jews receive? What was the role of scholarship during this period?
4. What did Jewish people wear in the Greek and Roman periods?
5. What tactics and weapons of warfare were unique in the intertestamental and New Testament period?
6. Describe the diseases, treatments, and burial practices of this period.
7. How did improved trade routes change the Jewish world of the New Testament?
8. Describe commerce and trade in the Greek and Roman periods.
9. What were the unique characteristics of the Pharisees' practice of Judaism? Of the Sadducees'? Of the Essenes'? Of the Zealots'?
10. What was the role of Herod's temple in New Testament times?
11. What was the role of synagogues during the intertestamental and New Testament period?

Glossary

Aelia Capitolina
Roman-style city built by the emperor
Hadrian in 130 A.D. on the site of the
destroyed Jerusalem to help prevent the
rise of Jewish nationalism

agora
marketplace

anachronism
element that fits into a different time
period than that of the narrative

Apocrypha
Deuterocanon; fifteen books authored as
late as the second century A.D.; additions
to the canon, conventionally closed with
the time of Ezra; dealt with events
surrounding the Maccabean revolt, or
provided traditional material related to
books already included in the canon, such
as the Additions to Esther and 1–2 Esdras

apotropaic rite
ritual to ward off evil

ashlar masonry
building practice that incorporated
dressed stones that were worked smooth
on all six sides in the Canaanite-
Phoenician style

Babylonian Talmud
so named for the location of the oral
commentary on the legal treatises of the
Torah (Pentateuch); collected and written
down over the mid-fourth through mid-
sixth centuries A.D.

bullae
hardened clay impressions made of the
emblem, symbols, or words of an official
seal

burnt offering
of animals; burnt whole to serve as an
atonement sacrifice

canon
officially accepted Scriptures

casemate wall
two parallel walls connected by short
perpendicular walls forming a series of
rooms, or casemates; sometimes filled
with rubble to strengthen the structure;
also used for storage, as back rooms for
houses built just inside the wall, or for
warehouses and shops

confederation
loosely-organized league of tribes;
provides social and political organization
at the tribal level, with village elders
settling local issues of law

Covenant Code
Exodus 21–23; law given at Sinai

covenant renewal ceremony
rite in which the epic history of the
people is recited and people are
instructed to stop religious practices
other than the worship of Yahweh and to
recommit to the sole worship of Yahweh

Dead Sea Scrolls
sacred books hidden by Essenes in
mountain caves near Qumran; discovered
in 1947; among the most important
modern tools for studying the biblical
text

Decalogue
Exodus 20:1–17; the Ten Commandments;
law given to the covenant community at
Sinai

Deuterocanon
Apocrypha; fifteen books authored as late
as the second century A.D.; additions to
the canon, conventionally closed with the
time of Ezra; dealt with events
surrounding the Maccabean revolt, or
provided traditional material related to
books already included in the canon, such
as the Additions to Esther and 1–2 Esdras

Deuteronomic Code
Deuteronomy 12–26; collected and
implemented during Josiah's late
seventh-century B.C. reforms; proposed
significant revisions of the laws found in
earlier codes

Diaspora
scattering of the Jews throughout
Mediterranean and European countries;
starting with the Assyrian deportation in
721 B.C., continuing with the Babylonian
deportation from Jerusalem in 587 B.C.,
and including the dispersal in later
periods under Greek and Roman rule

divination
practice of communicating with the dead,
often ancestors, or with the gods

dowry
money or its equivalent that is
contributed to a bride's personal wealth
by her family

early date
possible date of the exodus of Israel from
Egypt; suggested by the biblical account,
which places the exodus 300 years before
the period of the judges and 480 years
before the fourth year of Solomon;
around 1447 B.C. during the reign of
Pharaoh Amenhotep I

Early Iron Age
1200–1000 B.C.; also called Iron I

eleph
designation for a military unit; often
translated as "thousand"

Elohim
name for Israel's deity

endogamy
marriage within the kinship or social
group

ephod
garment worn by Israelite priests; term
also designates a garment used to adorn
idols in Canaanite worship

Essenes
group founded to protest the usurpation
of the high priesthood by Jonathan
Maccabaeus (152 B.C.); separated from the
temple's sacrificial cult; believed in the
resurrection and in rewards for a
righteous life; resided in separate
settlements in order to be free from
contamination by less ritually pure Jews,
to live strict and regimented lives, to
share wealth with the community, and to
practice celibacy; or resided in cities
where they practiced rituals of
purification and performed private
sacrifices

exogamy
marriage outside the kinship or social
group

Fertile Crescent
region that begins on the eastern shore of
the Mediterranean Sea and curves like an
inverted quarter moon ending at the
Persian Gulf; includes the major river
valley cultures of Egypt and
Mesopotamia; developed high
civilizations around 3000 B.C.

first fruits
offering of a portion of the first gleanings
from a harvest; brought to the priest, who
would ceremonially raise it to God on the
first day after the Sabbath

freewill offering
of animals or cereal; sometimes called
"thank offering"; only a portion burned
on the altar; the remainder eaten by the
one making the offering or contributed to
the priest(s) performing the sacrifice

glacis
fortification of clay and stone slope built
up against the face of the wall and
sometimes plastered over to present a
smoother, less scalable surface

Hapiru
also 'Apiru or Habiru; tribes mentioned in
Egyptian texts (from 2000 to 1200 B.C.);
generic term for stateless people or tribal
groups who lived on the fringes of the
settled areas of the ancient Near East;
sometimes served as surplus labor or
mercenaries; linguistically not directly
connected to the term "Hebrew"

Hasmonean
Maccabean leaders; claimed civil and
religious authority

Hasmonean kingdom
Maccabee kingdom; independent Jewish state (165–63 B.C.); succumbed to the ambitions of its rulers and was absorbed into the Roman domain

headers
uniform stones placed lengthwise along the width of a wall; alternated with stretchers

Hellenistic
Greek influence on Near Eastern cultures

Hellenizers
Jews who supported the importation of Greek culture

henotheism
recognizing a supreme god as well as a number of lesser divinities

hieroglyphics
pictorial symbols of Egyptian or Hittite script

Holiness Code
Leviticus 17–26; compilation and reworking of the priestly material; interprets priestly legislation for those living in exile

Holy of Holies
innermost room of the tabernacle and temple; housed the ark of the covenant

Hyksos
eighteenth-century B.C. raiders that invaded Egypt and set themselves up as pharaohs at Avaris

Iron I
1200–1000 B.C.; also called Early Iron Age

Jamnia
Yavneh; scholarly and commercial community that served as a center of revived Judaism after the Bar Kochba Revolt in 135 A.D.; traditional site of a group of rabbis who deliberated from 75 to A.D. 135, compiling manuscripts and exhaustively debating to determine which books should be included in the canon of Scripture

Josephus
Jewish historian of the first century A.D.

Late Bronze Age
1550–1200 B.C.; historical period which spanned Israel's exodus and settlement

late date
possible date of the exodus of Israel from Egypt; suggested by evidence of the use of forced labor to construct the Egyptian storehouse cities during the rule of Seti I and Rameses II (ca. 1300–1250 B.C.), and by thirteenth-century layers of destruction found in some Canaanite sites, which may be attributed to the conquests in Joshua and Judges

Levant
geographical term describing the lands that border the Mediterranean Sea from modern Turkey to Egypt

levirate marriage
obligation of a brother or closest male kin to marry, or at least impregnate, the widow of a man who died without an heir;

male child born of this union becomes the legal heir of the dead man

Maccabean revolt
so called after the war name of Judas "the hammer," one of the family of leaders in the revolt; concerned with temple purity, the practice of Judaism, and an independent Jewish state; 167–164 B.C.

Masoretes
group of scholars who, after A.D. 500, formalized the text of the Hebrew Bible that had been nearly set by the end of the first century A.D.

material culture
archaeological discoveries that reflect a people's beliefs and practices

Mesha Inscription
thirty-five-line tribute praising the Moabite god Chemosh for delivering his nation from its neighbor Israel; parallels 2 Kgs 3

Middle Bronze Age
2200–1500 B.C.; historical period characterized by political and social upheaval throughout the ancient Near East

Midrash
"commentary"; covers non-legal material, including legendary narratives of the lives of the major biblical figures in the Hebrew canon; also contained in the Talmud.

Mishnah
second-century A.D. Jewish compilation of sixty-three tractates or treatises of written commentaries on the Torah (Pentateuch); known as the "Oral Torah"; consensus of rabbinic opinion on how the laws of the Pentateuch related to aspects of everyday life in their time such as agriculture, marriage, and ritual purity

Mithraism
mystery religion of the first century B.C. to the third century A.D.; adopted by Roman legionnaires and spread by soldiers, merchants, and traveling philosophers

narratives
stories (v. prophecy, Wisdom literature, letters, etc.) in the biblical text

offset-inset construction
sometimes called "redans"; intentionally incorporated alternating protrusions and indentations in the construction of a wall, making it difficult for attackers to use battering rams and scaling ladders, and providing defenders more protection, a better view, and a broader field of fire from the battlements

oral tradition
passed from one generation to the next by word of mouth rather than in writing; accepted by the Pharisees as equal to the Torah for the interpretation of the law

ostraca
plural of ostracon; inscribed potsherds

ossuary
jar for the storage of bones; used in secondary burial

Palestinian Talmud
Jerusalem Talmud; oral commentary on the legal treatises of the Torah (Pentateuch); collected and written down over the mid-fourth through mid-sixth centuries A.D.; so named for the location of the copy

pastoral nomadism
in the ancestral narratives; a combination of fixed agriculture and herding practices

patronage
individual acts, usually involving the construction or repair of a building, city, or monument, by the wealthy and powerful for the purpose leaving a permanent memorial to their own service to the people

Pentateuch
Torah; Law; first five books of the Bible

Pharisees
200 B.C. to A.D 100. group that advocated the free use of the interpretive material such as the oral tradition and the Mishnah as the equal of the canonical works; sat on the Sanhedrin council; accepted the idea of a resurrection of the dead, and free will and fate as factors influencing human lives

Philo of Alexandria
Jewish writer who mixed the study of Greek literature with the study of Hebrew Scriptures during the first century A.D.

phylactery
tephillim; black leather box, containing four passages of Scripture; attached to the forehead and the left arm by leather straps; based on injunctions in Exod 13:9 and Deut 6:8 to keep the law constantly in the mind and heart; worn by devout men in the time of Jesus

pillared house
four-room house; style of house common during the biblical period; two-story dwelling with a ground floor made up of a long central room with a ceiling two stories high, surrounded by partitioned rooms on three sides

polis
political community of the Greek city-state; primary vehicle for the transmission of Greek culture to the rest of the ancient world

primary burial
deceased entombed permanently in one place

prophetic sign act
symbolizing the words of a prophecy by acting it out

Pseudepigrapha
sixty-five books dating to the Hellenistic and Roman periods; denied a place in the canon due to its contents of fictional commentary and theological ideas not acceptable to the Jewish community; includes Testaments of the Twelve Patriarchs, 1 Enoch, Jubilees, and Testament of Job

Ptolemies
Macedonian dynasty founded by Ptolemy, a general under Alexander the Great; ruled in Egypt, Syria, and Palestine from the fourth to first century B.C.; lost control over Palestine and Jerusalem in 200 B.C. when the Seleucid king Antiochus III won the battle of Panias in northern Galilee

Qumran
desert settlement of Essenes

rabbi
"teacher"; authority on the law and its interpretation
Rabbinic Judaism
Diaspora Judaism after the destruction and expulsion of the Jews from Jerusalem; emphasized synagogues as focal points for worship and the study of both the Hebrew canon of Scripture and Jewish commentaries on Scripture
relief
large, two-dimensional stone carvings; part of the archaeological record

Sadducees
200 B.C. to A.D. 100 group that argued for strict and exclusive use of the canonical books of the Torah to answer religious questions; rejected the idea of a resurrection of the dead; sat on the Sanhedrin council; drew most support from wealthy and influential families; generally supported the policies of the Romans as a way of preventing violent conflict
Sanhedrin
council of seventy-one chief priests, scribes, and leaders of the people; chaired by the high priest; organized during the Hasmonean period; duties originally involved hearing criminal cases; eventual jurisdiction only over religious matters; included Sadducees and Pharisees
satrap
provincial governor in the Persian Empire
secondary burial
corpse placed in a tomb until the flesh decomposes and the bones are gathered to the side or rear of the cave or placed in a bone jar to create space for the bodies of those who die in following generations
Seleucids
Macedonian dynasty founded by Seleucus, a general under Alexander the Great; ruled in Asia and Asia Minor from the fourth to first century B.C.; gained control over Palestine and Jerusalem in 200 B.C. when the Seleucid king Antiochus III won

the battle of Panias in northern Galilee
semi-nomadic pastoralism
almost constant herding activity, marked by periodic change of pastures
Septuagint
LXX; first translation of the Hebrew text of the Bible; Greek version of the Old Testament books; completed in Alexandria, Egypt some time after 200 B.C.; incorporated the fifteen Deuterocanonical books of the Apocrypha; used by most of the New Testament writers
Shasu
described in Egyptian records as tribes of lawless nomadic herders and sedentary farmers known to be rebellious and quarrelsome; inhabited land from the eastern Delta region to Gaza between 1500 and 1150 B.C.
shekel
unit of measurement that weighed 11.4 grams; originally a weight used on one side of a scale to balance against portions of a product on the other side; primary measuring unit in Israel
shema'
Deuteronomy 6:4–5; confession of faith
Sheol
deep and shadowy abode described in the biblical text as inhabited by the dead, both the good and the evil; not a place of punishment, but cut off from "the living God"; closely connected to the grave
Shephelah
"lowland"; hilly region east of the plain and the Mediterranean Sea; occupied by the Philistines
sicarii
hired assassins; so named for the short, curved sword they carried
stratum
level or layer of an archaeological dig, representing a unique phase in the life history of an ancient city
stretchers
uniform stones placed crosswise along the length of a wall; alternated with headers
synagogue
"gathering"; non-sacrificial worship developed during the Babylonian exile as a response to the loss of the temple in Jerusalem; involved recitation of the *shema'*, Scripture readings from the Law and the Prophets, prayer, thanksgiving, and individual exhortations; open to all people, including Gentiles
syncretism
mixing of religious and other cultural practices
Syria Palestina
"land of the Philistines"; the new name given to the province of Judea by the

Roman emperor Hadrian after the final Jewish revolt and the fall of Jerusalem

tabernacle
tent of meeting; Israel's place of worship during the desert wanderings
Tel Dan Inscription
inscription created around the time of the demise of Aram and the rise of Israel (ca. 800 B.C.); references the "House of David"
tell
mound created by successive layers of occupation as cities were rebuilt on top of previously-destroyed buildings
tent of meeting
tabernacle; Israel's place of worship during the desert wanderings
teraphim
household sacred images to be passed from a father to his heir along with paternal authority as head of the family
Tetragrammaton
"four-letter name"; YHWH or Yahweh; name for Israel's deity
theophany
a physical manifestation of God's person
Torah
Law; Pentateuch; first five books of the Bible
transhumance
herding by select members of a family on pastures both near and far from their settlement, while the majority of the population is occupied primarily with agriculture

Yahwist
J (for the German spelling of Yahweh); tenth- or ninth-century B.C. compilation of the biblical text; found primarily in Genesis; so named because of its almost exclusive use of the term "Yahweh" when speaking of Israel's deity
Yehud
Judea; Persian province established by the exiles returning to Jerusalem and distinguished from the province of Samaria
YHWH
Yahweh; four letters representing Israel's deity

Zealots
religious and political faction founded in A.D. 6 by Judas of Galilee in response to the imposition of a Roman census; closely affiliated with the Pharisees and their beliefs, but more extremist in violent opposition to Roman taxation; conflict culminated in the ill-fated defense of Masada in A.D. 74.

Select Bibliography

Introduction

Aharoni, Y. *The Land of the Bible.* Philadelphia: Westminster, 1967.

_____, and M. Avi-Yonah. *The Macmillan Bible Atlas,* 3d ed. New York: Macmillan, 1993.

Beitzel, B. *Moody Atlas of Bible Lands.* Chicago: Moody Press, 1985.

Brandon, S. R. "Archaeology and the Biblical Text." *Biblical Archaeology Review* 14, no. 1 (1988): 54–59.

Brisco, T. C., and V. Brisco. *Holman Bible Atlas: A Complete Guide to the Expansive Geography of Biblical History.* Nashville: Broadman & Holman, 1999.

Brodsky, H. "The Shephelah-Guardian of Judea." *Bible Review* 3, no. 4 (1987): 48–52.

Cohen, Shaye J. D. *The Beginnings of Jewishness.* Berkeley: University of California Press, 1999.

Currid, J. D. *Doing Archaeology in the Land of the Bible: A Basic Guide.* Grand Rapids: Baker, 1999.

Dever, W. G. *Recent Archaeological Discoveries and Biblical Research.* Seattle: University of Washington Press, 1990.

DeVries, L. F. *Cities of the Biblical World.* Peabody, Mass.: Hendrickson, 1997.

Dorsey, D. A. *The Roads and Highways of Ancient Israel.* Baltimore: Johns Hopkins University Press, 1991.

Hayes, J. H., and J. M. Miller, eds. *A History of Ancient Israel and Judah.* Philadelphia: Westminster, 1986.

_____. *Israelite and Judean History.* Philadelphia: Westminster, 1977.

Kenyon, K. M. *Archaeology in the Holy Land.* New York: Praeger, 1960.

King, P. J. "The Contribution of Archaeology to Biblical Studies." *Catholic Biblical Quarterly* 45 (1983): 1–16.

Knapp, A. B. *The History and Culture of Ancient Western Asia and Egypt.* Chicago: Dorsey, 1988.

Levy, T. E. "From Camels to Computers: A Short History of Archaeological Method." *Biblical Archaeology Review* 21, no. 4 (1995): 44–51, 64–65.

Matthews, V. H. *A Brief History of Ancient Israel.* Louisville: Westminster John Knox, 2002.

_____. *Old Testament Themes.* St. Louis: Chalice Press, 2000.

May, H. G., ed. *Oxford Bible Atlas.* 3d ed. New York: Oxford University Press, 1985.

Mazar, A. *Archaeology of the Land of the Bible 10,000–586 b.c.* New York: Doubleday, 1990.

Meyers, E. M., ed. *The Oxford Encyclopedia of Archaeology in the Near East.* 5 vols. New York: Oxford University Press, 1997.

Miller, J. M. "Approaches to the Bible through History and Archaeology: Biblical History As a Discipline." *Biblical Archaeologist* 45 (1982): 211–16.

_____. "Old Testament History and Archaeology." *Biblical Archaeologist* 50 (1987): 55–63.

Pritchard, J. B. *The HarperCollins Concise Atlas of the Bible.* San Francisco: HarperSanFrancisco, 1997.

Rasmussen, C. G. *Zondervan NIV Atlas of the Bible.* Grand Rapids: Zondervan, 1989.

Rast, W. E. *Through the Ages in Palestinian Archaeology.* Philadelphia: Trinity Press International, 1992.

Rehm, M. D. "Levites and Priests." Pages 297–310 in vol. 4 of *Anchor Bible Dictionary.* Edited by David Noel Freedman. 6 vols. New York: Doubleday, 1992.

Rogerson, J. W. *Anthropology and the Old Testament.* Sheffield: JSOT Press, 1984.

Sauer, J. A. "Syro-Palestinian Archaeology, History, and Biblical Studies." *Biblical Archaeologist* 45 (1982): 201–9.

Snell, D. C. *Life in the Ancient Near East.* New Haven: Yale University Press, 1997.

Whitelam, K. M. "Recreating the History of Israel." *Journal for the Study of the Old Testament* 3 (1986): 45–70.

Wright, G. E. *Biblical Archaeology.* 2d ed. Philadelphia: Westminster, 1962.

1. Ancestral Period

Ben-Barak, Zafrira. "Inheritance by Daughters in the Ancient Near East." *Journal of Semitic Studies* 25 (1980): 22–33.

Clifford, Richard J. *The Cosmic Mountain in Canaan and the Old Testament.* Harvard Semitic Monographs 4. Cambridge: Harvard University Press, 1972.

Frymer-Kensky, T. "Patriarchal Family Relationship and Near Eastern Law." *Biblical Archaeologist* 44 (1981): 209–14.

Hall, Robert G. "Circumcision." Pages 1025–1031 in vol. 1 of *Anchor Bible Dictionary.* Edited by David Noel Freedman. 6 vols. New York: Doubleday, 1993.

Hallo, W. W. "The Oldest Cookbooks in the World." *Bible Review* 9, no. 4 (1993): 26–31, 56.

Hendel, Roland S. *The Epic of the Patriarch: The Jacob Cycle and the Narrative Traditions of Canaan and Israel.* Decatur, Ga.: Scholars Press, 1987.

King, Philip J. and Lawrence E. Stager. *Life in Biblical Israel.* Louisville: Westminster John Knox, 2001.

Levenson, Jon D. *Sinai and Zion: An Entry in the Jewish Bible.* San Francisco: HarperSanFrancisco, 1985.

_____. *The Death and Resurrection of the Beloved Son: The Transformation of Child Sacrifice in Judaism and Christianity.* New Haven: Yale University Press, 1993.

Luke, J. T. "Abraham and the Iron Age: Reflections on the New Patriarchal Studies." *Journal for the Study of the Old Testament* 4 (1977): 35–47.

Matthews, Victor H. "Nomadism, Pastoralism." Pages 971–72 in *Eerdmans Dictionary of the Bible.* Edited by David Noel Freedman. Grand Rapids: Eerdmans, 2000.

_____. *Pastoral Nomadism in the Mari Kingdom, ca. 1830–1760 B.C.* Cambridge, Mass.: American Schools of Oriental Research, 1978.

_____. "Pastoralists and Patriarchs." *Biblical Archaeologist* 44 (1981): 215–18.

_____. "The Wells of Gerar." *Biblical Archaeologist* 49 (1986): 118–26.

_____, and J. C. Moyer. *The Old Testament: Text and Context.* 2d ed. Peabody, Mass.: Hendrickson, 2005.

_____, and D. C. Benjamin. *Old Testament Parallels: Laws and Stories from the Ancient Near East,* 3d ed. Mahwah, N.J.: Paulist, 2006.

McKane, W. *Studies in the Patriarchal Narrative.* Edinburgh: Handsel, 1979.

Millard, A., and D. J. Wiseman, eds. *Essays on the Patriarchal Narratives.* Leicester: InterVarsity, 1980.

Morrison, M. "The Jacob and Laban Narrative in the Light of Near Eastern Sources." *Biblical Archaeologist* 46 (1983): 155–64.

Oden, Robert A. "Jacob As Father, Husband, and Nephew: Kinship Studies and the Patriarchal Narratives." *Journal of Biblical Literature* 102, no. 2 (June 1983): 189–205.

Perdue, L. G., et al., eds. *Families in Ancient Israel.* Louisville: Westminster John Knox, 1997.

Rowton, M. C. "Autonomy and Nomadism in Western Asia." *Orientalia* 42 (1973): 247–58.

_____. "Dimorphic Structure and the Parasocial Element." *Journal of Near Eastern Studies* 36 (1977): 181–98.

Rubens, A. *A History of Jewish Costume.* New York: Funk & Wagnalls, 1967.

Sarna, N. M. *Understanding Genesis.* New York: Shocken, 1966.

Thompson, T. L. *The Historicity of the Patriarchal Narratives.* Berlin: de Gruyter, 1974.

_____. "A New Attempt to Date the Patriarchal Narratives." *Journal of the American Oriental Society* 98 (1978): 76–84.

Van Seters, J. *Abraham in History and Tradition.* New Haven: Yale University Press, 1975.

Vaux, R. de. *Ancient Israel: Social Institutions.* 2 vols. New York: McGraw-Hill, 1965.

Warner, S. M. "The Patriarchs and Extra-Biblical Sources." *Journal for the Study of the Old Testament* 2 (1977): 50–61.

Westermann, C. *The Promises to the Fathers: Studies on the Patriarchal Narratives.* Philadelphia: Fortress, 1980.

Yadin, Y. *The Art of Warfare in Biblical Lands in the Light of Archaeological Discoveries.* London: Weidenfeld and Nicolson, 1963.

Yamauchi, Edwin M. "Cultural Aspects of Marriage in the Ancient World." *Bibliotheca Sacra* 135 (1978): 241–52.

2. Exodus–Settlement Period

Avalos, H. "Ancient Medicine: In Case of Emergency, Contact Your Local Prophet." *Bible Review* 11, no. 3 (1995): 27–35, 48.

Beebe, H. K. "Ancient Palestinian Dwellings." *Biblical Archaeologist* 34 (1971): 38–58.

Benjamin, D. C. "Israel's God: Mother and Midwife." *Biblical Theology Bulletin* 19 (1989): 115–20.

Ben-Tor, A. "Tell Qiri: A Look at Village Life." *Biblical Archaeologist* 42 (1979): 105–13.

Biggs, R. D. "Medicine, Surgery, and Public Health in Ancient Mesopotamia." Pages 1911–24 in vol. 3 of *Civilizations of the Ancient Near East.* Edited by Jack M. Sasson. 4 vols. New York: Charles Scribner's Sons, 1995.

Bimson, J. J., and D. Livingston. "Redating the Exodus." *Biblical Archaeology Review* 13, no. 5 (1987): 40–53, 66–68.

Callaway, J. A. "A Visit with Ahilud." *Biblical Archaeology Review* 9, no. 5 (1983): 42–53.

Coote, R. B., and K. W. Whitelam. "The Emergence of Israel: Social Transformation and State Formation Following the Decline in Late Bronze Age Trade." *Semeia* 37 (1986): 107–47.

Davey, C. "The Dwellings of Private Citizens." *Buried History* 13 (1977): 21–37.

Dever, W. G. "Ceramics, Ethnicity, and the Question of Israel's Origin." *Biblical Archaeologist* 58 (1995): 200–213.

_____. *What Did the Biblical Writers Know and When Did They Know It? What Archaeology Can Tell Us about the Reality of Ancient Israel.* Grand Rapids: Eerdmans, 2001.

Farber, G. "Another Old Babylonian Childbirth Incantation." *Journal of Near Eastern Studies* 43 (1984): 311–16.

Finkelstein, I. *The Archaeology of the Settlement of Israel.* Jerusalem: Israel Exploration Society, 1988.

_____. "Ethnicity and Origin of the Iron I Settlers in the Highlands of Canaan: Can the Real Israel Stand Up?" *Biblical Archaeologist* 59 (1996): 198–212.

Fritz, V. "Conquest or Settlement? The Early Iron Age in Palestine." *Biblical Archaeologist* 50 (1987): 84–100.

Gens, C. H. L. de. *The Tribes of Israel.* Assen/Amsterdam: VanGorcum, 1976.

Gottwald, N. K. *The Tribes of Yahweh: A Sociology of the Religion of Liberated Israel 1250–1050 B.C.* Maryknoll, N.Y.: Orbis, 1979.

Halpern, B. "Radical Exodus Redating Fatally Flawed." *Biblical Archaeology Review* 13, no. 6 (1987): 56–61.

Hepper, F. N. *Baker Encyclopedia of Bible Plants.* Grand Rapids: Baker, 1992.

Hoerth, Alred J. *Archaeology and the Old Testament.* Grand Rapids: Baker, 1998.

Holladay, John S., Jr. "House, Israelite." Pages 308–18 in vol. 3 of *Anchor Bible Dictionary.* Edited by David Noel Freedman. 6 vols. New York: Doubleday, 1993.

Hoffmeier, J. K. *Israel in Egypt.* New York: Oxford University Press, 1997.

Hopkins, D. S. *The Highlands of Canaan.* Decatur, Ga.: Almond, 1985.

_____. "Life on the Land: The Subsistence of Struggles of Early Israel." *Biblical Archaeologist* 50 (1987): 178–91.

Houwink ten Cate, Philo H. J. "Hittite, History." Pages 219–25 in vol. 3 of *Anchor Bible Dictionary.* Edited by David Noel Freedman. 6 vols. New York: Doubleday, 1993.

King, P. J. and L. E. Stager. *Life in Biblical Israel.* Louisville: Westminster John Knox, 2001.

Lang, B. "Afterlife: Ancient Israel's Changing Vision of the World Beyond." *Bible Review* 4, no. 1 (1988): 12–23.

Lemche, N. P. *Ancient Israel: A New History of Israelite Society.* Sheffield: JSOT Press, 1988.

Lewis, T. J. *Cults of the Dead in Ancient Israel and Ugarit.* Atlanta: Scholars Press, 1989.

Malamat, A. "Let My People Go and Go and Go and Go." *Biblical Archaeology Review* 24, no. 1 (1998): 62–66, 85.

Matthews, V. H., and D. C. Benjamin. *Social World of Ancient Israel, 1250–587 B.C.* Peabody, Mass.: Hendrickson, 1993.

McNutt, P. *Reconstructing the Society of Ancient Israel.* Louisville: Westminster John Knox, 1999.

Mendenhall, G. E. "The Relation of the Individual to Political Society in Ancient Israel." Pages 89–108 in *Biblical Studies in Memory of H. C. Alleman.* Edited by J. M. Myers, et al. Locust Valley, N.Y.: Augustin, 1960.

Meyers, C. *Discovering Eve: Ancient Israelite Women in Context.* New York: Oxford University Press, 1988.

_____. "Of Drums and Damsels: Women's Performance in Ancient Israel." *Biblical Archaeologist* 54 (1991): 16–27.

Millard, A. "How Reliable Is Exodus?" *Biblical Archaeology Review* 26, no. 4 (2000): 50–57.

Miller, J. M. "The Israelite Occupation of Canaan." Pages 213–84 in *Israelite and Judean History.* Edited by J. H. Hayes and J. M. Miller. Philadelphia: Westminster, 1977.

Muhly, J. D. "How Iron Technology Changed the Ancient World and Gave the Philistines a Military Edge." *Biblical Archaeology Review* 8, no. 6 (1982): 40–54.

Parrot, A. and G. Dossin. *Archives royales de Mari.* Paris: Impr. Nationale, 1950–.

Reviv, H. *The Elders in Ancient Israel.* Jerusalem: Magnes, 1989.

Silberman, N. A. "Who Were the Israelites?" *Archaeology* 45 (1992): 22–30.

Stager, L. E. "The Archaeology of the Family in Ancient Israel." *Bulletin of the American Schools of Oriental Research* 260 (1985): 1–35.

Thompson, J. A. "Farming in Ancient Israel." *Buried History* 20 (1984): 53–60.

_____. "The Israelite Village." *Buried History* 19 (1983): 51–58.

Ussishkin, D. "Lachish: Key to the Israelite Conquest of Canaan?" *Biblical Archaeology Review* 13, no. 1 (1987): 18–39.

Vaux, R. de. *Ancient Israel: Social Institutions.* Vol. 1. New York: McGraw-Hill, 1965: 19–61.

Willis, T. M. *The Elders of the City: A Study of the Elders-Laws in Deuteronomy.* Atlanta: Society of Biblical Literature, 2001.

Wright, Christopher J. H. *God's People in God's Land: Family, Land, and Property in the Old Testament.* Grand Rapids: Eerdmans, 1990.

Xella, Paolo. "Death and the Afterlife in Canaanite and Hebrew Thought." Pages 2059–70 in vol. 3 of *Civilizations of the Ancient Near East.* Edited by Jack M. Sasson. 4 vols. New York: Charles Scribner's Sons, 1995.

Yadin, Yigal. *The Art of Warfare in Biblical Lands in Light of Archaeological Discovery.* London: Weidenfeld and Nicolson, 1963.

Zevit, Z. *The Religions of Ancient Israel: A Synthesis of Parallactic Approaches.* New York: Continuum, 2001.

Zohary, M. *Plants of the Bible.* Cambridge: Cambridge University Press, 1982.

3. Monarchy Period

Ahlstrom, G. W. "Where Did the Israelites Live?" *Journal of Near Eastern Studies* 41 (1982): 133–38.

Alt, A. *Essays in Old Testament History and Religion.* Oxford: Blackwell, 1966.

Beebe, H. K. "Ancient Palestinian Dwellings." *Biblical Archaeologist* 31 (1968): 38–58.

Benjamin, D. C. *Deuteronomy and City Life.* Lanham, Md.: University Press of America, 1983.

Bleibtreu, E. "Grisly Assyrian Record of Torture and Death." *Biblical Archaeology Review* 17, no. 1 (1991): 53–61, 75.

Blenkinsopp, Joseph. *A History of Prophecy in Israel.* Louisville: Westminster John Knox, 1996.

Bloch-Smith, E. and B. A. Nakhai. "A Landscape Comes to Life: The Iron Age I." *Near Eastern Archaeology* 62, no. 2 (June 1999): 62–92, 101–127.

Boecker, H. J. *Law and the Administration of Justice in the Old Testament and Ancient East.* Minneapolis: Augsburg, 1980.

Borowski, O. *Agriculture in Iron Age Israel.* Winona Lake, Ind.: Eisenbrauns, 1987.

———. "Five Ways to Defend an Ancient City." *Biblical Archaeology Review* 9, no. 2 (1983): 73–76.

Bunimovitz, S. and A. Faust. "Ideology in Stone: Understanding the Four-Room House." *Biblical Archaeology Review* 28, no. 4 (2002): 33–41, 59–60.

Clancy, F. "Shishak/Shoshenq's Travels." *Journal for the Study of the Old Testament* 86 (1999): 3–23.

Cogan, M. *Imperialism and Religion: Assyria, Judah, and Israel in the Eighth and Seventh Centuries B.C.* Society of Biblical Literature 19. Missoula, Mont.: Scholars Press, 1974.

———. and H. Tadmor. *II Kings: A New Translation with Introduction and Commentary.* New York: Doubleday, 1988.

Coggins, R., A. Phillips, and M. Knibb, eds. *Israel's Prophetic Tradition: Essays in Honour of Peter R. Ackroyd.* New York: Cambridge University Press, 1982.

Cole, D. P. "How Water Tunnels Worked." *Biblical Archaeology Review* 6, no. 2 (1980): 8–29.

Cordwell, Justine M. and Ronald A. Schwarz, eds. *The Fabrics of Culture: The Anthropology of Clothing and Adornment.* New York: Mouton, 1979.

DeVries, L. F. "Cult Stands: A Bewildering Variety of Shapes and Sizes." *Biblical Archaeology Review* 13, no. 4 (1987): 26–37.

Edelstein, G. and Gibson, S. "Ancient Jerusalem's Rural Food Basket." *Biblical Archaeology Review* 8, no. 4 (1982): 46–54.

Frick, F. S. *The City in Ancient Israel.* Missoula, Mont.: Scholars Press, 1977.

———. *The Formation of the State in Ancient Israel.* Sheffield: Almond, 1985.

Fritz, V. "What Can Archaeology Tell Us about Solomon's Temple?" *Biblical Archaeology Review* 13, no. 4 (1987): 38–49.

Hanson, P. D. *The People Called: Growth of Community in the Bible.* San Francisco: Harper & Row, 1986.

Haran, M. *Temples and Temple Service in Ancient Israel.* Oxford: Clarendon, 1970.

Hasel, G. F. "Health and Healing in the Old Testament." *Andrews University Seminary Studies* 21 (1983): 191–202.

Hauer, C. "From Alt to Anthropology: The Rise of the Israelite State." *Journal for the Study of the Old Testament* 36 (1986): 3–15.

Heaton, E. W. *Solomon's New Men.* New York: Pica, 1974.

Herrmann, S. "King David's State." Pages 261–75 in *In the Shelter of Elyon: Essays on Ancient Palestinian Life and Literature in Honor of G. W. Ahlstrom.* Edited by W. B. Barrick and J. R. Spencer. Journal for the Study of the Old Testament: Supplement Series 31. Sheffield: JSOT Press, 1984.

Hurowitz, V. "Inside Solomon's Temple." *Bible Review* 10, no. 2 (1994): 24–37, 50.

Keel, O. and C. Uehlinger. *Gods, Goddesses, and Images of God in Ancient Israel.* Minneapolis: Fortress, 1998.

Kinnier Wilson, J. V. "Medicine in the Land of Times of the Old Testament." Pages 337–65 in *Studies in the Period of David and Solomon and Other Essays.* Edited by T. Ishida. Winona Lake, Ind.: Eisenbrauns, 1982.

Lang, B. "Afterlife: Ancient Israel's Changing Vision of the World Beyond." *Bible Review* 4, no. 1 (1988): 12–23.

Lemche, D. "David's Rise." *Journal for the Study of the Old Testament* 10 (1978): 2–25.

Liebowitz, Harold A. "Late Bronze II Ivory Work in Palestine: Evidence of a Cultural Highpoint." *Bulletin of the*

American Schools of Oriental Research 265 (1987): 3–24.

MacKenzie, R. A. F. "The City and Israelite Religion." *Catholic Biblical Quarterly* 25 (1963): 60–70.

Matthews, V. H. "Entrance Ways and Threshing Floors: Legally Significant Sites in the Ancient Near East." *Fides et Historia* 19 (1987): 25–40.

———. "The King's Call to Justice." *Biblische Zeitschrift* 35 (1991): 204–16.

——— and D. C. Benjamin. *Old Testament Parallels: Laws and Stories from the Ancient Near East.* Rev. and exp. ed. New York: Paulist, 1997.

McCarter, P. K. "The Historical David." *Interpretation* 40 (1986): 117–29.

Milgrom, J. "Of Hems and Tassels." *Biblical Archaeology Review* 9, no. 3 (1983): 61–65.

Na'aman, N. "The Contribution of Royal Inscriptions for a Re-evaluation of the Book of Kings as a Historical Source." *Journal for the Study of the Old Testament* 82 (1999): 3–17.

Neufeld, E. "Hygiene Conditions in Ancient Israel (Iron Age)." *Biblical Archaeologist* 34 (1971): 42–66.

Patrick, D. *Old Testament Law.* Atlanta: John Knox, 1984.

Platt, E. E. "Jewelry of Bible Times and the Catalog of Isa 3:18–23." *Andrews University Seminary Studies* 17 (1979): 71–84, 189–201.

Pritchard, J. *Ancient Near Eastern Texts Relating to the Old Testament.* Princeton: Princeton University Press, 1969.

Prouser, O Horn. "Suited to the Throne: The Symbolic Use of Clothing in the David and Saul Narratives." *Journal for the Study of the Old Testament* 71 (1996): 27–37.

Rahmani, L. Y. "Ancient Jerusalem's Funerary Customs and Tombs." *Biblical Archaeologist* 45, no. 1 (1982): 43–53.

Redford, D. B. *Egypt, Canaan, and Israel in Ancient Times.* Princeton, N.J.: Princeton University Press, 1992.

Roth, M. T. *Law Collections from Mesopotamia and Asia Minor.* Atlanta: Scholars Press, 1995.

Rubens, A. *A History of Jewish Costume.* New York: Funk & Wagnalls, 1967.

Shanks, H., ed. "David's Jerusalem: Fact or Fiction?" *Biblical Archaeology Review* 24, no. 4 (1998): 24–44, 62–63.

Shiloh, Y. "The Four-Room House: Its Situation and Function in the Israelite City." *Israel Exploration Journal* 20 (1970): 180–90.

Smith, M.S. *The Origins of Biblical Monotheism: Israel's Polytheistic Background and the Ugaritic Texts.* New York: Oxford University Press, 2001.

Soggin, J. *A History of Ancient Israel.* Philadelphia: Westminster, 1985.

Thompson, J. A. "The 'Town' in Old Testament Times." *Buried History* 19 (1983): 35–42.

Ussishkin, D. "King Solomon's Palaces." *Biblical Archaeologist* 36 (1973): 78–105.

Vaux, R. de. *Ancient Israel: Its Life and Institutions.* London: Darton, Longman and Todd, 1973.

Weinfeld, M. *Social Justice in Ancient Israel and in the Ancient Near East.* Minneapolis: Fortress, 1995.

Whitelam, K. W. *The Just King: Monarchical Judicial Authority in Ancient Israel.* Journal for the Study of the Old Testament: Supplement Series 12. Sheffield: JSOT Press, 1979.

_____. "The Symbols of Power: Aspects of Royal Propaganda in the United Monarchy." *Biblical Archaeologist* 49 (1986): 166–73.

Wilkinson, J. "Leprosy and Leviticus: The Problem of Description and Identification." *Scottish Journal of Theology* 30 (1977): 153–69.

Wilson, R. R. *Prophecy and Society in Ancient Israel.* Philadelphia: Fortress, 1980.

Yadin, Y. *The Art of Warfare in Biblical Lands in the Light of Archaeological Discovery.* London: Weidenfeld and Nicolson, 1963.

Zias, J. "Current Archaeological Research in Israel: Death and Disease in Ancient Israel." *Biblical Archaeologist* 54 (1991): 146–159.

4. Exile and Return

Ackroyd, P. R. "Archaeology Politics and Religion: The Persian Period." *Iliff Review* 39 (1982): 5–23.

_____. *Exile and Restoration: A Study of Hebrew Thought of the Sixth Century B.C.* Philadelphia: Westminster, 1968.

Berquist, J. *Judaism in Persia's Shadow: A Social and Historical Approach.* Minneapolis: Fortress, 1995.

Bossman, D. "Ezra's Marriage Reform: Israel Redefined." *Biblical Theology Bulletin* 9 (1979): 32–38.

Bresciani, E. "The Persian Occupation of Egypt." Pages 502–28 in *The Cambridge History of Iran.* Vol. 2 of *The Median and Achaemenian Periods.* Edited by I. Gershevitch. Cambridge: Cambridge University Press, 1985.

Carter, C. E. *The Emergence of Yehud in the Persian Period: A Social and Demographic Study.* Journal for the Study of the Old Testament: Supplement Series 294. Sheffield: Sheffield Academic Press, 1999.

Coggins, Richard J. "The Origins of the Jewish Diaspora." Pages 163–81 in *The World of Ancient Israel.* Edited by R. Clements. Cambridge: Cambridge University Press, 1989.

Cohen, Shaye J. D., ed. *The Jewish Family in Antiquity.* Atlanta: Scholars Press, 1993.

Collins, J. J. *The Apocalyptic Imagination: An Introduction to Jewish Apocalyptic Literature.* Grand Rapids: Eerdmans, 1998.

_____. *Jewish Wisdom in the Hellenistic Age.* Louisville: Westminster John Knox, 1997.

Coogan, M. D. "Life in the Diaspora: Jews at Nippur in the Fifth Century B.C." *Biblical Archaeologist* 37 (1974): 6–12.

Cook, John M. *The Persian Empire.* London: Dent, 1983.

Dumbrell, W. J. "Kingship and Temple in the Post-Exilic Period." *Reformed Theological Review* 37 (May–August 1978): 33–42.

Freedman, D. N. "'Son of Man, Can These Bones Live?'" *Interpretation* 29 (April 1975): 171–86.

Grabbe, L. L. *Judaism from Cyrus to Hadrian.* 2 vols. Minneapolis: Fortress, 1992.

Harrison, R. "Hellenization in Syria-Palestine." *Biblical Archaeologist* 57 (1994), 98–108.

Hoglund, K. G. *Achaemenid Imperial Administration in Syria-Palestine and the Missions of Ezra and Nehemiah.* Society of Biblical Literature Dissertation Series 125. Atlanta: Scholars Press, 1992.

Japhet, S. "Sheshbazzar and Zerubbabel: Against the Background of the Historical and Religious Tendencies of Ezra-Nehemiah." *Zeitschrift für die alttestamentliche Wissenschaft* 94 (1982): 66–98; 95 (1983): 218–29.

Klein, R. *Israel in Exile.* Philadelphia: Fortress, 1979.

Koch, K. "Ezra and the Origins of Judaism." *Journal of Semitic Studies* 19 (1974): 173–97.

Kuhrt, A. "The Cyrus Cylinder and Achaemenid Imperial Policy." *Journal for the Study of the Old Testament* 25 (1983): 83–97.

Lipschits, O. "The History of the Benjamin Region under Babylonian Rule." *Tel Aviv* 26 (1999): 155–90.

Matthews, V. H. "The Social Context of Law in the Second Temple Period." *Biblical Theology Bulletin* 28 (1998): 7–15.

Mazar, B. *The Mountain of the Lord.* Garden City, N.Y.: Doubleday, 1975.

McCullough, W. S. *The History and Literature of the Palestinian Jews from Cyrus to Herod 550 B.C. to 4 B.C.* Toronto: University of Toronto Press, 1975.

McEvenue, S. E. "The Political Structure in Judah from Cyrus to Nehemiah." *Catholic Biblical Quarterly* 43 (1981): 353–64.

Meyers, C. "The Elusive Temple." *Biblical Archaeologist* 45 (1982): 33–41.

Miller, J. M., and J. H. Hayes. *A History of Ancient Israel and Judah.* Philadelphia: Westminster, 1986.

Moore, C. A. "Archaeology and the Book of Esther." *Biblical Archaeologist* 38 (1975), 62–79.

Myers, J. M. "Edom and Judah in the Sixth and Fifth Centuries B.C." Pages 377–92 in *Near Eastern Studies in Honor of W. F. Albright.* Edited by H. Goedicke. Baltimore: Johns Hopkins Press, 1971.

Stern, E. *The Material Culture of the Land of the Bible in the Persian Period 538–332 BC.* Warminster: Aris & Phillips, 1982.

_____. *Archaeology of the Land of the Bible: The Assyrian, Babylonian, and Persian Periods (732–332 B.C.).* New York: Doubleday, 2001.

Stohlmann, S. "The Judaean Exile after 701 B.C." Pages 147–76 in *Scripture in Context II: More Essays on the Comparative Method.* Edited by W. W. Hallo, J. C. Moyer, and L. G. Perdue. Winona Lake, Ind.: Eisenbrauns, 1983.

Ussishkin, D. "Lachish." Pages 317–23 in vol. 3 of *The Oxford Encyclopedia of Archaeology in the Near East.* Edited by Eric M. Meyers. 5 vols. New York: Oxford University Press, 1997.

Vaux, R. de. *Ancient Israel: Its Life and Institutions.* New York: Mcgraw-Hill, 1961.

Widengren, G. "The Persian Period." Pages 489–538 in *Israelite and Judaean History.* Edited by J. H. Hayes and J. M. Miller. Philadelphia: Westminster, 1977.

_____. "Yahweh's Gathering of the Dispersed." Pages 227–45 in *In the Shelter of Elyon: Essays on Ancient Palestinian Life and Literature in Honor of G. W. Ahlstrom.* Edited by W. B. Barrick and J. R. Spencer. Journal for the Study of the Old Testament: Supplement Series 31. Sheffield: JSOT, 1984.

Yamauchi, E. M. "Daniel and Contacts between the Aegean and the Near East before Alexander." *Evangelical Quarterly* 53 (1981): 37–47.

_____. *Persia and the Bible.* Grand Rapids: Baker, 1990.

Zadok, R. *The Jews in Babylonia during the Chaldean and Achaemenian Periods.* Haifa: University of Haifa Press, 1979.

_____. "Notes on the Early History of the Israelites and Judeans in Mesopotamia." *Orientalia* 51 (1982): 391–93.

5. Intertestamental and New Testament Period

Avalos, H. *Health Care and the Rise of Christianity.* Peabody, Mass.: Hendrickson, 1999. Arav, R., R. A. Freund, and J. F. Shroder. "Bethsaida Rediscovered." *Biblical Archaeology Review* 26, no. 1 (2000): 44–56.

Avigad, N. "Jerusalem Flourishing: A Craft Center for Stone, Pottery, and Glass." *Biblical Archaeology Review* 9, no. 6 (1983): 48–65.

Avi-Yonah, M. "The Development of the Roman Road System in Palestine." *Israel Exploration Journal* 1 (1950–51): 54–60.

Berlin, A. M. "What's for Dinner? The Answer Is in the Pot." *Biblical Archaeology Review* 25, no. 6 (1999): 46–55, 62.

Best, T. F. "The Sociological Study of the New Testament: Promise and Peril of a New Testament Discipline." *Scottish Journal of Theology* 36 (1983): 181–94.

Broshi, M. "Estimating the Population of Ancient Jerusalem." *Biblical Archaeology Review* 4 (1978): 10–15.

Collins, J. J. *Between Athens and Jerusalem: Jewish Identity in the Hellenistic Diaspora.* New York: Crossroads, 1983.

Court, J., and K. Court. *The New Testament World.* Englewood Cliffs, N.J.: Prentice-Hall, 1990.

Derrett, J. Duncan M. *Law in the New Testament.* London: Darton, Longman and Todd, 1970.

deSilva, D. A. *Honor, Patronage, Kinship and Purity: Unlocking New Testament Culture.* Downers Grove, Ill.: InterVarsity, 2000.

Dowley, T., ed. *Discovering the Bible.* Grand Rapids: Eerdmans, 1986.

Feldman, L. H. "The Omnipresence of the God-Fearers." *Biblical Archaeology Review* 12, no. 5 (1986): 58–69.

_____ and G. Hata, eds. *Josephus, the Bible, and History.* Detroit: Wayne State University Press, 1989.

Finegan, J. *The Archaeology of the New Testament: The Life of Jesus and the Beginning of the Early Church.* Princeton, N.J.: Princeton University Press, 1969.

Gallagher, E. V. "The Social World of Saint Paul." *Religion* 14 (January 1984): 91–99.

Gowen, D. E. *Bridge between the Testaments.* Pittsburgh: Pickwick, 1980.

Grabbe, L. L. "Betwixt and Between: The Samaritans in the Hasmonean Period." *SBL Seminar Papers* (1993): 334–42.

Gutmann, J., ed. *Ancient Synagogues: The State of Research.* Missoula, Mont.: Scholars Press, 1981.

Hanson, K. C., and D. E. Oakman. *Palestine in the Time of Jesus: Social Structures and Social Conflicts.* Minneapolis: Fortress, 1998.

Harris, O. G. "The Social World of Early Christianity." *Lexington Theological Quarterly* 19, no. 3 (1984): 102–14.

Hengel, M. *Judaism and Hellenism.* Philadelphia: Fortress, 1981.

Hirschfeld, Y., and G. Solar. "Sumptuous Roman Baths Uncovered near Sea of Galilee." *Biblical Archaeology Review* 10, no. 6 (1984): 22–40.

Horsley, Richard A. *Archaeology, History, and Society in Galilee: The Social Context of Jesus and the Rabbis.* Valley Forge, Pa.: Trinity Press International, 1996.

Jeremias, J. *Jerusalem in the Time of Jesus.* Philadelphia: Fortress, 1969.

Koester, H. *Introduction to the New Testament: History, Culture, and Religion of the Hellenistic Age.* 2 vols. Philadelphia: Fortress, 1980.

Lemaire, A. "Burial Box of James the Brother of Jesus." *Biblical Archaeology Review* 28, no. 4 (2002): 24–33, 70.

Magness, J. *The Archaeology of Qumran and the Dead Sea Scrolls.* Grand Rapids: Eerdmans, 2002.

Malherbe, A. J. *Social Aspects of Early Christianity.* Baton Rouge: Louisiana State University Press, 1977.

Malina, B. J. *Christian Origins and Cultural Anthropology.* Atlanta: John Knox, 1986.

_____. *The New Testament World: Insights from Cultural Anthropology.* Atlanta: John Knox, 1993.

Matthews, Victor H. *A Brief History of Ancient Israel.* Louisville: Westminster John Knox, 2002.

Meeks, W. A. *The First Urban Christians: The Social World of the Apostle Paul.* New Haven: Yale University Press, 1983.

Meshorer, Y. *Ancient Jewish Coinage.* New York: Amphora, 1982.

Meyers, E. M. "The Challenge of Hellenism for Early Judaism and Christianity." *Biblical Archaeologist* 55 (1992): 84–91.

_____. "Early Judaism and Christianity in the Light of Archaeology." *Biblical Archaeologist* 51 (1988): 69–79.

Murphy-O'Connor, J. "The Corinth That Saint Paul Saw." *Biblical Archaeologist* 47, no. 3 (1984): 147–59.

Neusner, J. *From Politics to Piety: The Emergence of Pharisaic Judaism.* Englewood Cliffs, N.J.: Prentice Hall, 1973.

Osiek, C. *What Are They Saying about the Social Setting of the New Testament?* New York: Paulist, 1984.

Osiek, C., et al, eds. *Families in the New Testament World.* Louisville: Westminster John Knox, 1997.

Peters, F. E. "Hellenism and the Near East." *Biblical Archaeologist* 46, no. 1 (1983): 33–39.

_____. *Jerusalem.* Princeton, N. J.: Princeton University Press, 1985.

Porath, Y. "Herod's 'Amphitheatre' at Caesarea: A Multipurpose Entertainment Building." Pages 15–27 in *The Roman and Byzantine Near East: Some Recent Archaeological Research.* Edited by J. H. Humphrey. Journal of Roman Archaeology: Supplementary Series 14. Ann Arbor, Mich.: Journal of Roman Archaeology, 1995.

Powell, M. "Weights and Measures." Pages 897–908 in vol. 6 of *Anchor Bible Dictionary.* Edited by David Noel Freedman. 6 vols. New York: Doubleday, 1992.

Rahmani, L. Y. "Ancient Jerusalem's Funerary Customs and Tombs, Part Three." *Biblical Archaeologist* 45, no. 1 (1982): 43–53.

_____. "Ossuaries and *Ossilegium* (Bone-Gathering) in the Late Second Temple Period." Pages 191–205 in *Ancient Jerusalem Revealed.* Edited by H. Geva. Jerusalem: Israel Exploration Society, 1994.

Reinhardt, W. and A. Warren. "The Population Size of Jerusalem and the Numerical Growth of the Jerusalem Church." Pages 237–65 in *The Book of Acts in Its Palestinian Setting.* Edited by R. Bauckham. Grand Rapids: Eerdmans, 1995.

Rivkin, E. *A Hidden Revolution: The Pharisee's Search for the Kingdom Within.* Nashville: Abingdon, 1978.

Roetzel, C. J. *The World That Shaped the New Testament.* Atlanta: John Knox, 1985.

Rousseau, J. J., and R. Arav. *Jesus and His World.* Minneapolis: Fortress, 1995.

Saldarini, A. J. *Pharisees, Scribes, and Sadducees in Palestinian Society: A Sociological Approach.* Grand Rapids: Eerdmans, 2001.

Scott, R. B. Y. "Weights and Measures of the Bible." *Biblical Archaeologist* 22, no. 2 (1959): 22–40.

Smallwood, E. M. *The Jews under Roman Rule: From Pompey to Diocletian.* Leiden: Brill, 1976.

Stambaugh, J. E., and D. L. Balch. *The New Testament in Its Social Environment.* Philadelphia: Westminster, 1986.

Stieglitz, R. R. "Long-Distance Seafaring in the Ancient Near East." *Biblical Archaeologist* 47, no. 3 (1984): 134–42.

Tcherikover, V. *Hellenistic Civilization and the Jews.* Peabody, Mass.: Hendrickson, 1999.

Theissen, G. *Sociology of Early Palestinian Christianity.* Philadelphia: Fortress, 1978.

Thompson, J. A. *Life in Bible Times.* Downers Grove, Ill.: InterVarsity, 1986.

VanderKam, J. "People and High Priesthood in Early Maccabean Times." Pages 205–24 in *The Hebrew Bible and Its Interpreters.* Edited by V. Propp, et al. Winona Lake, Ind.: Eisenbrauns, 1990.

_____. *The Dead Sea Scrolls Today.* Grand Rapids: Eerdmans, 1994.

Van Der Woude, A. S., ed. *The World of the Bible.* Grand Rapids: Eerdmans, 1986.

Wilkinson, J. *Jerusalem As Jesus Knew It: Archaeology As Evidence.* London: Thames & Hudson, 1978.

Subject Index

Personal Names Index

Place Names Index

Ancient Texts Index

252